Perspectives on Purpose

Perspectives on Purpose and its sister book, *Perspectives on Impact*, bring together leading voices from across sectors to discuss how we must adapt our organizations for the twenty-first century world. *Perspectives on Purpose* looks at the shifting role of the corporation in society through the lens of purpose; *Perspectives on Impact* focuses on the recalibration of social impact approaches to tackle complex humanitarian, social, and environmental challenges.

Margarita ('Nina') S. Montgomery is an archaeologist–turned–strategist currently working at IDEO. A PhD candidate at Oxford, she holds a fellowship at TRIPTK and has spoken on organizations and society at Harvard Business School and Oxford's Saïd Business School, among others. Nina received a BA in Classics from Dartmouth and a master's in Classical Archaeology from Oxford as a Reynolds Scholar.

"Climate change, once imminent, has arrived in force. The world, once without end, has shrunk to the size of a nest. We now have to accept our responsibilities to salvage and create a heritable world. First among these responsibilities is the conduct of economic life – how to do business to good purpose and solve the problems, however unintentional, of our own creation. This book shows us how."

— Vincent Stanley, Director of Philosophy at Patagonia

"Ms. Montgomery's inspirational work is a rally cry and reminder that we're not playing a zero-sum game here, but a win-win. And when we structure ourselves not to compete, but to collaborate under one shared conceptual framework for purpose-led business, the possibilities for meaningful and lasting social impact are endless."

— Jessica Alba & Christopher Gavigan,
Co-Founders at The Honest Company

"To build a great company, purpose is not a nice-to-have; it's a must-have. This book brings together a range of thoughtful voices on how to develop and communicate that purpose."

— Adam Grant, *New York Times* bestselling author
of *Originals* and *Give and Take*

"With so many brands proclaiming their 'purpose' today, this book offers clear-eyed, pragmatic views on how companies can authentically make the world better in some way – not through philanthropy and certainly not through marketing campaigns, but through their profit-making core business. Indeed, it shows that 'profit or purpose' is a false choice and that an increasing number of companies and their leaders are getting it right."

— Jon Iwata, Former Chief Brand Officer at IBM, and
Executive Fellow at Yale School of Management

"It is undeniable that of all the words that purport to bind endeavors and organizations (Vision; Mission; Plan; Brand to name a few), Purpose is the most powerful. It sits above the others. It is fundamental. For a singular purpose creates freedom and enfranchisement. When history is written about the changes which took place at the beginning of the twenty-first century, it will be the growing understanding of the importance of Purpose which is documented. This excellent book is the start of that history."

— Michael Birkin, CEO at kyu

"The problems of today and tomorrow demand collective action and creative solutions. The first step in developing the necessary culture of community-based problem-solving is to convene diverse leaders from industry and academia whose imagination and experience help us see with new, more inclusive eyes. The Perspectives book series, and especially the volumes on Impact and Purpose, does just that by amplifying the voices of underrepresented thought innovators whose perspective is vital to the future success, stability, and security of our society."

— Dan Porterfield, President and CEO at the Aspen Institute

Perspectives on Purpose

Leading Voices on Building Brands and Businesses for the Twenty-First Century

Edited by Nina Montgomery

Routledge
Taylor & Francis Group

LONDON AND NEW YORK

First published 2019
by Routledge
2 Park Square, Milton Park, Abingdon, Oxon OX14 4RN

and by Routledge
52 Vanderbilt Avenue, New York, NY 10017

Routledge is an imprint of the Taylor & Francis Group, an informa business

British Library Cataloguing-in-Publication Data
A catalogue record for this book is available from the British Library

Library of Congress Cataloging-in-Publication Data
A catalog record for this book has been requested

ISBN: 978-0-8153-8724-4 (hbk)
ISBN: 978-0-367-11237-0 (pbk)
ISBN: 978-1-351-17356-8 (ebk)

Typeset in Bembo
by Apex CoVantage, LLC

cui dono lepidum novum libellum?

To my parents, Katherine and David Montgomery, the ultimate nurturers of purpose.

And to my siblings – Cece, Will, Sophie, and Tommy – who make even the less purpose-ful moments worthwhile.

Contents

Acknowledgements

This book has grown far beyond any scope I ever imagined for it. It was made possible by a number of people to whom I'm very grateful and forever indebted.

First, to the wonderful contributors, especially those who agreed to participate early on in the process, I am honored and grateful that you took a chance on a young, excitable editor. Any value this book offers is derived entirely from you and your willingness to share your perspectives with the world.

To Jessica Alba and Christopher Gavigan – thank you for adding your voice to this conversation. I hope our readers are as inspired by your foreword as I was when I first I read it!

Beyond written contributions, this project and its overall framing has benefited greatly from early and continued conversations with Sam Hornsby, Maryam Banikarim, Alex Dimiziani, Matthew Quint, Frank Oswald, and Tom Andrews. There were also many, many other mentors and friends who offered advice over coffees and phone calls along the way; you know who you are, and I'm very appreciative of your endless support.

As this project grew, it became clear that to deliver on the potential of the book I needed support. I'm grateful for the amazing army of assistant editors who were up for the task. The word-smithing genius and editorial advice of Caela Murphy, Deirdre Dlugoleski, Summer Modelfino, and Natalie Shell were invaluable, and these volunteers are responsible for making many of these chapters sing. A special thanks also must go to English Taylor and Margo Manocherian, who have been masterful sounding boards. And to Professor Justin Jones – I couldn't have asked for a more supportive PhD advisor – on academics and side projects alike! Thank you.

I'm also incredibly thankful for my brilliant publishers – Amy Laurens and Alex Atkinson. You two were the dream team for a first time editor/author, from first proposal through to final proofs.

A special thanks also to TRIPTK and Havas for their support as we continue the purpose conversation beyond the pages of this book; you've both have been wonderful partners, committed to building meaningful brands for this new era.

And finally, to my family. From Poppop's ancient history lessons and Yaya's Spanish charm to G-dad's emphatic, sociological curiosity and Grammie's principled devotion – you have all left such a significant impression on my sense of self and modes of thinking. I'm so proud of this personal heritage. To my parents, who encouraged me to study Latin and wander a bit before finding my way, you both are such incredible listeners, cheerleaders, educators, and nurturers. I hope to be half the parent and person you each are. And to my siblings – Cece, Will, Sophie, and Tommy. I love and am so proud of all four of you. You're my favorite people and best friends.

Figures and boxes

Figures

Boxes

Foreword

The Honest Company was born of a simple purpose: to bring health and happiness to people everywhere. We were in search of safe options for our babies and our families but there were so many questions. We needed one place that we could go to for trusted products and information. And when we couldn't find what we were looking for – and realized we were just two in a community of parents seeking the same – we decided to create it. We simply had to.

As we built Honest and our incredible community, it was with the firm belief that – similar to the butterfly effect – all the small choices we made could add up to something quite big. Our hope was to re-define the family brand. For good. And we've spent every day since working to live up to that promise.

The living up is not without its challenges. With success comes not only the ability to further your purpose, but also a host of inevitable questions. Why, how, and at what cost should we scale? And how do we optimize for the benefit of the business, our consumers, and the greater good?

In working to answer these questions, there will always be a tension between purpose and profit, content and commerce. And though the filter of a mission might add complexity, it also adds clarity and simplicity. When you're grounded in what is your unique DNA from day one – when you know *exactly* who you are and what you're about – it takes some of the charge and the struggle out of that search for balance.

No, it's not always easy – but today, it's not only worth it, it's necessary. In a time when people are seeking ideals over ideas and when trust is such a significant commodity, it's our job to be responsible for the communities we serve. It's our job to be disciplined enough to ask hard questions and make harder decisions. And it's our job to draw a line in the sand and say we stand for something.

That's why a book such as this is so important – a bringing together of today's socially minded business leaders to say 'this is the future.' Adopt now or later, but thankfully, this is the new paradigm. We're as invigorated by this shift as we are by those leading its charge, many of whom are women and minorities. It's a beautiful thing to know we're on the right side of history.

Ms. Montgomery's inspirational work is a rallying cry and reminder that we're not playing a zero-sum game here, but a win-win. And when we structure ourselves not to compete, but to collaborate under one shared conceptual framework for purpose-led business, the possibilities for meaningful and lasting social impact are endless.

Jessica Alba and Christopher Gavigan,
Founders, The Honest Company

Introduction

Nina Montgomery

This book started with a simple observation: companies are questioning whether the priorities that enabled them to compete and prosper in decades past will continue to serve them in decades to come.[1] The target of this reflection is the long-held business emphasis on maximizing profits for stakeholder and owners above all else.[2] What part did past corporate activity, guided by this priority, play in creating the good, bad, and ugly of today's world? And what path does its continued practice pave for our future?

Others with more years notched in the business world have similarly pointed to this need for a fundamental – existential, even – questioning of our very notion of business. In their influential book *Built to Last: Successful Habits of Visionary Companies*, Jim Collins and Jerry Porras suggest that "enduring great companies of the twenty-first century will need to have radically different structures, strategies, practices, and mechanisms than in the twentieth."[3] Echoing this sentiment in an open letter that launched a thousand think pieces, BlackRock's Larry Fink calls for a new model of corporate governance. He warns that without a serious commitment to change, businesses "will lose the license to operate from key stakeholders . . . [they] will succumb to short-term pressures to distribute earnings, and, in the process, sacrifice investments in employee development, innovation, and capital expenditures that are necessary for long-term growth."[4]

These are just a few voices in a growing chorus calling for a recalibration of business priorities to meet the realities of the twenty-first century.[5] Beyond stock price and shareholder value, there is emerging consensus that competitive business will require more human-centered and socially aware models.[6]

'Purpose' has become the lens and language used to reckon with this changing blueprint of business. The idea is most commonly framed as an organization's belief about the value it creates, beyond its bottom line.[7] A purpose-led company asks how it can create both economic and social prosperity, and in so doing positively impact people's lives and the planet more broadly. This aspirational north star creates efficiencies by aligning a range of stakeholders and bringing long-term strategic clarity. And it serves as a guide for the design of a business' hard and soft structures – everything from its supply chain to its culture. Purpose, by this view, is not about business doing good out of a sense of responsibility or altruism; it's about weaving purpose into the profit-making core of business, and linking doing well with doing good.

When I pitched this book on organizational purpose in late 2017, I had hopes and dreams about its relevance but few expectations for what it might become. As I first reached out to the contributors featured here, I was overwhelmed by their interest – and continued to be astonished by the energy they poured into this project over months of developing it together.

From our many conversations, it was clear that this topic hit a nerve. As much promise as each contributor felt the idea of north star purpose had, they were also frustrated by how purpose has been co-opted across industry. Many exclamations of "purpose!" today are conflated with superficial social activations like cause marketing, corporate activism, or charitable giving.[8] This wave of 'do good' appeals feels increasingly calculated and contrived, leading skeptics to ask how purpose is any different from the soup of mission, vision, values, and other higher-minded business buzzwords of decades past. Admittedly, it's hard not to raise an eyebrow when greeted by yet another article, or in our case book, with the term in its title.

The contention of this book, however, is that dismissing purpose as business buzz is throwing the baby out with the bathwater. When properly conceived, purpose is a powerful tool to do the much needed work of building, or rebuilding, organizations to meet the realities of the twenty-first century. The problem, in other words, is not with purpose itself, but with how we practice it. How do we meaningfully alchemize purpose into every aspect of the organization, dissolving it into the texture of everyday culture and conduct? How can we design purpose into a business' profit-making core? How can purpose inform the way we activate brands across the globe?

While there are many valuable and provocative perspectives that engage with these questions in isolation, they tend to be drowned out by the pop-purpose buzz. By inviting perspectives on purpose into dialogue, our hope is to substantiate what purpose is, how it's practiced today, and where its room for future development lies – and by extension comment on the state of the changing business blueprint.

In the chapters assembled here, we'll learn from the wisdom and experiences of C-suite executives and agency leaders, academic powerhouses and young entrepreneurs, 'corporate clients' and their 'purpose partners.' We'll see how purpose is being brought to life across a range of categories – including technology, beauty, hospitality, food and beverage, and retail – and organization types – from heritage business and new-to-world brands to non-profit organizations. And we'll hear how purpose is guiding the decisions companies make about their supply chains and innovation pipelines; about how they hire, fire, and promote people; about how they engage partners and express their brands in the world; about the way they communicate and community build with stakeholders (including employees *and* consumers); and about the way they impact and integrate into society at large. As you read, I hope these chapters encourage you to craft your own perspective on purpose and inspire you to join the conversation.

Moving purpose forward

Forward movement requires acknowledging what's holding us back. As you read you'll notice that our contributors don't agree on everything. Sometimes our terminologies vary. Sometimes we disagree on how 'social' purpose has to be. Sometimes we have different ideas about how to discover and deploy purpose within our organizations. I've chosen not to smooth over these apparent discrepancies because I believe they are part of this collection's value. They point to the critical, ongoing conversations we must have and acknowledge the points of tension that require our thoughtful acupuncture as we continue to practice purpose.

But what struck me most as this project progressed was contributors' remarkably consistent belief in the critical importance of a genuinely purpose-centered future for business. They share a strong desire to reclaim the concept from diluted popular invocations and in so doing, push the conversation around purpose forward. The case studies, stories, and best practices shared across these chapters evolve the popular understanding of purpose in several interconnected ways. These are the four driving themes of this shift that I found to be most pervasive:

From responsible business to good business

Whether explicitly stated or not, much of the rhetoric around pop-purpose is about a corporation's altruistic duty to improve society: 'with great power comes great responsibility,' the maxim goes. The problem is that this view separates purpose from profit, relying on the morality of business to 'do the right thing'. But businesses are not moral entities. Business will always be about commerce, and commerce will always be about growth. When purpose and profit are separated, in the moments where they are at odds a company can, and will, opt out of purpose in favor of profit. Purpose is therefore best when part of the profit-making core of business and integral to the growth of a company. It becomes about good – as in smart – business, rather than a sense of moral responsibility.

From ideology to accountability

Purpose will always have an important ideological component. But ideology can quickly become empty promises or worse, blind optimism that overlooks any unintended consequences of corporate activity done in the name of higher purpose. Both of these scenarios leave even the most well-intentioned companies open to criticisms of not practicing what they preach. Our contributors strongly point to a concept of purpose that emphasizes *accountability* over ideology. This shifted focus requires a consideration of at least two critical questions: to whom are we accountable, and what are we accountable for? The former asks who our stakeholders are, beyond our stockholders, and the latter interrogates how we deliver on purpose, to what ends, at what cost, and with what results. There are many examples throughout this book of companies grappling with these questions and embedding accountability to purpose throughout their organization's design.

From corporate activism to collective action

One popular narrative bound up in purpose is that broken governments have abdicated their responsibility to make society better, so corporations − "liberating their heroic spirit" − must step in and take up this mantle as change-maker.[9] While our contributors are indeed optimistic about the corporation's ability to make positive impact in society, they are also cautious about framing business as the activist crusader. Rather than privatizing change, many of our contributors are defining a role for businesses as *collaborators* in change-making. They recognize that many of our most pressing social problems − from climate change to social inequality − arise from the interplay of private, public, and social sector actors. If all are part of the problem, then surely all must play a critical role in building sustainable, systemic solutions.

From leadership's mantra to everyone's movement

While much of the existing conversation on activating an organization's purpose is written by business leaders for business leaders, a central theme of this book is that purpose is everyone's business. Meaningful incorporation and maintenance of purpose requires participation not just from senior executives (though their buy-in and leadership is indeed critical), but from all employees − regardless of role, rank, and tenure at an organization. Everyone has an essential role in shaping and influencing purpose.

As we continue to experiment with the lengths and limits of organizational purpose in the coming years, even decades, I suspect these themes will become increasingly relevant to our work. Purpose doesn't need to be about saving the world. But a raised consciousness about the ecosystems and communities corporations touch will become an integral part of business-as-usual.

About this book

The thread of this book's narrative is strung across three sections. The first provides framing thoughts on purpose-led business, digging deeper into many of the themes I raise here. Freya Williams begins this section with a discussion of how orbiting around the north star of purpose can drive bottom-line positive growth. Sam Hornsby then demonstrates why purpose is imperative for modern brand-building given the changing contract between consumers and companies. Next Matthew Quint breaks down the challenges of measuring the business impact of purpose and the necessity to tailor metrics to the depth and breadth of an organization's commitment to it. Continuing on the theme of accountability, Frank Oswald helps us consider the ethical implications of being purpose-led – what should leaders do when wrestling with tough choices that the tension between purpose and profit can expose? The last word in this section belongs to Maryam Banikarim, perhaps one of the most seasoned practitioners of purpose in industry, having led four businesses – Hyatt, Gannett, NBC Universal Comcast, and Univision – through the purpose journey from her seat at the executive table. She shares insights on how to be a "champion of purpose" within an organization, and how to empower others to join the movement, as champions, too.

With this foundation set, section two sketches a process for designing a purpose-led business. The shared point of view here is that purpose-led brands are built, or rebuilt, from the inside out, and the progression of chapters mirrors this centrifugal process. Sharing stories from established companies and startups, Heidi Hackemer and Ambika Gautam Pai start by discussing how organizations discover their purpose. With this north star set, Tom Andrews helps us think about how we use it to transform the culture and infrastructure of a business. Drawing on her experience at Airbnb, Alexandra Dimiziani then shares how values can serve as a useful guide for activating purpose, both inside and outside the organization. The section's remaining chapters transition to external activations of purpose, beginning with Jorge Aguilar's deep dive into how organizations can deliver on purpose through the living brand and product experiences they create for consumers. Thomas Ordahl then shares a new brand management model based on cultivating and nurturing a community, united by shared purpose. Taking her work at Sephora as an example, Corrie Conrad concludes the section with a perspective on how to build a social impact program that uses a company's strengths for greater good.

The third section aims to tie the book's themes together through four case studies. Haley Rushing and Letitia Webster share how VF Corporation – the $12 billion apparel, footwear, and accessory powerhouse with brands like The North Face, VANS, Timberland, and more – is rebuilding its hundred-year-old portfolio around a centralized purpose. Ila Byrne and Ryan Hunter then recount how Diageo, one of the biggest spirits portfolios in the world, built a vodka brand from scratch to address and bring awareness to a broken food system. Sam Liebeskind and Sarah Potts offer the inspiring oral history of how Thorn – a non-profit technology company dedicated to stopping child abuse – and its partners at the branding agency Wolff Olins harnessed the power of purpose to focus their mission and mobilize partners to joint action. Finally, Rob Michalak shares how the 'grandfather' of purpose-led business, Ben & Jerry's, continues to raise the bar for how companies link their own prosperity to that of the world around them.

The book concludes with a powerful note penned by leading young voices to those at the helm of business. Jonathan Jackson curates a discussion between Millennial entrepreneurs, scholars, and community leaders who point toward what meaningful corporate engagement with communities should look like – and where many corporations fall short today.

For all the nuances in these perspectives and for all the questions we still need to work through, I hope this book can get us on the same page about the utility of purpose for designing twenty-first century brands and businesses. As Jessica Alba and Christopher Gavigan so eloquently put in their foreword, we have a lot to learn from each other and a huge opportunity to grow together. It's a win-win to open the doors of our organizations and share perspectives on purpose.

I

Framing thoughts on purpose

1

The business case for purpose

Friedman, Fink, and the battle for the soul of business

Freya Williams

Freya Williams has advised organizations including Unilever, the United Nations, REI, Target, VF Corporation and many others on how to convert sustainability and social purpose into competitive advantage for their business and brand. Co-founder of OgilvyEarth and former lead of Edelman's Business + Social Purpose practice in New York, today Freya is the North American CEO of Futerra, the global sustainability change agency. Freya is best known for her work in making sustainability relevant to mainstream audiences. She captured many of her learnings in her 2015 book Green Giants: How Smart Companies Turn Sustainability into Billion-Dollar Businesses, *which has been profiled in* The Economist, Fortune, *and* Forbes. *Her work has also been featured in* The Financial Times, Newsweek *and even* The Onion. *Freya lives in New York with her husband and kids.*

★ ★ ★

I'm going to share two sets of corporate purpose statements with you.[1] As you read, I'd like you to guess which ones you think would be more likely to build business results. Okay, here we go:

1. To build shareholder value by delivering pharmaceutical and healthcare products, services, and solutions in innovative and cost-effective ways.
2. To maximize long-term stockholder value, while adhering to the laws of the jurisdictions in which we operate and at all times observing the highest ethical standards.
3. Create value for shareholders through the energy business.
4. To earn money for our shareholders and increase the value of their investment through growing the company, controlling assets, and properly structuring the balance sheet, and thereby, increasing EPS, cash flow, and return on invested capital.

Got those? Okay, now here's the second set:

1. To create a better everyday life for the many people.
2. To bring inspiration and innovation to every athlete in the world. (If you have a body, you are an athlete).
3. To help expedite the move from a mine-and-burn hydrocarbon economy toward a solar electric economy.
4. To make sustainable living commonplace.

Which set of statements do you think is more likely to have driven business results? The first set, the one that envisions shareholder value as the primary, or indeed sole, focus of business? Or the second set, that see business as an engine to achieve positive social or environmental outcomes?

If you're like the majority of business thinkers, you will easily pick the first set. But you will be wrong.

Because this little quiz cuts to the heart of a battle being waged in real time in the global marketplace today – a battle for the soul of business. This battle is over no less a question than this: why does business exist? What is the purpose, not just of an individual business or brand, but of business *as an institution*?

An increasing number of fascinating enterprises are proving that business has so much more to offer than generating returns for shareholders. And in the process, they are proving out what I call the Purpose Paradox: the surprising fact that businesses that pursue a purpose beyond profit are more profitable than those that pursue profit alone.

This will strike many traditional business minds as touchy feely mumbo jumbo. I should know: I've spent the past twelve or so years of my career trying to persuade them otherwise. More often than not, I've been met with skepticism and a wry 'Bambi, come in from the woods' raise of the eyebrow. That's why about five years ago I set out to quantify the business case in terms the business establishment might find more persuasive. The result was my book, *Green Giants: How Smart Companies Turn Sustainability into Billion Dollar Businesses*. I went for the billion dollar thing because there's something about that billion. In the language of business it holds a certain mystique. As it should. Less than 0.00006 percent of businesses ever make it to the billion dollar mark. So I felt that if I could prove that sustainability, social responsibility, and purpose could drive a company to achieve those results, it might enable a new kind of conversation within the business community.

In the book, I catalogue nine companies that have built billion-dollar-plus businesses with sustainability or social good at their core and outline the six factors they share in common. One of the factors is a purpose beyond profit. Their higher purpose is a direct driver of their billion dollar success. The second set of purpose statements from the opening of this chapter are pulled from four of these Giants: (1) IKEA, (2) Nike, (3) Tesla, and (4) Unilever. These statements outline a purpose for the business beyond profit – and not just any purpose, but a *social* purpose, one that sees the business as part of society, with the potential to be a positive force in the world.

A word on the term 'purpose.' Often, the term functions as a catchall for anything that could be classified as good, whether a campaign marketing a cause, corporate philanthropy, a citizenship program, a CSR program, or not-for-profit branding. Purpose has become the latest business buzzword. One study shows that 88 percent of current business leaders and 90 percent of future leaders believe business should have a social purpose, while another study shows that 90 percent of business leaders understand the business importance of purpose.[2]

But what is this mythical purpose? Is it really any different from a vision or mission statement, things business leaders have been creating forever?

Since there's no universally agreed upon definition of the term, here's mine: purpose-driven business envisions business as a force for good, a force with the power to change the world around it and to deliver tangible improvement to human life and the environment. It doesn't just deliver a rational or emotional benefit to an individual customer or consumer; it also contributes to the collective good. It delivers profit, as it delivers value to all of a company's stakeholders – not just shareholders.

It's not that these Giants don't care about profit; on the contrary, they absolutely do. But they regard profit as an outcome of achieving their purpose, not as the reason they exist. And a mounting body of evidence suggests that this philosophy is part of what *enables* them to outperform their profit-oriented counterparts on multiple measures including – you guessed it – profitability (they also delivered for shareholders, with their share price on average outperforming a set of conventional comparison companies by 11.7 percent per year every year over five years).[3]

But it's not just my nine study companies. In their book *Built to Last*, Jim Collins and Jerry Porras documented that organizations driven by purpose and values outperformed the market 15 to one and outperformed comparison companies six to one.[4] More recently, a study by the consulting firm EY found that businesses that prioritize purpose outperform those that don't across multiple measures including innovation and growth.[5]

So where did it all go wrong? Why are we so convinced that purpose and profit are fundamentally competing forces? The answer can be traced to 1970 when Nobel Prize-winning economist Milton Friedman published his seminal essay 'The Social Responsibility of Business Is to Increase its Profits.'[6] In it, he described people who advocate for the social responsibility of business as "Socialists." Friedman's essay declared that the exclusive purpose of business is to increase its returns to shareholders and that employees should engage exclusively "in activities designed to increase its profits."[7] It dismissed the notion that business has any other social responsibility as "a fundamentally subversive doctrine."[8]

The publication of Friedman's essay is regarded as the moment at which the belief that social responsibility and profit are competing agendas hardened into fact in the minds of the business community. His legacy casts a long shadow. Today, growing profits and maximizing shareholder returns are (erroneously) taught as *the* purpose of the corporation in almost every leading business and law school in America (and to a lesser degree in Europe and beyond). Surveys show that after completing an MBA, students are even more likely to see shareholder value as the most important goal of the corporation.[9] This has become our dominant business ideology.

But what if Friedman was wrong?

Compare Friedman to the founder and CEO of one of my Green Giants, Ingvar Kamprad of IKEA. On December 20, 1976, about 30 years after he founded IKEA, Kamprad published *The Testament of a Furniture Dealer*. In the 14-page document, Kamprad committed his company's purpose to paper: "To create a better everyday life for the many people by offering a wide range of well-designed, functional home furnishing products at prices so low that as many people as possible will be able to afford them."[10]

Peppered with language like "democratization," "protest," and "mortal sin," and with exhortations to "contribute to the process of democratization," the *Testament* reads more like a political manifesto crossed with a religious tome than a private sector strategy document. The word "responsibility" appears 18 times. In the *Testament*, Kamprad boasts proudly, "A well-known Swedish industrialist-politician has said that IKEA has meant more for the process of democratization than many political measures put together."[11]

Kamprad is very pro-profit; "profit is a wonderful word!" he writes.[12] But in his world-view, profit is not created for its own sake but rather to enable IKEA to better pursue its purpose. "A better everyday life for the many people! To achieve our aim, we must have resources," writes Kamprad in the profit section of his *Testament*, which is titled "Profit gives us resources."[13]

How has this 'socialist' philosophy served Kamprad? In 2012, he was estimated to be the richest person in Europe and the fifth richest in the world (this has since been revised to the 495th richest, according to an IKEA spokesperson, because Kamprad created two foundations that now own the company groups, Inter IKEA Group and the IKEA Group, and foundation statutes bar him and his family from benefiting from its funds).[14] That must make him one of the most successful businessmen of all time. Take that, Professor Friedman.

Why purpose drives profits

With the philosophical piece out of the way, let's turn to the practical side of purpose: *why* it drives profits. There are three key reasons why a social purpose drives profitability:

1. Purpose = plan
2. Motivated people
3. Loyal customers

Purpose = plan

The problem with a north star of 'build profit' is that it doesn't tell you how you're going to do it. It's like me saying my purpose in life is to get really rich. Fine. But how am I going to get there?

Students of Jim Collins' *Good to Great* are familiar with the Hedgehog Concept. Collins writes that 'Good to Great' companies have "a simple, crystalline concept that guides all their effort" and he identifies having a clear concept as one of the key factors that "drives business greatness."[15] The 'Hedgehog' terminology is derived from an essay by Isaiah Berlin who compared the hedgehog to the fox. "Foxes pursue many ends at the same time . . . never integrating their thinking into one overall concept or unifying vision. Hedgehogs, on the other hand, simplify a complex world into a single organizing idea, a basic principle or concept that unifies and guides everything," Collins explains.[16]

The purpose statements of Green Giants function as their Hedgehog Concepts. They provide the clarity of the single organizing idea, and this clarity of concept guides clarity of action.

Tesla has a lofty purpose, but Musk made the purpose practical by translating it into a deceptively simple plan, which he summed up in a 2006 blog post '*The Secret Tesla Motors Master Plan*' as follows:[17]

1.   Build sports car
2.   Use that money to build an affordable car
3.   Use that money to build an even more affordable car
4.   While doing above, also provide zero emission electric power generation options

So far, barring several controversial delays, Tesla has stuck to the plan with uncanny discipline. Remember, this entry was posted over a decade ago, in 2006. In 2018, Tesla is in the midst of grappling with steps three and four (as I type, Tesla had just exceeded its self-defined goal of producing 5,000 units per week of mass-priced Model 3, a feat naysayers doubted it could pull off).[18] Tesla checked the box on steps one and two (the Roadster, with a price of $100,000, was followed in 2012 by the Model S, starting at $62,400 – certainly a more 'affordable car.') At the time of writing, Tesla's market cap was $5 billion greater than that of General Motors, despite selling many times fewer cars. It seems the plan is paying off.

IKEA is similar. *The Testament of a Furniture Dealer* captures IKEA's purpose and outlines the strategy that flows from it. It's all in there: the importance of low cost, the primacy of efficient design, the benefit that size brings to purchasing relationships, and the avoidance of waste – all packed into 14 pages, written almost 40 years ago. Even though IKEA has grown to a company with €34.1 billion in 2017 retail sales since the *Testament* was written, the document remains, quite recognizably, the operating system of the business.[19] IKEA has stayed the course with its purpose and remained absolutely faithful to the master plan – even outliving its author.

A plan alone is, of course, not enough. You have to stick to it with the kind of focused discipline Tesla and IKEA have displayed.

"There is nothing mushy about [purpose] – it is pure strategy," Harvard Business School Professor Hirotaka Takeuchi has said.[20] "Purpose is very idealistic, but at the same time very practical."[21]

Motivated People

At an advertising awards dinner in 2014, actor Jerry Seinfeld gave a speech. "Spending your life trying to dupe innocent people out of hard-won earnings to buy useless, low-quality, misrepresented items and services is an excellent use of your energy," he told the assembled representatives of the marketing industry, with only a hint of irony.[22]

The quote got a ton of buzz among my Facebook friends, many of whom are in the advertising industry, in part because it cut a little too close to the bone. It's the reason, back in 2006 when I was a brand planner at the agency, I asked the then-CEO of Ogilvy New York if I could build a sustainability practice. As I often say, I couldn't go on selling people stuff they didn't need for a living. I needed to find my purpose and pursue it through my work.

Today, many employers are unlocking the rewards purpose provides. A passionate purpose attracts – and retains – passionate people. Employees of purpose-led companies I've interviewed and worked with are more like disciples than staff members.

A mounting body of data backs this notion up. Employees who derive meaning and significance from their work were found to be more than three times as likely to stay with their organizations.[23] Employees who say they can make an impact while on the job report higher levels of job satisfaction than those who can't by a two to one ratio. And it's even more pronounced among the generation who became the majority of the workforce as of 2015: Millennials. A study found that 83 percent of graduate school students would take a 15 percent pay cut to have a job that seeks to make a social or environmental difference in the world; 97 percent want to work for a green company.[24] As the influence of Millennials grows, demands on employers to match their need for meaning will too.

When employees believe in your purpose, their motivation is intrinsic, not something you have to bribe them to have. I've watched clients at companies all over the world 'get religion' about their work once a purpose has been defined. They get that fire in the belly for which there's no substitute. They embrace your purpose because it's their purpose too and they want to succeed – together.

Loyal customers

In August 2014, a Long Island couple, describing themselves as "two VERY highly satisfied Tesla customers," took out a full-page ad in two Palo Alto, California, newspapers to publish an open letter to Elon Musk, whom they called an "Automotive Visionary."[25] "Thank you for building the great American car," they said, going on to offer suggestions to make the car even better, including moving the cup holder, addressing the car's blind spots, and running a marketing campaign to create "many additional enthusiastic Tesla owners." Musk responded to them on Twitter within the day, promising to address their requests.

Tesla's blog features posts from many passionate owners. On August 7, 2009, for example, a former U.S. Naval officer, John McEwan, posted an ode to his new Model S and its purpose, titled *'Promoting National Security Has Never Been So Much Fun.'*[26] In it, McEwan expresses his joy at being "liberate[d] from foreign oil and wild price fluctuations at the pump."[27] He compares his Model S to "the first horseless carriage or the first radio or first television or the advent of the personal computer, fax machine, cell phone, or even the Internet itself . . . It represents the fundamental paradigm shift that will define the twenty-first century."[28] He loves the car's performance but he loves that the performance comes with purpose even more.

A passionate purpose and the products it produces attract passionate consumers. I have a client who moved to Edinburgh, Scotland, from New York. He's a vegetarian, can't eat gluten, and is a hard-core sustainability advocate. When he visits New York, he heads straight to Chipotle for a veggie burrito bowl (they don't have Chipotle in Edinburgh). The team knows we'll be eating Chipotle every day for a week when he's in town, but I don't get too many complaints. My client loves Chipotle because it's delicious and has vegetarian and gluten-free options, and even more because its purpose aligns with his values.

He's not alone. There is a growing body of evidence that what people are looking for from brands has radically changed. We no longer want simply to buy products; we want to buy into a purpose. In fact, 90 percent of consumers around the world want the brands they do business with to share their core values.[29] In addition, 87 percent want a more meaningful relationship with brands, and 87 percent believe that business needs to place at least equal weight on society's interests as on business interests.[30]

Indeed, public relations firm Edelman's 2015 brandshare research identified what it called a "new need state": societal need. This is defined by behaviors like "uses its resources to drive change in the world," "takes a stand on issues I care about most," and "lets people know the company's mission and vision for the future."[31] The research found that meeting a societal need doesn't just contribute to making people feel warm and fuzzy; it actually drives hard business outcomes, delivering an eight percent increase in intent to purchase, a ten percent increase in likelihood to defend the brand to detractors, a 12 percent increase in likelihood to recommend, an 11 percent increase in likelihood to share personal information, and a 12 percent increase in sharing branded content.[32] Again, this is a trend that is more pronounced among Millennials.

And by the way, consumers have no problem with you making money out of purpose; 76 percent of global consumers believe it is acceptable for brands to support good causes and make money at the same time, a 33 percent increase globally from 2008. In fact, when quality and price are equal, the most important factor influencing brand choice is purpose, outpacing design and innovation and brand loyalty.[33]

Many other studies have yielded consistent findings. The bias is especially pronounced among a social group that one firm names the Aspirationals. Representing a third of the global population, Aspirationals are defined by their love of shopping (93 percent), their desire for responsible consumption (95 percent), and their trust in brands to act in the best interest of society (50 percent).[34] "Aspirationals represent a powerful shift in sustainable consumption from obligation to desire," says Raphael Bemporad, cofounder and chief strategy officer at brand innovation consultant BBMG, one of the report's authors.[35] In other words, people want to buy from purpose-driven companies. These people can also be powerful advocates; nine in ten Aspirational consumers also say they encourage others to buy from socially and environmentally responsible companies.[36]

Customers of purpose-led brands are believers, allies, and advocates – not just consumers. A purpose confers crucial competitive advantage in an otherwise prevalent culture of brand ennui. In a world of marketing where one study found that people around the world would not care if 73 percent of brands disappeared tomorrow (the figure is 92 percent in the United States), and think only one in five brands make a meaningful difference in people's lives, purpose can mean the difference between commercial success and complete irrelevance.[37]

Conclusion: Friedman versus Fink

A social purpose is anything but anti-business. Done right, purpose can be a driver of profitability for brands, not a barrier to it. It can be a spur to innovation of both new product lines and new business models. It can build trust and foster authenticity in an age when people have lost faith in a business world they see as out to screw them. It can give brands in commodity categories new stories to tell while unlocking new target markets. Consumers feel the vibe and respond by granting brands greater emotional resonance.

In today's world, purpose = profits.

The Purpose Paradox proves there is nothing sacred about the Friedman ideology, a doctrine that holds profit and social good as competing objectives. Friedman's thesis is just that – an ideology – and business dogma changes all the time. It is changing now.

Consider this: In 1981, legendary former GE CEO Jack Welch gave a speech at New York's Pierre Hotel entitled *'Growing Fast in a Slow-Growth Economy.'*[38] Welch did not use the specific term 'creating shareholder value' in the speech, but it was unabashedly profit-first, and it is viewed (along with the Friedman essay) as the other defining moment in the formation of the shareholder value movement. Shortly thereafter, Welch set GE's mission: to be the world's most valuable company.

He was wildly successful at it. During his tenure, GE's value rose 4,000 percent. One of his primary leadership directives was that GE had to be number one or number two in the industries it participated in. He fired the bottom-performing ten percent of managers every year. GE had 411,000 workers at the end of 1980, just before he took charge, and 299,000 at the end of 1985. His policies earned Welch the moniker 'Neutron Jack,' but *Fortune* magazine named him 'manager of the century' in 1999.[39] Welch maximized stock value, then retired, no doubt taking his retirement pay in stock.

Then, in 2009, about eight years after he retired from GE, Welch did what appeared to be an about-face, telling the *Financial Times* he never meant to suggest that boosting a company's share price should be the main goal of executives. "Shareholder value is the dumbest idea in the world," he said. "Shareholder value is a result, not a strategy."[40]

Welch did not go so far as to embrace purpose, and it's not entirely clear what precipitated his pivot. But when the guy credited with inventing shareholder value renounces it, it's probably time to look for a new business philosophy.

Then, in 2018, BlackRock's iconic and highly influential founder Larry Fink, and maybe the closest thing we have to a modern-day Welch, sent shockwaves through the business and shareholder communities with his annual shareholder letter. He wrote, "Society is demanding that companies, both public and private, serve a social purpose. To prosper over time, every company must not only deliver financial performance, but also show how it makes a positive contribution to society."[41]

There isn't a boardroom in America that didn't sit up and take notice. But Fink's stance is not motivated by morals alone. He's protecting his firm's and his clients' assets. Remember the Purpose Paradox: increasingly shareholder value and social and environmental value will be delivered via the same strategies. Fink has seen the data. And he's betting the farm on purpose. The rest of the shareholder community would do well to follow his lead.

We are in the midst of a battle for the soul of business. And while it's too soon to declare a winner, one day soon, we may wake up to discover that a new generation of billion dollar brands has taken over and that Milton Friedman's idea of business has gone the way of the dinosaurs.

2   The new brand-consumer contract

Tectonic shifts and new tenets

Sam Hornsby

Sam is founder and CEO of TRIPTK, a leading strategic insight and brand consulting firm that operates at the forefront of culture, commerce, and creativity. TRIPTK's global studios of researchers, strategists, designers, data scientists, and cultural theorists help brands to learn, grow, and transform. Sam's lifelong learning has woven anthropology and business, and his passion for human cultures has brought him to live and work across Europe, China, and America. He specializes in bringing businesses closer to the people and cultures they serve, creating true shared value with customers, and has partnered with dynamic companies across sectors including Diageo, Marriott International, VF Corporation, PepsiCo, Google, and Viacom. Sam sits on the board of Mission, the world's first philanthropic fashion media brand. An ocean lover, he will soon sail the Atlantic to raise funds for environmental projects. He lives in Brooklyn.

★ ★ ★

For a growing number of consumers, the foundation of trust upon which the big brand promise is predicated is eroding. To escape this accelerating crisis, brand owners must re-orientate to their 'consumers' as people and their 'markets' as communities, and they must engage these stakeholders as equal partners in the creation of shared value.

The old brand-consumer contract has been predicated on an 'us and them' mindset that still persists in many traditional brand-marketing organizations. It has bred all manner of structures and hierarchical assumptions reinforcing an unequal relationship between corporate 'producer' (up here) and the passive receiving 'consumer' (down there). The result to this day is a widespread cacophony of didactic brand messaging and willfully pernicious sentiment ("I wouldn't feed that to *my* kids, but then I'm not the target"), much of which is reinforced by subtle structural factors; from corporate HQs in affluent suburbs, to the cost-cutting shift to in-house creative agencies with an inevitable thirst for the Kool Aid.[1]

Increasingly, frustrated and skeptical individuals are no longer willing to engage with companies on this basis or take their promises at face value when exchanging precious dollars for goods and services. The same marketing-media complex that has given rise to the 'almighty brand' has cultivated a mighty consumer-lobbyist, all too happy to vote with their wallets, walk with their feet, and tweet-rally their constituents to negotiate a better and fairer deal.

To succeed in striking this new deal, the purposeful brand owner must rigorously enact a contract of shared value creation with people and their communities, one built on actions not words and guided by an organizational culture of empathy. Re-writing the contract requires brave leaders and a humanistic approach, one increasingly embraced by successful brands in which employees and customers, not just shareholders, are the focus of value creation – for the sustainable enrichment of all.

The tectonics impacting the contract

It's no coincidence that the widespread call for 'purpose-led' and 'social-impact' brands has arisen alongside the slow but unmistakable dawn of a modern socio-political crisis.

Why, we might wonder, is so much of contemporary brand marketing so overtly political? Today it's not uncommon for household goods brands to tackle political topics from gender inequality and gay rights, to social-health issues like mental illness, in their campaigns. While some of this work is substantiated by action (and undoubtedly plenty of good intent), much is cause-related bandwagon branding with little integrity – or little integration into the business itself. A case in point: Audi's 2017 Super Bowl ad declared the need to put more women in the metaphorical driver's seat, only for the company to then be exposed as having no women on their board.

The cultural underpinnings of this phenomena represent a pronounced shift. We are experiencing a deep deficit of trust in our institutions, wrought by the information age and an atomized society. In the absence of alternative moral or political touchstones, brands are – quite ironically and opportunistically – filling the void, walking the tightrope of consumer backlash in the hope of accruing good will in a post-modern ideological free-for-all.

The trust-deficit that's turning brands into soap-box political players has been decades in the making. If much of the twentieth century was marked by the exercise of statecraft and the tolls of war, our current era represents one of market-craft in which the corporate conglomerate – and the brand – reigns supreme. The gains have been gargantuan. Almighty brands contribute billions of dollars of value to the market caps of industry disruptors and incumbents alike.

Yet after flourishing largely uncontested for years, the dominant economic-political narrative and its mantra 'let the markets decide' has stumbled on an inescapable dilemma: that compound growth and endless, blind consumption could well spell our downfall as a human community. We're now emerging from decades of economic growth and its significant benefits on one side, with a host of challenging issues on the other; weakened national and community institutions, dire social alienation, record inequality, an abundance of 'stuff,' and, for many, an inability to respond to the crisis around us with anything other than resigned hedo-nihilistic consumption.

Meanwhile, in brand marketing meetings the world over, discussing these 'trends' has been a frenzied preoccupation. Sat atop the conference table in these conversations has been a consistent scapegoat, 'The Millennial.' A tremendous glut of data, statistics, and heavily researched papers now highlights the changing values of the Millennial consumer: their unprecedented marketing exposure and savviness ("they receive 5000 brand messages a day!"), their preference for brands that demonstrate positive values ("84 percent of them do!"), their desire for 'transparency' and 'authenticity' and so on across thousands of PowerPoint decks. (Respite from the implications of these traits usually involves the gleeful observation of idiosyncrasies amongst a whole generation reduced to themes: "they profess to care about social issues, but look – they don't give more to charity!").

This preoccupation with generational 'trends' has obscured the view of brand organizations and their agencies from the truly tectonic undercurrents at play in the changing brand-consumer contract, and their own role in forging an environment in which brand promises are no longer worth the packaging or billboards they're written on.

Demonstrating purpose and practicing socially minded corporate governance is thankfully now coming to be recognized in the C-suites of major businesses as a mission critical mandate.[2] Yet this powerful and necessary impetus runs serious risk of becoming mere internal-speak or re-cast CSR unless approached wholeheartedly and earnestly as the creation of true shared value. Creating this shared value requires investment in insight functions, in deeply understanding community priorities and challenges, and in the holistic utilization of resources: not just financial, but cultural and creative. In this, brands obtain elevated value – in people's lives, in the cultural and social world, and in their bottom line. To realize this value, we must admit that the brand-consumer contract is not just broken, but beyond repair. We don't need more trends reports, we need a new contract.

The tenets of a new brand-consumer contract

When approaching brand endeavors, brand operators can choose to recognize the following six tenets as a basic Heads of Terms.

1. Partnership > promises

The brand recognizes that the consumer is a genuine partner in the creation of the contract, not merely a person to be persuaded. Instead of focusing on promissory messaging, the brand will identify and generously cultivate value for the consumer by improving their lives.

2. *Co-creation > creation*

The brand recognizes that offerings and experiences are more likely to meet real needs when co-created with end users, partners, and key stakeholders. Instead of innovating in a vacuum, the brand will practice systematic and continuous co-creation, which recognizes participants as agents in a process of value creation.

3. *Community citizen > co-opting*

The brand recognizes that it is embedded within an interconnected and diverse community that includes employees, consumers, and interest groups. Instead of treating people as cohorts to be co-opted, the brand will act as a positive community citizen.

4. *Solving > selling*

The brand recognizes that it possesses unique resources able to help solve real challenges; not only financial but assets of intellectual and cultural capital. Instead of superficial or myopic problem resolution, the brand will strive to solve genuine problems and meet true unmet needs.

5. *Actions > words*

The brand recognizes that the meaning of words and brand messages without accompanying, substantiating actions perpetuates mistrust in it and all brands. Instead of taking action to be 'claimed,' the brand will take meaningful actions with the goal of building affinity and equity in the long term.

6. *Windows > mirrors*

The brand recognizes that audiences expect and deserve a window into the brand organization and its operating principles. It subscribes to the 'if it can't be shared, it should be changed' mentality. Instead of holding up aspirational mirrors to the consumer, the brand will offer transparency and honesty.

Re-writing the contract

The brand marketing industry is in no shortage of talent that can rebuild the consumer contract and have a positive impact – indeed it continues to attract creative and ambitious minds in droves. In my career and role at TRIPTK I've been fortunate to partner with some of the most powerful and forward-looking brand organizations in the world, including those featured in this book, on initiatives to enliven legacy brands and create new ones fit for our times. A consistent theme in successful initiatives has been the presence of brave brand owners and managers with the backbone to resist short-cuts, the vision to build brands beyond quarterly targets, the genuine empathy for their brand community, and the deep felt trust that no good action goes unrewarded.

In practice, these brand leaders live the tenets of the new contract and embrace the fact that striking this new deal represents much harder work than business-as-usual. When recognizing the consumer as a partner they prioritize feedback loops across the brand development cycle. When innovating they co-create holistically to bake community value into product and service DNA. When solving problems they take inspiration from the tool-kits of grassroots organizations. They realign budgets and strategic emphasis from words towards actions and brand behaviors, and when messaging is important they celebrate brand content that has rich, semiotic value and tells layered, meaningful stories. These leaders push their brands to break the bubble of the brand-media complex and show up in the real places and environments that matter to their communities. As clients, they value insights and engage consultancies as objective partners in the short-and long-term maintenance of a consumer contract.

The impact of these brand leaders should be lauded, and followed. Increasingly, we can see the commercial success of brands that over-index on re-writing the contract, even if short-termist industry data and tracking have not caught up.[3] Of course, change is constant and these new tenets can be always improved on. I propose the new tenets of the consumer contract not as a check-list but as ideas that can inform the activities of an ongoing organizational culture. Adopting these ideas will take significant investment of time and capital as well as an overdue evolution of outdated industry infrastructures (a process that will surely come with growing-pains). But the tectonics that have brought us here are not reversing any time soon, and we must adapt.

Conclusion: the power and perils of purpose

The tendency of the big brand complex can be to confuse semantics with substance. This is no less true of the recent notion of 'purpose.' Purpose has excited the industry, in part because it acts as a short-cut to the tenets of the new consumer contract – it responds to the same cry for more responsible corporate brand governance – and it can be a hugely motivating and powerful single-minded concept to galvanize the employee community. Because it provides this neat vehicle for business owners to bake positive corporate values into brand development, every brand seemingly *must* have a purpose today.

But as with any new concept, we must ensure that we employ purpose for its substance, not its semantics. In particular, purpose falls flat when it is undertaken without understanding of the tectonic undercurrents that make it essential.

Without this context, purpose – an evergreen mission that can guide all organization activity, including brand-building – can all too easily end up as mere words on a page, confused with a myriad of other brand frameworks (especially 'positioning') and trotted out and claimed as 'proof' of brand values in communications. Building a purposeful brand is categorically not the same as running ads with a social purpose message, and at TRIPTK we've been fortunate to help many companies identify, enshrine, and apply their purpose as an organizational operating system. This is the difference between jumping on trends and responding to tectonics, the difference between a broken and a strong consumer contract, and the difference between failure and success in our new social reality.

3 Ethical dilemmas and purpose-led decision-making

Do the right thing for whom?

Frank J. Oswald

Frank J. Oswald has been on the faculty of Columbia University's Master of Science Strategic Communication program since 2010, where he currently teaches classes in communications ethics and persuasion. Oswald has led the development of corporate, investor, and marketing communications programs for leading brands for more than 35 years. His clients have included a broad range of global companies, from Accenture to Yahoo!, as well as startup businesses, academic institutions, and nonprofit organizations. He has an M.S. in strategic communication from Columbia University, and a B.A. in journalism from the University of Wisconsin – Madison, where he was a Harry J. Grant Milwaukee Journal scholar.

★ ★ ★

Though it may now sound strange, you once needed to obtain a blood test to apply for a marriage license. My heart begins to race just writing that sentence, because I suffer from vasovagal syncope, which is a fancy way of saying that I get lightheaded, and have even passed out, at the sight of a hypodermic needle. My condition is so extreme that I had to make three trips to a blood-testing center before I had the nerve to 'go through with it' before my own wedding.

So I remember feeling emancipated in the summer of 2014 when I first read that Theranos, a Palo Alto-based company I had never heard of before, was launching a revolutionary technology that could perform comprehensive blood tests with a tiny finger prick instead of an intravenous blood draw. Elizabeth Holmes – the company's enigmatic 30-year old founder – envisioned a day in the not-too-distant future where there would be "a Theranos center within five miles of almost every American and within one mile of every city dweller."[1]

Holmes' story was compelling: Theranos' technology would not only help healthcare providers and patients save billions of dollars in expensive lab costs, but it also had the potential to save millions of lives by helping to diagnose diseases earlier and more reliably. She referred to the company's compact and sleekly designed miniLab as "the iPod of blood-testing equipment" and started dressing in black turtlenecks and slacks, earning her the nickname "the next Steve Jobs." Former U.S. Defense Secretary William Perry – a member of Theranos' megastar-studded Board of Directors – one-upped that comparison: "She has a social consciousness that Steve never had. He was a genius; she's one with a big heart."[2]

Although Holmes quickly became known as the youngest self-made female billionaire in the world, it was her altruistic DNA ("this is about being able to do good") that impressed me.[3] I was preparing course material for a communications ethics course and Theranos sounded like one of a new breed of companies that embraced 'conscious capitalism' – a catchy term that John Mackey, the founder of Whole Foods, helped popularize in a book by the same title. Describing what he called an "awakening," Mackey wrote, "I have learned that we can channel our deepest creative impulses in loving ways toward fulfilling our higher purposes, and help evolve the world to a better place."[4]

In increasingly glowing media profiles, Holmes explained that her father had always instilled a higher purpose in her, too. "I would much rather live a life of purpose than one in which I might have other things but not that," she told the New Yorker.[5] Holmes further personalized that pitch at a TEDMED conference in the early fall of 2014, telling a story about a beloved uncle who died suddenly, and without warning from cancer. "We see a world . . . in which no one ever has to say, 'if only I'd known sooner'" she told the audience, "A world in which no one ever has to say goodbye too soon."[6]

Holmes' message resonated far beyond the conference hall. Her purpose-led appeal helped recruit more than 800 employees (including top talent from Apple and other tech giants) to work at Theranos at its peak in 2015, as well as a who's who list of venture capitalists and board members. The company won multi-million-dollar contracts with Walgreens and Safeway and began rolling out its blood-testing systems to pharmacies and grocery stores across the United States. A virtual unknown only the summer before, Holmes became one of the most widely lauded CEOs in America. In April 2015, Time named her in its list of the 100 most prominent people in the world.

Behind the scenes, however, a very different story was playing out, as John Carreyrou began reporting in The Wall Street Journal in October of that same year. Theranos' technology could only perform a fraction of the blood tests that Holmes had publicly claimed and the company was actually conducting a majority of testing on equipment made by other manufacturers. To make things worse, tests conducted on Theranos' own equipment were often inaccurate, potentially putting patients' health and lives at risk. Employees who spoke out were told to toe the line, quit, or be fired. "If anyone here believes you are not working on the best thing humans have ever built or if you're cynical, then you should leave," Holmes said in a speech to employees.[7]

Holmes' eventual undoing (she was indicted of defrauding investors, banned from operating laboratories, and barred from serving as an officer or director of a public company for ten years) was almost as fast as her rise to fame. I was stunned by the sudden turn of events and by how easy it was for Holmes to deceive me and other far smarter people. It was a genuine 'wait . . . what?' moment that pierced the perception that today's new breed of purpose-led companies, by their very nature, operate on a higher ethical plane than those of previous generations. Over the next two years, controversial decisions and actions at a wide range of purpose-led companies from Airbnb to Unilever further deflated that notion.

For the leaders of these businesses – and those who aspire to be like them – the lesson should be clear: while purpose commands great power, it demands even greater responsibility. Purpose-led companies and brands are not immune to ethical dilemmas; in fact, they may be even more vulnerable to them due to conflicting demands from multiple stakeholders, including the public. This chapter will examine that dynamic and offer an ethical decision-making framework to help you achieve the promise and avoid the perils of managing a purpose-led brand.

Everyone is talking about purpose. What does it mean?

"Life is never made unbearable by circumstances, but only by lack of meaning and purpose."

—Viktor E. Frankl

Viktor Frankl's *Man's Search for Meaning* – a meditation on the power of human will, drawing on Frankl's experience as a concentration camp prisoner during the Holocaust – helped me get through college in the late 1970s. One passage, in particular, is as meaningful to me today as it was then: "The more one forgets himself – by giving himself to a cause to serve or another person to love – the more human he is and the more he actualizes himself."[8]

As personally inspiring as that sentiment was, it was far from the business world I entered in 1979. Back then, a majority of companies still abided by Nobel Prize-winning economist Milton Friedman's famous dictum: "There is one and only one social responsibility of business – to use its resources and engage in activities designed to increase its profits so long as it stays within the rules of the game, which is to say, engages in open and free competition without deception or fraud."[9] Displays of corporate social consciousness – like handing out giant bank checks at charity events – were often done for what many cynically called 'PR purposes.'

While the terms 'mission' and 'purpose' were used back then, most corporate missions were interchangeable axioms about 'exceeding expectations' and 'building shareholder value.' The first time I recall the word purpose being used in a more inspiring way was in 1994 when James C. Collins and Jerry I. Porras published the book *Built to Last*. Defining what they called "visionary companies," the consulting team wrote: "Yes, they seek profits, but they're equally guided by a core ideology – core values and a sense of purpose beyond just making money. Yet, paradoxically, the visionary companies make more money than the more purely profit-driven comparison companies."[10]

Collins and Porras defined purpose as "the set of fundamental reasons for a company's existence beyond just making money" and led the movement, still in vogue today, for companies to develop short, pithy purpose statements.[11] Walt Disney, for example, defined its purpose in just four words: "to make people happy." According to the authors, successful companies needed to "export" their purpose and values to all of their operations around the world. While those concepts sound commonplace today, they were groundbreaking in the late 1990s. Business strategy meetings were often dominated by discussions about the organization's BHAG (Big Hairy Audacious Goal), another term that Collins and Porras coined.

Entering the new millennium, fueled by increasing concerns about climate change, the rise of green consumerism and an influx of young, dynamic leaders at successful startups, a new business mindset began to form and along with it a greater social conscience. Companies of all sizes and across all industries started talking about Corporate Social Responsibility and triple-bottom-line reporting with growing seriousness. B Corporations (a private certification) and Benefit Corporations (a for-profit legal entity) took social responsibility one step further, requiring organizations that seek those designations to include making a positive impact on society, workers, communities, and the environment among their explicit goals.

Today, I believe the *denotation* of being 'purpose-led' remains generally true to what Collins and Porras defined more than two decades ago. But the *connotation* (what we perceive the phrase to mean) has evolved greatly to include this rise in social consciousness. To unscientifically gut-check that supposition, I emailed a dozen colleagues, from both business and academia, and asked them to define what a purpose-led brand means. Though the responses varied more than I even expected, there were several common threads that weave nicely into a single definition:

- A purpose-led brand is one that can "clearly articulate the relevant role it plays in addressing society's needs" and "whose integrity is affirmed by its ability to improve the world."
- These brands understand that, above all, "their cause is at their core." That cause should guide their "strategic vision and decision-making" and employees must "work to ensure that their every action supports that direction."
- Purpose-driven brands "focus first on helping people versus producing profit" and "recognize their impact on the world transcends the immediacy of their products, benefiting mankind in explicit ways."
- The constituents of purpose-led brands – employees to consumers to fans – "can participate in the pursuit of that role and relevance through their interactions with the brand."

This was the 'ideal company' I was searching for when I began my career. Based on my teaching experience, I also know that these are also the kinds of companies that smart, talented young people want to work for today. Furthermore, it's been shown that when consumers share the same purpose and values as a brand, it influences their purchase decisions;[12] there's even research that suggests that people with a strong purpose live longer.[13]

But the popularity of purpose (Amazon sells more than 30,000 books with 'purpose' in the title) has led to the misappropriation of the word by many people and companies. The proliferation of purpose experts, purpose conferences and puffy, say-nothing purpose statements (e.g., 'helping to improve tomorrow's world today') have exacerbated the problem. Brand marketers beware: consumers who felt deceived by greenwashing can become just as distrustful about 'purpose-washing,' too.

Bottom line: as inspiring as being purpose-led sounds, purpose is not a panacea, and purpose-led organizations are prone to the same kinds of ethical challenges as profit-led ones. Purpose-led brands that claim to benefit society but appear to act in a contrary fashion not only risk their own reputations but can fuel consumer skepticism about whether purpose is just the latest business buzzword or, worse, a marketing ruse. Recognizing why many of these ethical dilemmas arise is the first step toward avoiding them.

The feel-good cliché that masquerades as a moral compass

Shortly after Google was founded, the company adopted the swashbuckling motto "Don't Be Evil." Larry Page and Sergey Brin reiterated that pledge in a refreshingly conversational letter that preceded Google's IPO:

> Don't be evil. We believe strongly that in the long term, we will be better served – as shareholders and in all other ways – by a company that does good things for the world even if we forgo some short-term gains. This is an important aspect of our culture and is broadly shared within the company.[14]

Although not everyone fell in love with the phrase, it stuck, and the uniqueness of its tone added authenticity to Page and Brin's promise that Google would not be a conventional company. That all changed in 2014 when Google became Alphabet and replaced its quirky moral compass with the prosaic "Do the Right Thing."

In fact, once you start looking, you'll find those same four words employed by growing numbers of companies. Wells Fargo, for example, integrated "We do the right thing, in the right way, and hold ourselves accountable" into the bank's Code of Ethics and Business Conduct after being exposed for widespread customer account fraud. Likewise, when Uber sought to polish its image after ousting CEO Travis Kalanick in 2017, the ride-sharing giant released an ad that featured new chief executive Dara Khosrowshahi saying, "One of our core values as a company is to always do the right thing." Uber codified that statement in the company's revamped cultural norms with the emphatically punctuated "We Do the Right Thing. Period." The ubiquitous axiom was echoed by Salesforce's Chief Equality Officer, Tony Prophet, in an interview for *Fast Company*: "We're an institution in society and we have a responsibility to do the right thing. Over the long arc of time, when you do the right thing for the planet, it will be good for you as a business."[15]

As uncompromising as these statements may sound, the tough question they often ignore is "do the right thing for whom?" (Figure 3.1) For shareholders? For employees? For customers? For society and the common good? The collar-tugging conundrum that senior leaders have to face every day is that 'the right thing' for one constituency is the 'wrong thing' for another.

Figure 3.1 Profit-led companies can always default to shareholder needs and demands; purpose-led companies have far more complicated decisions to make.

When those conflicts arise, companies that operate on a profit-led model can always default to defending shareholder value and their bottom lines; purpose-led companies have far more complicated decisions to make. Every time a constituency feels wronged by a decision, it creates an opportunity for that group to inflict damage to the company's brand by wielding its commitment to 'do the right thing' like a double-edged dagger.

In the spring of 2018, Google employees challenged the company's vow "to make the world better" after word spread that the tech giant was developing artificial intelligence (AI) tools for the U.S. military. More than 4,000 employees signed a letter urging Google CEO Sundar Pichai to cancel the project, stating "We believe that Google should not be in the business of war."[16] Googlers reportedly pasted "Do The Right Thing" bumper stickers throughout the company's New York office; many refused to work on the project and more than a dozen outright quit. Acceding to employee concerns, Google developed a set of AI development principles, including a pledge to only work on AI projects that are "socially beneficial" and not develop AI applications for use in weapons.[17] Shortly thereafter, employees at Microsoft and Amazon protested their respective employers' contracts with the U.S. Immigration and Customs Enforcement agency (ICE), directly pitting the demands of employees against those of customers, investors, and the government.

Following the fatal shooting of students and faculty at a Florida high school in February 2018, Dick's Sporting Goods stopped selling assault-style firearms and urged the U.S. Congress to embrace "the right thing to do" by passing effective gun-violence legislation.[18] A number of companies followed suit; among them, Bank of America announced it would cut ties with manufacturers of assault-style weapons, earning widespread praise. A month later, it was BofA in the crosshairs when the company participated in a loan to help struggling gun maker Remington Outdoor Co. out of bankruptcy. While the loan had been in the works prior to the bank's pledge, vocal gun-control advocates accused the bank of lying and putting people's lives in danger, while shareholder advocates argued it was BofA's obligation to make profitable loans. The bank closed the deal and then quietly sold the loan.

Non-profit organizations with social missions increasingly face similar conflicts. Should an organization committed to the public good take money from companies or individuals that aren't? Should you accept sponsorships from groups whose politics or views on social issues differ significantly from those of your membership? For some organizations, these questions are beyond consequential, they are existential because they need every possible dollar of support to keep their doors open.

The inconvenient truth is that while purpose-led brands often earn greater public recognition, they're also subject to far greater public scrutiny. Even what appears to be the most insignificant decision on paper can have an insurmountable impact when played out in public. Meeting these higher social expectations requires an ethics-based decision-making process.

An ethical decision-making framework for purpose-led brands

The first thing you learn when you begin teaching an ethics course is that no one thinks they need to take an ethics course. The second thing you learn is that because there are so many different ethical models, students often simply choose the one they find most personally advantageous and then develop rationalizations for their decisions. The same is true in business.

For example, while most people instantly agree that it's wrong to lie, they're just as quick to point out that there are exceptions, like not wanting to hurt a friend's feelings or protecting a family member from harm (the subject of countless debates about Kant's Categorical Imperative). Parallel reasoning may have been employed at Theranos, as lying about its blood-testing technology became akin to protecting its own child. Furthermore, Holmes may have rationalized that 'fake it until you make it' was just the way that all Silicon Valley startups operated.[19] Applying a utilitarian argument, she also could have persuaded herself and others that the promise of saving millions of lives tomorrow far outweighed the risks posed to far fewer patients today.

In situations like these, decision-makers often fail to recognize the myriad ethical dimensions of their actions. Some even cling to their rationalizations after they're exposed. An early Theranos investor who lost $500,000 continued to call Elizabeth Holmes a "great icon" long after the founder's dramatic downfall and chastised critics by saying, "we're eventually going to change healthcare as we know it, and she will have had a huge hand in making that happen."[20]

The fact is any single-lens method of ethical analysis can mislead decision makers – and that includes the single lens of purpose. To avoid that problem, purpose-led brands should consider adopting a decision-making process (Figure 3.2) that integrates different ethical models to analyze and resolve potential issues from multiple perspectives. Without delivering a weighty lecture on competing ethical philosophies here, I've broken that system down into five sequential steps:

1. Employ empathy

As Max H. Bazerman and Ann E. Tenbrunsel illustrated in their excellent book *Blind Spots*, we fail to recognize many of the ethical dilemmas embedded in a given decision. That's why it's crucial to begin any decision-making process by asking: 'Who are all the different people or groups who could be impacted by this?' By expanding your aperture of empathy in this way, you'll often discover your decisions impact far more people than you first considered. Employing empathy doesn't mean you need to concede to the concerns or demands of all of these audiences. It merely means acknowledging without judgment that your actions could impact the lives of many others – potentially significantly.

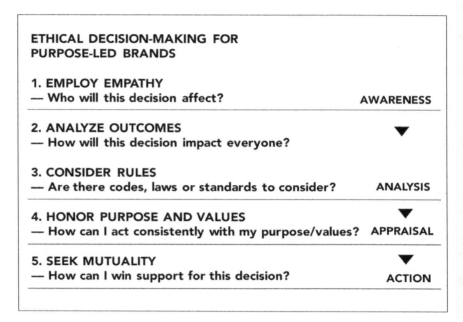

Figure 3.2 To avoid ethical blind spots, purpose-led brands must consider the impact of decisions on all of their constituencies – and then analyze that impact from a variety of perspectives.

2. Analyze outcomes

What are the potential positive and negative consequences of your decision on the groups you've identified? This includes short-term and long-term consequences, which are especially crucial for purpose-led brands that promote a long view of their impact on society and the world. Once again, it is imperative to keep this analysis objective and independent of your own needs. Imagine, for instance, sitting behind a "veil of ignorance" (a term coined by American philosopher John Rawls) and you don't know to which of the groups from Step 1 you belong. The purpose of this step is only to identify and analyze different potential outcomes, not to draw conclusions from them.

3. Consider rules

In my four decades in business, no five words have been a bigger red flag to me than, 'We're not doing anything illegal.' Purpose-led brands have to think far beyond what the law requires them to do and evaluate everything from professional and human rights codes to rapidly evolving social and cultural norms. The 'rules' that companies must play by today go far beyond avoiding "deception and fraud," as Milton Friedman once evangelized. In addition to failing that simple litmus test, it is unsettling to acknowledge that Theranos' management did not even abide by the centuries-old medical oath: "first, do no harm."

4. Honor purpose/values

The very term 'purpose-led' can suggest 'purpose first,' as if purpose absolves your organization from considering its other responsibilities. But that auto-drive manner of decision-making can often lead to unintended results. Instead, the purpose-led decision maker needs to weigh all of the considerations in the previous steps and then ask: 'How can we best honor our purpose and values in this situation?' If this process is conducted with a creative problem-solving mindset, it can often generate group solutions that go far beyond the binary alternatives that individuals and organizations consider when managing a conflict.

5. Seek mutuality

There's no such thing as an everyone-wins solution, especially for purpose-led organizations. But you can involve affected parties, both during and after the decision-making process, to seek buy-in or, at the very least, common ground. This is especially important for public companies that must continually balance meeting 'this quarter's expectations' with the much longer-term needs of their organizations and society.

If you've ever taken a course in ethics, you're likely to associate elements of each of these steps with different ethical models: Step 1 (Ethics of Care), Step 2 (Utilitarianism and Egalitarianism), Step 3 (Deontological Ethics), Step 4 (Virtue Ethics), and Step 5 (Dialogical Ethics). But rather than seeing these as competing philosophies, which is how they are often taught, I believe they can be used as complementary analysis tools, helping purpose-led companies evaluate all dimensions of an issue before making a decision.

Putting purpose-led decision-making to the test

Published more than 20 years ago, Howard Schultz's *Pour Your Heart Into It* is still one of the best books on branding I've ever read. Early in the book, Schultz discusses how Starbucks aimed from the outset to become the 'Third Place' in people's lives – "a comfortable, sociable gathering spot away from home and work, like an extension of the front porch."[21]

In April 2018, that purpose was put to the test when two African American men were handcuffed by police and removed from a Starbucks in Philadelphia's Center City following a complaint from the store's manager that the men, who had not made a purchase, refused to leave. The men had also asked to use the bathroom but were turned down, consistent with the store's policy of only admitting paying customers. The incident, which was captured on video and shared on social media, made Starbucks an instant target for protests about social injustice and racial discrimination in America. The company was also attacked by critics across media, including Twitter users who launched a global #BoycottStarbucks movement.

Rather than merely issuing a corporate apology (which it did), Starbucks acted in a far more purpose-driven way by recognizing that the issue impacted many groups – including employees, customers, and local communities – and not just shareholders. Perhaps most importantly, it had become a societal issue and a flashpoint for tensions that extended far beyond the brand's stores. To better understand those issues, the company engaged in discussions with those affected parties and worked with prominent authorities (including former Attorney General Eric Holder and Sherrilyn Ifill, the president of the NAACP Legal Defense and Education Fund) to begin addressing the issue in a comprehensive way.

Openly admitting its failure to live up to its long-held purpose as a Third Place, Starbucks acted on a variety of fronts, including redefining 'customer' as any guest (regardless of whether they make a purchase), changing its store policy regarding bathroom use, and closing 8,000 stores in the United States for an afternoon (at an estimated cost to shareholders of $12 million) to conduct racial sensitivity training it aptly titled "The Third Place: Our Commitment Renewed."[22] Going one step further, Starbucks made those materials available to everyone online and the company continues to engage in dialogue with experts and customers alike for how it can improve its operations and help engender a more civil society.

Other purpose-led brands, including many featured in this book, are employing similar holistic decision-making processes to resolve issues and make tough choices in situations when their values are challenged. Before Airbnb launched its Community Commitment to address discrimination by hosts on its platform, the company's management critically evaluated its own culture and initiated sweeping changes to increase diversity of its own workforce and suppliers (see Chapter 8). This type of process can also be used to avert issues, rather than merely respond to them, which Hyatt demonstrated in deciding to release a poignant but potentially controversial ad that featured the Rev. Martin Luther King just days after a white nationalist rally turned violent in Charlottesville, Virginia (see Chapter 5).

Purpose-led decisions, like these, aren't without risks or consequences. For example, while Starbucks' actions were applauded, critics and customers alike have questioned whether the company's new policies could compromise their own Third Place experience if tables and bathrooms fill up with unpaying guests, which could alienate paying customers and negatively impact sales. Rather than a rebuttal of purpose-led decision-making, this new challenge serves as a prominent reminder that brands that pursue this path must continuously monitor both the intended and unintended consequences of their actions across constituencies. Without this ongoing commitment, purpose-led brands can fall victim to questionable behavior just as easily as profit-led ones.

4 Measuring purpose
From organizational commitments to social impact

Matthew Quint

Matthew researches, writes, and shares knowledge on a wide range of issues critical to building a strong brand, including marketing ROI, strategies for marketing in the digital age, and how to develop creative and effective brand communications. He is also thrilled to produce and host the acclaimed BRITE Conference which brings together big thinkers from industry and academia to discuss how innovation and technology help organizations build and maintain strong brands.

★ ★ ★

While growing up, Legos were *the* toy for me.[1] I spent countless hours crafting and re-crafting houses, cars, space ships, and dozens of other things. The basic building blocks from any Lego set could be turned into anything one's mind could imagine, and that made them incredibly special.

At age 11, I used all of my holiday money to purchase a new Lego castle set. Upon opening it, I discovered that not every piece was a standard building block. And there weren't just new types of building blocks, but pieces that were fully shaped items: a drawbridge door, a turret spire, and even a section of the castle wall. I was crushed. It was the last Lego set I ever bought or asked for as a gift.

I didn't know it at the time, obviously, but this was the first crystalized brand experience of my life; an experience tied directly into one part of this new, multi-dimensional business term, purpose. The purpose of Legos, I would argue, was 'creative re-construction' but this set, and almost every other set I would see in the store from then on, had pieces that served only one function.

This, and other moves of the company, seemed prudent as globalization, the rise of cable television, and the growth of video games were occurring in the 1980s and 1990s. Lego continued to do well financially – despite the shock of losing me as a customer. From standard business measurements of the time, the company saw no near-term indicators that straying somewhat from its purpose might hurt the brand.

Thirty years ago, most companies had no way to measure the nuanced impacts of a commitment to, or a straying from, purpose. They couldn't, for example, effectively track individual customers and see from this data if historically loyal customers, or if certain customer types, were starting to slip away despite strong overall sales figures. There was no Twitter, Facebook, or Reddit to monitor for insights on customer and public sentiments about a product or a brand. And, there wasn't the same level of rubric among human resource departments and top management to examine employee satisfaction and engagement.

In 1998, however, traditional business metrics let Lego know something was afoot as year-over-year profit and revenue declines began. By 2004 the situation had become so drastic that, for the first time since its founding in 1932, the company hired a non-family member as CEO, Jorgen Vig Knudstorp.

Not surprisingly, Knudstorp laid off staff as an initial effort to help stem Lego's losses. But, as the *Daily Mail's* James Delingpole reported in his 2009 article, there was much more at the core of Knudstorp's strategy:[2]

> Besides staff, Lego reduced by half the number of Lego components. While once there were nearly 7,000, they're now down to around 3,000.
>
> Above all, though, Knudstorp's plan meant trying to rediscover the essence of Lego – and remembering that it's a toy. To this end he wrote down what he calls his Moments of Truth:
>
> 1. When it's advertised, does it make a child say 'I want this?'
> 2. Once he opens the box, does it make him go 'I want more of this?'
> 3. One month later, does he come back to the toy, rebuild it and still play with it? Or does he put it on the shelf and forget about it?

In other words, Knudstorp was trying to get the company to rediscover its purpose – that idea of 'creative re-construction' – and use that to drive profit. In doing this, he went on a 13-year run of year-over-year sales and profit increases.

How do we know this recommitment to Lego's core purpose drove more than a decade of financial success? We don't, exactly. But in this chapter, my purpose (sorry, had to do it) is to provide guidelines around three ways purpose is incorporated into an organization and what techniques could be applied to measure its impact. I will not offer a detailed and specific methodology to be followed by all firms. Nor will I highlight a 'golden' metric to evaluate the effect of purpose. What follows is an examination of a range of metrics that can be connected together to help a purpose-led organization or brand evaluate how these commitments are impacting its stakeholders.

The value of purpose

In a recent *Harvard Business Review* piece on connecting profit and purpose, CMOs from Lyft, SAP, HP, Clorox, Juniper, Sephora, and Visa all expressed the value purpose can provide to a company.[3] They cite the benefits of streamlining decision-making, inspiring employees, and meeting customer expectations. In 2015, Ernst & Young, in partnership with the *Harvard Business Review*, released a study on 'The Business Case for Purpose,' which surveyed 474 executives on 'shared purpose' and 89 percent agreed that it would drive employee satisfaction, 80 percent agreed it would create greater customer loyalty, and 85 percent would be more likely to recommend a business with a shared purpose to others.[4]

What is valued must be measured. But in considering metrics around purpose, one of the biggest challenges is that term – like so many marketing, branding, or business buzzword terms – hasn't had the benefit of a concise and formal definition; hence the creation of this book. But no matter how much more precisely one tries to define the term, we must recognize that it will be used, or interpreted, slightly differently by every organization.

Take, for example, the multi-part definition of purpose in the E&Y/HBR study – one that I believe encompasses the broad industry use of the term and the way it is generally formulated in this book: "an aspirational reason for being which inspires and provides a call to action for an organization and its partners and stakeholders and provides benefit to local and global society."[5] Such a definition presents measurement implications for how "aspirational" the purpose is, whether it truly drives "organizational action," assessing which stakeholders are affected by it and how much, and under what rubric is the organization "benefiting local and global society."

In addition, most CEOs or CFOs who commit to being more purpose-led will also require seeing metrics that correlate the effect of purpose on big picture KPIs such as year-on-year revenue growth, profit growth, customer growth, market share, firm valuation, etc. One of the first attempts at offering a shareholder value assessment of purpose-led brands came from Jim Stengel's collaboration with Millward Brown and its BrandZ data in his 2011 book, *Grow*. With this data, Stengel identified 50 high growth brands – outpacing the S&P 500 by 400 percent from 2001–2011 – and found that "each brand was built on an ideal of improving lives in some way, irrespective of size and category."[6] However, in a 2017 editorial piece in *The Drum*, a further analysis of the 26 brands with stock offerings among the Stengel 50 showed that from 2012–2017 only nine of the companies beat the S&P 500.[7] And here we see the value of examining purpose-related metrics. Did these companies stray from their purpose? Is purpose less impactful than Stengel argues? Or, were other factors at play affecting investor commitments to these companies? Possibly a commitment to purpose required a near-term management sacrifice from some of these companies – forgoing new market entry, switching a supply chain, adjusting a product price, etc. – that worried investors.

To develop effective measurement thinking for a term with such nuance, I believe it is beneficial to consider three levels in which purpose is used by organizations:

- *Purpose as an organizational aspiration*, historically defined through terms like vision/mission/values, that guides decision-making about management decisions, employee actions, and partner expectations
- *Purpose as a higher order commitment* to benefit local, regional, or global society, and assessing possible trade-offs to revenue or profit necessary to accomplish this
- *Purpose as executed more narrowly* within a specific brand, service, product, or social initiative

On measuring purpose as an organizational system

In many circles, the 'aspirational reason for being' (or 'North Star,' or 'Why,' etc.) is the core element of purpose that organizations develop. As Montgomery notes in the introduction to this book, businesses have long defined elements of "purpose" already through "mission, vision, values" statements. What is different now, driven by the accessibility of information in the digital age, is a commitment to be simultaneously inward-and outward-facing in formulating a core purpose of an organization.

To envision this transition to purpose, think of a company placing its 'mission, vision, values' beliefs – its functional and emotional components – into a crucible to bond them together into a more streamlined organizing principle that makes it easier for the company *and* its stakeholders to evaluate its products, services, and experiences against. In some cases, companies have now added a top-level purpose statement to their traditional 'mission, vision, values' statements. In other cases, slight adaptations have been made to 'mission' or 'vision' statements to reflect a more purpose-driven sentiment for all stakeholders.

Just how meaningful, distinguishing, and society-driven are these 'purpose statements?' Looking at a few corporate examples, many 'purpose statements' offer only subtle, but potentially important, distinctions from the table-stakes requirements that a company offer great products or services to its customers:

- Amazon's mission is to be Earth's most customer-centric company where people can find and discover anything they want to buy online.[8]
- [Apple's] products connect people everywhere, and they provide the tools for our customers to do great things to improve their lives and the world at large.[9]
- Facebook's mission is to give people the power to build community and bring the world closer together.[10]
- Southwest's purpose is to connect people to what's important in their lives through friendly, reliable, and low-cost air travel.[11]
- Over 23 years later, Chipotle's devotion to seeking out the very best ingredients we can – raised with respect for animals, farmers, and the environment – remains at the core of our commitment to Food With Integrity. And as we've grown, our mission has expanded to ensuring that better food is accessible to everyone.[12]

Each of these companies clearly note some aspirational drive – "discover anything," "improve their lives and the world at large," "bring the world closer together," "connect people to what's important in their lives." Importantly, though, we see here that only Chipotle has included more precise terms about benefiting society as part of its purpose via phrases like "raised with respect for animals, farmers, and society" and "ensuring that better food is accessible to everyone."

Measuring the effects of a purpose commitment at this aspiration level doesn't require inventing too many new metrics, but rather coordinating many standard business metrics to connect to purpose-related evaluations. Firms must also remember that the value of a commitment to purpose is not always apparent in the short-term, but is more often delivered over the long haul of an organization. So measurement evaluations of purpose must look at year-over-year-over-year trends.

At the organizational level, the primary area of purpose analysis should be employee metrics – recruitment, satisfaction, retention, decision-making – since this 'aspirational' part of purpose is most tangible internally.

As Carol Cone, CEO of Carol Cone ON PURPOSE, notes from her 30 years working with brands of all kinds on CSR and now purpose, "This business impact element of Purpose is strongly focused towards employee engagement, recruitment, and retention. Yet even more so, activating an authentic purpose and embedding it into organizational behaviors can inspire employees to maximize their commitment to their work."[13]

For companies focused on recruiting top young talent, Deloitte's Millennial Survey notes that,

> Over the past six years, Millennials – and now Gen Z – are acutely attuned to business' wider role in society . . . However, when asked what their organizations focus on, they cited generating profit, driving efficiencies, and producing or selling goods and services – the three areas they felt should have the least focus.[14]

Consumer metrics are a secondary area to track and financial metrics a tertiary element to examine. It is, of course, important to examine the impact of purpose beyond its effect on employees. A firm's important KPIs around consumer attitudes and behaviors, and their resulting business impacts, should also be connected to purpose-led decisions and communications as much as possible. There are many more confounding factors to consider when evaluating consumers and financial metrics, however, which is why they follow in importance to employee and recruiting metrics. If a purpose-led company delivers a product with superb functionality, that functionality may drive much more purchasing impact than any purpose-related elements of the organization. Or, for example, a change in fuel costs may have a much greater effect on profits even amidst a corporate purpose effort. As with measurements around brand that have developed over the past 20 years, the contribution of purpose to traditional KPIs must be teased out from the various other factors that affect sales and profit. See Box 4.1 for a summary of some of the key metrics that may be useful for any organization interested in evaluating how purpose is impacting the organization.

Box 4.1 Aligning business metrics with purpose

Some metrics around purpose should aim to specifically examine employee and external stakeholder understanding of a company's brand purpose and its delivery on that purpose. But, the true value of high-level organizational commitments must also be examined via traditionally important business impacts on customer growth and retention, revenue growth, and profit measures. Because of the confounding factors involved in other core business measures, it is valuable for firms to consider how much weight to give to each of these metrics in evaluating how much they are impacted by purpose – e.g., stronger weighting for direct perception metrics about purpose (among employees or customers), and most likely weaker weighting for financial metrics, such as revenue growth, which are often impacted by other measures (price changes, new market entrants, marketing spend, etc.).

Of course, as with any measurement effort, it is necessary to establish a baseline state (e.g., current employee churn rate or current customer sentiment to the company or brand). Then you must establish clear quantitative and qualitative purpose goals you want to achieve over a specific time period. Then, the use of many standard metrics will provide business guidance against which a firm can evaluate its commitment to purpose and the effects of that commitment. Where are trade-offs being made to follow brand purpose? And how are these trade-offs correlated with revenue growth, profit growth, etc.?

Employee, consumer, and business metrics are among a few to consider.

Employee metrics

- Survey of employee understanding of organization's purpose – using both aided and un-aided recall – and the ability to describe how the firm's purpose is executed in their role
- Employee satisfaction and willingness to recommend the workplace (e.g., placing in Fortune's Most Admired Places to work, rankings on Glassdoor and LinkedIn)
- Employee engagement in various firm-led content and experience offerings (e.g., reading newsletters from the firm, socially sharing content, attending firm social activities, attending firm volunteer activities, etc.)
- Employee decision-making – a survey analysis of choices made and their connection to purpose (i.e., were any top-line or bottom-line trade-off decisions influenced by purpose?)
- Employee recruitment and retention – is the firm able to hire and hold on to top talent?

Consumer metrics

- Consumer awareness of the firm's purpose – both via direct survey to customers, social listening analytics, and, if appropriate, proprietary brand analytics tools (i.e., Y&R's Brand Asset Valuator, Millward Brown's BrandZ, Interbrand's Best Global Brands, etc.)
- Consumer perceptions – brand lift, purchase intent, willingness to switch, etc.
- Customer willingness to recommend
- Customer acquisition and churn
- Changes in customer lifetime value – e.g., the rate of change in purchases from loyal customers
- Changes to brand sentiment among the public – e.g., press coverage, social media dialogue, reputation

Business metrics

- Revenue – adjusted for relevant increases in offerings and price
- Market share
- Market cap change or investor valuation change

CVS Health provides an interesting example to look at in terms of thinking about these purpose metrics, and the importance of considering a long-term view. In 2014, CVS made a conscious effort to view itself as a 'healthcare company' rather than merely a pharmacy, changing its name to CVS Health. The company now states its corporate purpose as, "Helping people on their path to better health."[15] How might the company then look at metrics around this purpose change?

On the employee end, there would be immediate opportunities to do surveys on the understanding of this new change (ideally, employee input would have been sought before the change to help ease the change management process as well, of course). Quantitative measures would be kept for employee engagement with any new online, or in-person, training or communications materials. Tracking would be set up in advance to look at online sources about workplace satisfaction (Fortune, Glassdoor, Indeed, etc.). And any employee-related social media posts, whether organic or suggested by the company, could be monitored.

An immediate decision-making metric was applied when the company announced in February 2014 (before the name change to CVS Health) that it would stop selling cigarettes and tobacco because it was incongruous with its developing new purpose commitment. In taking such a decision, leadership knew that the company would be hit with a few billion dollars a year in lost revenue.[16] This specific decision, and the broader purpose effort could then be analyzed against key consumer and financial KPIs.

In this case, the company had the benefit of getting so much press for the decision that Gallup did it a favor by running a poll on consumer awareness and attitudes weeks after the announcement to find that,

> More than eight in 10 respondents (81 percent) – including CVS shoppers and non-CVS shoppers – reported that they were aware of the company's proposed action. More than half of the respondents either agreed or strongly agreed that the decision helped them better understand CVS' mission and purpose (58 percent) and that the announcement helped them better understand what makes CVS different from its competitors (53 percent).[17]

From a financial perspective, CVS Health did bear a cost in the first year of the effort and generated a net income growth of just one percent in 2014. In 2015, however, the company was back to more than 12 percent growth in net income. In addition, shareholders appeared encouraged by the move with CVS jumping its stock price from roughly $67 on February 1 2014, to a peak of over $110 per share in July 2015. The company's shares in the summer of 2018 had dipped back down to the $60 – $70 per share range, however. Such a metric then allows the company to look at whether it is straying from its new purpose, whether it is still trying to fully realize this purpose (e.g., a pending merger of CVS Health and Aetna first announced in December 2017), or whether other factors in the retail and healthcare environment are affecting CVS Health and its category independent of its purpose commitment.

One other important distinction should be made here as well. Very often 'brand' and 'purpose' are tied together, and Montgomery even discusses the impact of corporate and consumer attentions to brands as drivers of this push towards more purpose-led organizations. For some organizations the corporate brand and sub-brand are heavily intertwined. But of course, there are other brand architectures in which sub-brands are named and managed as distinct units within an organization. Depending on such governance decisions purpose can be a trickier path to walk for an organization.

Take, for example, the path of Unilever over the past 15 years. Via its Dove brand, the company was one of the very first to drive purpose into a brand via its 'Campaign for Real Beauty' launched in 2004. The effort aimed to break the beauty care mold by highlighting the fact that the category had defined unrealistic beauty standards for almost all women. But amidst the Campaign for Real Beauty, another well-marketed Unilever brand, Axe, was simultaneously airing commercials full of young men using Axe and then getting the attention of the young and trim 'models' that Dove was critiquing as an unrealistic standard for women. Purpose can be quite powerful, but also difficult to maintain across every brand, initiative, and partner of large organizations.

But, it is clear that Unilever's leadership was influenced by its success in maintaining the purpose commitment of Ben & Jerry's (purchased in 2000) and making a category-risky commitment to launch the Campaign for Real Beauty. The 'Sustainable Living Plan' was launched by Unilever in 2011, and tracks corporate and brand commitment to improving health and hygiene, environmental impact, and workplace fairness.[18] It continues to bring more and more brands into its 'Sustainable Living Brands' portfolio – with 26 of 40 plus brands as of May 2018, including the Certified B Corporation brands Ben & Jerry's, Seventh Generation, and Pukka Herbs. It has noted consistently faster growth, in the 40–60 percent range, for the past four years among Sustainable Living Brands compared to others in the company's portfolio. Of course, this is exactly where tracking purpose metrics is important, as it allows the company to uncover the contribution of purpose to corporate and brand success amidst other factors like marketing spend, broad consumer purchase changes, new market entrants, overall category lift, etc.

On measuring purpose as social impact

Firms that follow through and connect purpose to delivering benefits to society and the environment represent a true change in business mentality. While Corporate Social Responsibility (CSR) is decades old, such measures have often been conducted completely independently of the core mission of a business – e.g., a philanthropic contribution from an energy company to the performing arts, rather than to an environmental sustainability effort. When CSR and business operations are fully entwined we see the realization of a purpose that provides "benefit to local and global society" as defined above.

The critical phrase assigned for years to CSR efforts was 'greenwashing.' Firms accused of greenwashing were attentive to a very limited social or environmental cause, touting such commitments as part of their marketing, but ignoring a full analysis of their overall impacts on society. While not yet universal, over the past 10–15 years, the corporate world – and much of the startup community – has been focused on providing a deeper analysis to every impact the firm has on society. For example, there are presently 980 participant companies, and another 3,000+ signatories, in the UN Global Compact, which has ten specific principles around human rights, labor, and the environment that these businesses pledge to follow.[19] Among these firms are many familiar multi-national enterprises like L'Oreal, Fuji-Film, Nestle, Bayer, Nike, Credit Suisse, etc. The Global Compact is, however, a voluntary commitment, and the UN does not have the resources to monitor these companies' performance on these principles.

One of the most robust metrics and measurement efforts in this area has been developed by the non-profit B Corporation (see Box 4.2). In collaboration with a standards advisory body made up of members of NGOs, academia, and corporations, B Corporation has built an assessment and analysis tool that examines how a company is performing in four areas; governance, workers, community, and environment. Undertaking an analysis of all of these measures can truly tie together the aspirational elements of being purpose-led with a detailed analysis of the company's success in benefiting society.

Presently there are around 2,500 'certified B corporations' in over 50 countries that have completed the assessment, with accompanying documentation of proof,

Box 4.2 B Corporation measurements

For organizations making the 'all-in' commitment to purpose, the metrics that are considered by B Corporation provide an interesting look at the level at which a company needs to incorporate social and environmental impact analysis and governance efforts. Sample questions from B Corporation's assessment tool regarding governance, workers, community, and environment include:[20]

- What portion of your management is evaluated in writing on their performance with regard to corporate social and environmental targets?
- Has the company worked within its industry to develop social and environmental standards for your industry?
- Based on referenced compensation studies, how does your company's compensation structure (excluding executive management) compare with the market?
- What is the minimum number of vacation days/sick days/personal days/holidays offered annually to full-time tenured workers (tenured defined as with the company for more than two years or life of the company)?
- Based on the results of your employee satisfaction assessment (conducted within the past 2 fiscal years), what percent of your employees are 'Satisfied' or 'Engaged?'
- What percentage of management is from underrepresented populations? (This includes women, minority/previously excluded populations, people with disabilities, and/or individuals living in low-income communities.)
- Are full-time employees explicitly allowed any of the following paid or non-paid time-off hours or options for community service?
- What percentage of energy (relative to company revenues) was saved in the last year for your corporate facilities?
- What percentage of energy used is from renewable on-site energy production for corporate facilities?

Other consulting organizations exist to help companies develop equivalent analyses as well, and organizations can develop such metrics themselves. There are numerous trade-offs – both challenges and opportunities – to this deep a level of commitment: communications decisions, partnership decisions, supply chain decisions, point-of-sale decisions, etc.

and scored well enough to be certified – relative to their firm size, industry, and geographic locations. Familiar brands with certification include Ben & Jerry's, Patagonia, Cabot Creamery, Etsy, Method, and Seventh Generation. What the folks at the B Corporation are most proud of, however, is the increasing number of companies using their assessment tools. Over 15,000 companies have completed a formal submission, and the organization notes that tens of thousands more have filled out the assessment tool.[21]

Another key point of the B Corporation effort was to incorporate the social impact efforts a company undertakes into its governance structure. As an example of how important this factor is, Warby Parker lost its certified B corporation status when its leadership and board decided not to go through the legal process to become a Benefit Corporation. Such a commitment "provides legal protection to balance financial and non-financial interests when making decisions – even in a sale scenario or as a publicly traded company."[22] These are the kinds of trade-offs required for purpose to represent a full commitment to societal and environmental impacts.

There are other examples of such analyses being done on the business impact of social purpose. In 2015, for example, Nielsen conducted its third Global Corporate Sustainability Report which analyzed the sustainability practices (via product claim on packaging and/or marketing tactics) for over 1,300 global brands and found that, "sales of consumer goods from brands with a demonstrated commitment to sustainability have grown more than 4 percent globally, while those without grew less than 1 percent."[23] Recognizing these types of impacts, the FSG Consultancy (founded by Prof. Michael Porter and Michael Kramer) spearheaded the Shared Value Initiative, which is "a management strategy in which companies find business opportunities in social problems," and includes partners such as Nestle, Walmart, Novo Nordisk, BASF, and Chevron.[24]

On measuring purpose by initiative

The aspirational and 'all-in' social purpose impacts noted above are constant, high-level commitments that must be viewed with a long-term lens. However, there is also huge value in looking at purpose metrics for individual products, services, and initiatives offered by an organization.

In fact, this is probably where most organizations can begin an analysis of their purpose efforts. The specificity of looking at one execution or initiative of an organization helps to take out many confounding factors. In addition, as noted earlier in the chapter, many companies will struggle to implement holistic elements of purpose due to the burdens of revenue generation, profit expectations, and investor pressure. As the head of business development for B Corporation noted to me in 2016, "a lot of young companies are eager to become certified, but we caution them that it is a very intensive commitment with fiscal trade-offs. We remind them that early on it is most important to keep the lights on, to build stability, and then work to become fully certified when it is fiscally viable."[25]

A specific product, service, or initiative should involve a precise tailoring of the measurement. For example, an initiative by a food company to help feed the hungry (imagine the purpose-led Chipotle) would involve specific strategic metrics. First, the company would establish a baseline measurement around food availability among the population being served. Then it would track process measures such as the volume of food supplied, the number of people receiving food, the demographic details of recipient populations, overall community and consumer awareness of the effort, awareness of existing and recruited employees, etc. Next, it would look at near-term annual measures of success such as reductions in attendance at the food pantries, lower volumes of food needed to keep pantry shelves stocked, engagement of new organizations partnering in the project, etc. Finally, over the long-term, the ideal would be to work with community and health partners, to measure the outcomes on the recipient population's 'overall quality of life' – i.e., whether they have better school attendance rates, employment rates, etc.

At a large corporate level take, for example, Coca-Cola's 'We are the Coca-Cola Company' campaign launched in the fall of 2017. This represents the first corporate brand marketing effort for the company. The commercial ties together a range of Coca-Cola's brands – from Honest Tea to Odwalla to SmartWater – and also connects the company's commitment to replenish water supplies for its global sales volume. This is a CSR effort begun in 2010 and monitored regularly by the company, but is something that its stakeholders may not be fully aware of.[26] Conducting pre-and post-campaign consumer surveys, analyzing social media statements and sentiment, and looking at changes in market share and stock price can help drive a better understanding of the effectiveness of this specific purpose campaign and provide insights on how to adapt future initiatives and efforts.

Conclusion: moving forward

As purpose is becoming an element of competitive strategy, one future challenge is handling the backlash effect when a fully holistic purpose-based company fails to deliver on its promise. Look no further than Chipotle for such dangers. The company is just now beginning to right itself from considerable financial impacts created by its E. coli contamination incidents in 2015 and 2017 – some elements of which were just bad luck, and some of which were probably caused by poor food preparation practices. Such a case demonstrates how crucial measurement efforts are, as that which is measured can be better managed. While accidental E. coli incidents can hit any food company, had Chipotle better measured employee commitment to its quality management practices it might not have failed on its own 'Food With Integrity' promise.

Additionally, true measurement effects of purpose should undergo more 'test and control' efforts. Look at the aforementioned Coca-Cola ad campaign promoting its water sustainability efforts. Such a marketing campaign around purpose can only be measured properly if put in context against other types of marketing efforts. A company should run an ad like that in a few markets, run a non-purpose-driven ad in other similar markets, and run no ads in a few other similar markets. This can provide better statistical correlations of the impact of the purpose-campaign on sales increases and social discussion within those regions.

Teasing out the effects of aspirational purpose efforts from how companies operated under traditional mission/vision/values will continue to be difficult outside of the effects on recruitment, retention, and employee satisfaction/engagement. There are so many confounding factors concerning quality, price, social trends, and competitor impacts that affect consumer perceptions and a company's financials. And it is unlikely that many firms will become as social-impact-driven in their overall purpose as Chipotle. So, the most impact measurements will come from initiative-specific efforts towards bettering society and the environment. It will be crucial for organizations to measure a combination of the direct impacts of the initiative – e.g., gallons of water saved, carbon emissions reduced, number of patients treated, etc. – and the spin-out effects to be gained from incorporating such efforts into broader marketing campaigns and product/service innovations.

The truth is that many of the deepest corporate commitments to social and environmental purpose were driven by an analysis of their likely effects on the bottom line, usually through efficiency increases, and on some rare occasions, through top-line revenue growth. Walmart and Target would almost certainly not be the two largest corporate suppliers of solar power in the United States if government initiatives hadn't made the amortized purchase and development of solar arrays on its stores, warehouses, and parking lots cheaper than just getting energy from the existing power grid.[27]

The future is likely to drive more companies to be purpose-led as social and environmental trends continue to have deep effects on their business. As Robert Candelino, then general manager and VP of Marketing for Haircare at Unilever, noted at my 2015 BRITE conference, "without clean, reliable water our supply chain would start falling apart and we would have no products to sell." Such changes require an immediate commitment to create metrics around purpose-led efforts, as only through measurement can smarter strategic decisions be made over time by these companies and their employees.

5 How to be a champion of purpose

Maryam Banikarim

Maryam is creative, wicked smart, a fearless risk taker, and someone who gets things done. Her natural born agility has meant that she has thrived in a variety of organizations, from large-scale corporate to early stage startup. In each case she has imaginatively applied a wide breadth of marketing tools to move the organization forward, creating value and inspiring employees, partners, and clients alike. Most recently as the global CMO at Hyatt Hotels Corporation, Maryam was responsible for helping Hyatt become the most preferred hospitality brand, driving loyalty and community among high-end travelers with a portfolio of 13 global brand experiences. Prior to this role, Maryam was Gannett's first ever CMO where she is credited with repositioning the company and its brands (including USA Today), uncovering and executing the company's core purpose, reinvigorating employee morale, and establishing a national sales organization, resulting in topline growth. In a few short years, she and the management team saw the stock price go from $13 a share to over $30. Maryam's can-do attitude was also essential at 'making things come to life,' successfully unifying and transforming both Univision and NBC Universal during periods of rapid transformation. Maryam's achievements have been widely recognized from The New York Post's *'50 Most Powerful Women in NYC,' to* Fast Company's *'Top 10 Disrupters,' to* Advertising Age's *'Women to Watch.' Additionally, she is recognized as a Woman of Distinction by the League of Women Voters of the City of New York, was honored by the Girl Scouts Council of Greater New York, and is a recipient of the Ellis Island Medal of Honor. After graduating from Columbia University's Barnard College where she was their first ever Truman Scholar, Maryam moved to Buenos Aires, Argentina to work on her Spanish, become a journalist, and learn to Tango. Upon acceptance to a dual program at Columbia University's Business School and International Affairs School, Maryam returned to New York to apply her infectious energy and drive to bring a voice and purpose to great brands.*

★ ★ ★

My career thus far has taken a curvy road. I've worked across different types of industries, different types of brands, and different types of business problems. But the challenges I've jumped into have always required making up new rules and taking smart risks in the face of change. At Univision, we needed to find a way to accelerate growth as sales – while still strong – were beginning to slow. I went to NBC Universal just as it was merging with Comcast and we needed to figure out how the combined companies would operate as one. When I joined Gannett – known then as the largest American newspaper publisher and the owner of *USA Today* – we needed to help the company navigate the continued decline of the print journalism industry. And, at Hyatt, we needed to address the disruptive forces impacting the hospitality industry.

In each of these business challenges, I was brought in as a 'fixer.' In each I was obsessed with growth, as all marketers must be, and used the entire toolkit of marketing at my disposal to help drive the business into the future. And in each of these cases, 'purpose' was a highly effective tool in my toolbox.

What is purpose and why should I care?

'Purpose' is an idea that has gained traction recently, but the concept is not always clearly understood. I want to start by clarifying what purpose is not. Though I sit in a marketing role, purpose is different from marketing. Sure, purpose can (and should!) be the basis of a powerful brand platform, but it's not simply a tagline, or external-facing 'we believe' statement. Purpose is also different from Corporate Social Responsibility (CSR). Purpose can and should guide how you give back to the community. But Purpose is about something much bigger.

Purpose *is* a company's north star. It's the direction that the organization is going and the difference that the company wants to make in the world. In more familiar business terms, it's the overarching strategy of a company that holds the organization steady and provides a filter for making all business decisions. Purpose fosters innovation, rallies the troops, launches marketing creative, and provides long-term orientation for all constituencies involved in the business.

Purpose is sometimes conflated with words like 'mission' and 'vision' but I actually find it's helpful to pull these ideas apart. They all mean something slightly different and a company's 'mission' and 'vision' are best seen as ideas dimensionalizing the overarching purpose, rather than terms synonymous with it. We can break it down this way:

> *Purpose:* Why do we exist? For Gannett, it's about "serving the greater good of the nation and the communities we serve." For Hyatt, it's about "caring for people so they can be their best." These are big, accessible, yet lofty ideas about the difference you want to make in the world.

> *Mission:* How will we fulfill our purpose? Our purpose may be lofty but our mission is down to earth. Mission is the practical *modus operandi* for delivering on purpose. It's about 'how' we're going to make our purpose come to be. Going back to our examples, for Gannett we fulfilled our purpose by "being on a relentless quest to provide trusted news and information and to actively support the people and businesses in the communities we serve." For Hyatt, we fulfilled our purpose through our mission of "delivering distinctive experiences for our guests."

Vision: What does the world look like if your purpose is successful? Visions are the utopias that are worth striving for. Like all utopias, we might not live in it tomorrow or ever, but it's the striving that counts. Gannett's vision is to create a world where the communities we serve are growing and thriving because of the difference we make every day. Hyatt's vision is a world of understanding and care.

These ideas are all connected, but the higher principle is purpose. Everything stems from and ladders up to that.

I always turn to Southwest Airlines as an example of the power of purpose done right. The airline business is an extremely competitive, commodity-based one, in which Southwest is a relatively small, disadvantaged player. However, with a clearly defined purpose, Southwest was able to defy the odds and see their business soar. Their 'purpose' is to give people the freedom to fly – "to connect people to what's important in their lives."[1] Their 'mission,' or how they make purpose happen, is to operate the lowest-cost, highest-efficiency airline in the world delivered by the friendliest people in the industry. Their 'vision,' or what the world would look like if successful, is a day when the skies are democratized and when everyone can go see and do what they thought not possible. This purpose manifested itself as a useful filter for business decisions. Southwest decided to get rid of blackout travel days, despite the financial implications, because limiting travel is incongruous with their purpose of freedom. This purpose was also incredibly valuable in helping the organization hire and retain the right people – people whose personal beliefs align with Southwest's and who consequently act instinctively on those values.[2] And, this purpose inspired their famous advertising with "ding, you're free to move about the country." When laser-focused on growing a business, identifying and deploying purpose is a critical part of the equation – and so it should come as no surprise that Southwest has experienced many consecutive quarters of growth.

Author and business strategist Jim Collins has done a great deal of research on the value of purpose and has proven that organizations driven by purpose outperform general market companies 15 to one, and outperform comparison companies six to one.[3] If you look at the data he offers, companies with purpose create greater revenue and have more satisfied employees. This financial return is also supported by Jim Stengel's work tracking 50 companies – all purpose-driven – that consistently outperform the S&P 500.[4] So though it might sound New Age-y or 'fluffy' to its critics, purpose is ultimately about growing a business.

In each business transformation I helped navigate, I've seen the power of purpose first hand. Sometimes I brought purpose to the business, like with Univision, NBC Universal Comcast, and Gannett, and sometimes I helped deploy purpose, like with Hyatt which had already gone down the path of identifying their purpose before I arrived. Other contributors in this book will break down in more detail how to identify and deploy purpose across an organization. What I hope to add to this conversation is a point of view on how to be a champion of purpose. How does purpose get brought to the table? How does it get set in motion? Who are the players? And how do you ignite a purpose movement across the organization?

Getting the green light

The impetus for starting down the purpose path takes many forms, but it always centers around getting the organization headed in the same, clear direction. This was the case at Univision where I first learned about purpose. We were looking to do a first-ever corporate branding campaign to elevate the company and accelerate growth in the media marketplace. We connected with Roy Spence, the founder of creative agency GSD&M (today, Spence is also the founder at the Purpose Institute). When Jerry Perechino, the Univision Chairman and CEO at the time, and I shared the creative brief with Roy, he came back to us and said, "I don't think this is about advertising. I think you need to figure out your purpose as an organization and I can help you with that." Roy had done the original Southwest purpose work and pointed to the immense value to their business. Convinced, we decided to go down the purpose journey with him. Jerry gave the project the green light and after that meeting it was up to me to ensure that we championed and executed against it.

Other purpose journeys are kicked off because of a pressing necessity. At Gannett, the bulk of our business, a publishing business, was under immense pressure. Not only was the business dissipating, but we also had a very demoralized employee base. The business results were depressing enough, but we also heard time and time again the sentiment that whenever our employees went to a party and told people they worked in the newspaper business people would give them a sorrowful look because everyone thought publishing was dead or dying. With my experience from Univision and NBC Universal, I proposed a purpose project to CEO Craig Dubow and COO Gracia Martore. It was clear we needed a way to re-engage and re-motivate our greatest asset – our employees – and remind them of the difference they were making in the world every day. It was Gracia who said, "I get it. If we can solve the morale problem, we can increase productivity and improve the business. But we need this to work!" No pressure. Craig and Gracia signed off, and my team led the charge to find and bring to life our purpose.

I've also seen purpose work launched to provide clarity, unification, and direction in times of change. This can be change at the organizational level, like in the case of my time at NBC Universal. The company was in the process of being bought by Comcast and we needed to understand who we were going to be once we merged. I ran the corporate agency at the time and said to Jeff Zucker, then CEO of NBC Universal, that I thought purpose work would help us figure out our new sense of self post-merger and how we could communicate this to make integration smoother. Jeff gave me the go-ahead and my team spearheaded the effort that launched day one of the merger, and was carried on by Steve Burke, who became CEO of the combined company.

Purpose is also valuable for navigating change at the industry level. This was the case with Hyatt. CEO Mark Hoplamazian had already recognized the potential of purpose to inspire and orient the global hospitality organization facing disintermediation, new competitors, and other new pressures in the industry. As Mark said, "I need to help the organization see the pressures on our business, and reassure them that we have a way to compete and win – with purpose." Since Hyatt's purpose was already uncovered when I got there, my team's task was to figure out how to deploy it globally.

From these purpose 'origin stories' in each business I worked for, I hope you can see a pattern emerging. Though the impetus to purpose was slightly different in each case, CEO green-lighting and buy-in was consistently critical across them all. In my experience, Purpose is a CEO imperative. The CEO is the one who sets the company's north star. But then there are many who help execute on that purpose – to bring it to life across the organization – and this requires a Purpose Champion.

Purpose is a team sport

While I happen to have taken up the task of championing purpose from the Chief Marketing Officer seat, I've seen purpose led by human resource leaders, innovation leaders, operations leaders, and others depending on the company and its players. As long as it's someone senior enough to be directly connected to the CEO, someone who believes in purpose, someone who will chase it like their life depends on it – the Purpose Champion can come from any discipline.

There are a few characteristics I've seen that are particularly critical for Purpose Champions to possess. The first is an instinct for action. If the CEO plays the lead advocacy role, the champion, as their right hand, must be a lead 'doer,' or activator. The Purpose Champion mobilizes people, liaises with the agency partners involved, and raises their hand to say 'how does this align with purpose?' in critical decision-making conversations. Great champions of purpose are also great listeners. Purpose must be authentic to an organization's people, and the Purpose Champion needs to hear the language, sentiments, and themes bubbling up and be insistent that the organization's purpose represents these views. I've often found that being an 'outsider' new to a business has been immensely valuable here since I was able to serve as an objective, unbiased, and empathetic listener. Finally, Purpose Champions must also be top-notch leaders. Purpose requires all heads of business to deploy and advocate, and it requires all employees around the world to participate and own it. A great champion of purpose is a cheerleader – captain – coach. Sometimes you cheer others on from the sidelines. Sometimes you authoritatively call the shots. Sometimes you are on the field leading the play – rolling up your sleeves and doing. A good Purpose Champion knows when to wear each hat, and how to wear it successfully.

At the onset, you need this senior, dogged Purpose Champion who 'gets it' and has a mandate from the CEO to bring their purpose agenda to life. In other words, the Purpose Champion needs to 'own' purpose. We all know 'owners' – when you're in a business they pick up slack no matter how big or small. We also know 'renters' – who think it's not their job or wait for others to do the work before them. To make purpose a reality you need someone who is an owner. Someone who will make sure the ball doesn't get dropped no matter what. At NBC Universal, for example, even though we had the green light from CEO Jeff Zucker to do purpose work, it took dogged conviction to actually get it done at a time when the company was being bought and when leadership was transitioning. We had to not only navigate NBC Universal but also Comcast, because we were doing the purpose for the combined entity. We worked hand in hand with human resources and communications across both organizations, being conscious of the political dynamics that were in play but also staying true to representing every brand within the combined portfolio. The project started with Jeff Zucker who was the CEO at the time, but was finished for Steve Burke, who was the incoming CEO – a tricky dance to say the least! But an important one to ensure that the work of purpose would live on as the CEO mantle was being passed. My role as the Purpose Champion here was to ensure that no one dropped the ball when there were so many things competing for CEO attention during this time of organizational transition.

The Purpose Champion never does this alone; he/she is always working with others to make purpose happen. Purpose is a team sport and picking your team is critical. Over the years I've had the privilege to work with so many incredible owners on purpose work. The team included many – so many I can't possibly name them all here. In fact, it's probably more of a small army than a team. But two key people, Debbie Goetz and Sandra Micek, have been on several of these purpose journeys with me and I am grateful for these two fervent purpose owners and evangelists. They are truly incredible. Debbie, Sandra, and I all had different roles wherever we went – the purpose team should never be clones of each other – but brought our different perspectives and styles together. For example, at Gannett, while Sandra used purpose to overhaul the USA Today brand inside and outside the company, Debbie used purpose to galvanize over 100 local and digital portfolio companies to work together with partners in ways they never knew possible. At the same time, I worked with human resources and investor relations to reframe the way we hired and retained talent, and evolved our positioning from a value to a growth stock.

It's the combination of all these efforts that allowed for a successful turnaround at Gannett. And this would not have been possible without the core team. This core team is made up of early adopters who can help cascade purpose throughout the organization – because at the end of the day, success depends on bringing others into the fold. Think of purpose like a movement: you need to find the right, resonant message and get people to believe it, adopt it, and then to champion it themselves. You know your job is done when purpose can live on and grow without you.

Building the purpose movement

For purpose to be successful it needs to be a people-led movement. The biggest part of the Purpose Champion's role is to create this movement at scale within the organization. This is probably the hardest part of the job. At Gannett our 30,000 employees were spread over 100 locations across the country, and at Hyatt we were

100,000 employees across 750 locations worldwide. How do you build a purpose movement and mobilize people across distributed organizations like these? The short answer is, "with amazing teams, partners, and employees." The long answer is a bit more complicated.

In my view, movements require three critical factors: *Resonance* (deep connection with and relevance for an intended audience), *Momentum* (sustained energy and escalation over time), and *Institutionalization* (ideas of the movement get embedded into the cultural infrastructure of an organization and become an instinctive part of everyday life). Having now started four purpose movements in four different organizations, I hope to share some lessons and best practices I've learned for finding resonance, building momentum, and institutionalizing purpose within the organization.

Finding resonance

Purpose work is most authentic when it comes from the inside out. You can't invent purpose, you have to find or uncover a truth that already exists. Here are some best practices for uncovering and communicating a resonant purpose.

Look for purpose in all the right places

In any company, there will always be people who believe wholeheartedly in the power of purpose, people who will never be ardent believers, and everything in between. When working to uncover purpose, you want to talk to the cross-section of the employee base that is the most motivated – that group who is passionate about what they do and already live your purpose every day. General managers are great resources to help appoint these individuals, who range from new employees to veterans and often self-select. When setting out to uncover purpose at Univision, we learned that our community relations colleagues (who answered the phone calls of local viewers and listeners and helped them with every day issues, from filling out medical forms or navigating school issues) already lived the purpose of our organization. Though they had little to do with programming at Univision, they reflected the 'connection' that Univision provided for its community, and this became the foundational anchor of our company purpose. These colleagues were simply passionate about what they do, and speaking with them helped us truly understand who we were *at our best*. Not to mention – they become invaluable local champions of purpose down the road!

Stories help make purpose feel 'by our people, for our people'

When we were trying to pull apart the difference between 'service' and our purpose of 'care' at Hyatt, collecting stories from our employees was an incredibly effective tactic to dimensionalize that nuance. A favorite we heard was from an engineer at the Grand Hyatt in New York City who had been fixing something in a guest room at the moment the guest discovered that her mother had just passed away. Our employee told us that in that moment he was no longer just an engineer. He responded as any empathetic person would – offering condolences and empathetic care. One year later to the day, the same engineer sent a note to the guest, saying, "Please know that my family and I think of you often and keep your memory alive in our thoughts and prayers. Sincerely AS." The guest was so touched that she took it upon herself to share her appreciation with us in a note that read, "I wept at this kindness. I know you can't train people to be this sensitive and kind. You just have to hire these one-in-a-million people." Sharing stories like this helps bring purpose to life better than any formal document ever could. Plus, everyone has these kinds of stories, and telling one can inspire others to share theirs.

Manifestos matter

Once purpose is identified, making a resonant 'manifesto,' or a short statement of purpose shared by all people in the business is hugely important to make sure everyone understands and connects with the purpose. Our 'credo' at the new NBC Universal was the following:

> We are in business to create and deliver content so compelling it entertains, informs and shapes our world.
>
> We believe that the talent, creativity and diversity of our people is our greatest resource. We emphasize teamwork because we are smarter, more dynamic and better together.
>
> We believe in doing the right thing and treating people the right way. We think integrity and honesty are the foundation of a productive working environment. We take our business seriously, but do not take ourselves too seriously.
>
> We are passionate about what we do and take pride in what we create. We have a pioneering spirit and are willing to take risks and embrace new technologies. We like to keep score and win.
>
> As we grow our businesses together, we will not just anticipate the future, but rather create, invent and deliver it.

At Hyatt, we landed on the following manifesto:

> What do you need? What can I do? So you can be your best, what can I do for you?
>
> As members of the Hyatt family, this is what we do. We put ourselves in someone else's shoes and use our judgment to do whatever must be done . . .
>
> To lift someone's spirits and lighten their load.
> To help someone prepare for a really big day.
> To practice a random act of kindness that makes all the difference.

We listen with our ears, our eyes and our hearts.
We read between the lines and do what can be done.
We may not be perfect. But that's ok.
Being authentic beats being perfect every time.

We believe in seeing what someone truly needs.
Be they family or friends, colleagues or partners, neighbors or guests . . .
Because a little more care, a little more kindness, a little more thoughtfulness
allows us to go above and beyond so that we can connect in just the right way.

This is our passion. This is our Purpose:
We care for people so they can be their best.

These two manifestos look and feel very different, but they were designed to reflect the spirit of the purpose identified at each organization. In both cases, we debated every word endlessly to capture the right tone, personality, and intention, and this finessing is so critical to help purpose sing and come off the page. Manifestos become a 'constitution' of sorts. It's a text we go back to to reinvigorate and remember why we get up and go to work and what we want to deliver each day. Beyond the text itself, the sight, sound, and motion of video are also incredibly helpful tools to put each manifesto line in context and help make the manifesto a living, breathing symbol.

Building momentum

Once purpose has been uncovered, the next step is to bring people on board as new champions of purpose. To help design this phase, it is critical to involve a small core team who really know the organization and how to motivate it, and who can call bullshit if anything feels off. At Hyatt this included my team as well as key operations members, the head of human resources, and the former head of marketing who was retiring but had worked at the company for over thirty years and knew the company inside and out. Key to the success of this journey was also our agency, SYPartners, which was instrumental in thinking through the strategy for deployment and also in executing against it. Here are some things I've learned about effectively escalating momentum around the purpose movement.

Make the need for change visceral

For the purpose movement to take hold and grow, it often requires behavior change within the organization. Since people inherently don't want to change you need to give them a reason to do it – and to do it urgently. At Gannett, everyone knew that change had to happen because the writing was on the wall for the publishing industry. While employees were skeptical, they recognized their jobs and the company were at risk and change was everyone's mandate. In that case, since we didn't have to do much convincing on why, we instead focused on how. By contrast, the need for change at Hyatt felt less urgent to most colleagues: everyone was making their numbers and the business was doing well. When we launched purpose, we needed to make clear the very real need to change given what was on the horizon for the hospitality industry. To this end, our launch event featured an immersive, museum-like audio-visual experience – which we affectionately called the 'hall of hell' – that presented real and scary statistics about how the momentum of disintermediation was dire. This was an incredibly visceral experience and woke many up to the imperative to change.

Launch purpose like a grassroots campaign

The way you launch purpose is a hugely symbolic moment and can set the tone for the movement. In my mind, the most important thing to reinforce is that purpose is *all of ours*. If purpose is everyone's it can't be something launched only to leadership with pomp and circumstance; it has to reach each and every person directly. At Hyatt, we launched purpose at a three-day event with global business leaders in Orlando, but by also setting up a 'news room' where each employee around the world could watch live and take part in the event remotely, everyone felt included. After our July launch event, the effort to reach each person continued as our VP of Learning and Development, travelled to different regions and hotels, hosting workshops on the ground to help people really make the idea of 'care' their own. These aspects of the launch were designed to give people permission to take ownership of purpose and buy in to the purpose movement on their own terms, rather than hearing it as a mandate passed down through the chain of command.

Leveraging local Purpose Champions

My experience has always been that – if you've uncovered the right purpose shared by people within the organization – the more freedom you give people to put purpose into practice in a way that is instinctive to them, the better. Again, I think it's important to note that you'll never get every employee to be an ardent believer in purpose, but tapping into the network of people that *do* fervently believe on the ground is critical to spreading the purpose movement. Many of these local champions were part of the purpose discovery process, representing the cross-section of the organization that already has the organization's purpose in their DNA. They will often act on purpose instinctively and with no instruction. At Hyatt, for example, after launching the purpose platform in Orlando these local Purpose Champions did things like broadcast our Global Town Halls in the cafeteria and bring people together to participate in and celebrate these moments. Some even took pictures of these impromptu events and sent them back to us to share throughout the organization. The organic, unofficial nature of these efforts makes them some of the most powerful purpose movement catalysts. As business leadership, our role is to empower these local champions. We would often have global calls to arm them with different tools and to let them know what we were looking for – stories, pictures, etc. For Gannett's 'Make a Difference Day,' for example, we gave local champions the basic building blocks to make getting their teams to participate as turn-key as possible. Importantly, this didn't mean over-proscribing activities. Instead, we encouraged them to run with it in a way that was authentic to their particular office. The point is to not weigh down local champions with process, but to instead empower them to run with their passion.

Regular touchpoints keep purpose top of mind

After launch, the momentum of the purpose movement is built by a series of symbolic moments. The role of the Purpose Champion is to build crescendos and momentum, to get the adrenaline for purpose pumping through the organization through touchpoints of different shapes and sizes. Sometimes there are small touchpoints, like activities put on by local Purpose Champions, or leadership modelling behavior change or purposeful action. Other times these touchpoints can be bigger symbolic moments, like a large-scale global purpose launch event or the release of a global spot. Especially with these big moments since there are so few, it is important to build engagements that help viralize purpose within the organization. When Hyatt launched the 'World of Understanding' campaign at the Oscars, for example, we sent a note to the whole company along with the video. Because they were proud of the work and felt it represented them, our 100,000 employees in that moment became 100,000 advocates and helped amplify the message by sending it to their address book. It was a really inspiring moment of unity and pride in our shared purpose. Delivering various types of touchpoints helps keep momentum so people don't go back to doing the same thing they were doing before once routine settles back in. Though you can't over-orchestrate the movement's growth, the Purpose Champion must be conscious of the 'purpose pulse' within the organization at any given moment and stimulate it when they can by empowering local champions and offering a number of meaningful touchpoints.

Embedding institution

At the end of the day, institutionalizing purpose is the most powerful way to realize its value as a growth engine. It's the thing that makes purpose more than parties in the cafeteria – it entrenches purpose within an organizational culture and develops instinctive purpose-led behaviors. There are many ways to do this, which others in this book will share. But here are a few best practices I've learned throughout my journey:

Actually use purpose to make decisions

Purpose is not just a manifesto to be read and revisited every once in a while. It is a powerful business platform that can act as a guide for decision-making. A favorite example here is another Hyatt one. I was in Zurich with the marketing team and a team member told me that she did a 'day in the life' at one of our hotels and was struck by how difficult it was to get your hair in the bun required for the job (there are many, many bobby pins involved). I then heard a similar sentiment from one of our employees who actually got a scalp infection from the bun's pins. This story struck me because, if our purpose is about care, this bun situation felt quite uncaring. I brought the bun issue to the executive committee, the head of human resources, and the on-site manager, and we decided to disband the bun policy because it was so contradictory to our purpose. I wrote an email to the woman who had told me the story (whose scalp infection had recovered at that point) to let her know of the policy change with the subject line "the bun is dead." 'The bun is dead' became part of the lore that circulated within the company and made clear that the feedback loop was open: if someone brings an issue to Purpose Champions, something will change. This helps us demonstrate that purpose is a walk we're willing to walk, and that's powerful.

Bring purpose into your organizational role

I hope to have made clear throughout this chapter that purpose isn't just about marketing. But to help institutionalize purpose, every leader of the business must bring it into their discipline and embed it into the way their teams create and operate. For me, this means bringing purpose into the marketing function and using our consumer-facing activations as a way of communicating our purpose to the world. A favorite example is the Hyatt Regency, one of the biggest brands in the Hyatt portfolio known for its large convention-style hotels. The brand was about to have its 50th anniversary and we wanted to create a spot cementing our brand as one about bringing people together – here, Hyatt's purpose of 'care' came to life through the understanding that comes from bringing people together to exchange ideas. As we were brainstorming how to authentically communicate this brand idea, we discovered an incredible story from 50 years ago. When Martin Luther King and the Southern Christian Leadership Conference were looking for a place to hold their annual meeting, they were turned away by every single hotel – except for the Hyatt Regency. The hotel opened their doors when others wouldn't. We created a spot where a brilliant spoken word artist talked about how coming together leads to understanding and we planned to launch it on the 50th anniversary of the day when Martin Luther King gave his speech at the conference in the hotel. But then the riots at Charlottesville happened just days before our scheduled spot launch. We were met with the challenge of whether to release the ad because we didn't want to seem like we were taking advantage of a terrible moment in American history. It is in moments like these where purpose kicks in. We decided we would show the same bravery shown by the organization 50 years ago and run the spot on the original date as planned even though it was right after the riots took place. We got great feedback from the press generally, but also from our employees who told us they were proud to work for a company that has such a long history of caring about people and important issues. Our purpose of care was brought first into the spot we created and then into our decision-making about when to launch it. For purpose to be successfully institutionalized within an organization, all heads of business must lead holistically with purpose.

Aligning human resources to purpose

Though it's important for all divisions of a business to incorporate purpose into their work, I've found that purpose becomes most effective once built into the human resources function. How can we bring purpose into the hiring, review, and rewards processes? At Hyatt, HR was charged with figuring out how to build purpose into how we recruited new employees, and how we reviewed and incented current employees. This meant that as an organization we reviewed and amended things like compensation strategies to make sure that we were rewarding people in ways that aligned to our purpose and values. Formalizing purpose in this way is a huge undertaking and it takes time. But in the end it's the critical element to take purpose from a movement to a way of life – to a lived and breathed organizational culture that can fuel company growth.

Conclusion

I consider myself very fortunate. I was fortunate to have been at the meeting with Roy Spence, where I first learned about purpose. I was fortunate to read the work of Jim Collins and see the possibility. I have been incredibly fortunate to work with several CEOs who saw the potential for purpose to move their business forward, and empowered me to champion purpose to help achieve that. And I have been fortunate to work with fantastic partners like Sandra, Debbie, SYPartners, and many, many others.

We are now all part of a 'club' that believes deeply in the power of purpose to transform companies. We know what it takes to introduce purpose and inspire a movement. We are only too willing to share our journey with others who recognize purpose as a means of growth. We share our mistakes as well as our successes. Others did that for us when we started. We've seen it play out first hand, and know it makes the difference in a company's success. And we know anyone with the passion and conviction can do the same.

It's that belief that makes us all potential Purpose Champions. Welcome to the club.

II

Building purpose-led organizations, from the inside out

6 Setting the north star

Finding purpose and building instinct

Ambika Gautam Pai and Heidi Hackemer

Ambika Gautam Pai was formerly a Partner and Co-Head of Strategy at Wolf & Wilhelmine. She's a career-long strategist who has worked in both the B2C and B2C landscape with partners like Google, UNICEF, Target, and Nike, building brands that in turn build business, rethink categories, and connect deeply with people. Ambika has educated students on brand-thinking at Parsons, guest-lectured at Wharton, and spoken at length about the power of feminine leadership and cultivating real diversity and inclusion.

Heidi Hackemer is the Founder and Chairman of Wolf & Wilhelmine, a brand strategy shop that helps brave clients such as Nike, Oscar, and Airbus make real impact in the world. She previously led the Engagement team at the Chan Zuckerberg Initiative. Heidi also consulted with the Obama White House and co-founded the Creative Alliance, an organization that matches powerful initiatives with powerful creators to make a positive change in the country by activating communities. Heidi spent her early career working at top shops in the advertising and marketing world in both the US and Europe, working with clients such as Google to launch Chrome, Chromebook, and Glass and serve as the brand lead for Google's Advanced Technology and Projects group. In this capacity, she also collaborated with clients such as LEGO, the BBC, Coca-Cola, Unilever, and Sony to create award-winning work.

★ ★ ★

In a book on 'purpose' that has defined the idea as explicitly *not* about marketing, you might be wondering how we, the brand people, got the task of discussing how to find purpose. This worry probably stems from the fact that historically brand was the last step in the process – a 'shiny wrapper' slapped on top of a company and its products by the marketing department in the form of evocative commercials, eye-catching out-of-home billboards, or more recently, influencer-studded social media content.

With this heritage, it's no surprise that brand has a branding problem. Today, a company's brand has much more potential than just communications and marketing. Powerful brands articulate a business' purpose and values, serving as the north stars for entire organizations, giving employees the philosophy and framework to make decisions with integrity on behalf of an organization. When the brand then hits the marketplace, this integrity gives modern audiences thorough reasons – from company ethos and operations to the product itself – to buy into the brand. Brand, then, in the way we use it and build it is not about the 'shiny wrapper' at all. It is the internal and external expression of a company's central belief – its purpose.

There's often an implicit correlation between the success of organizations that think of brands in this way and the missteps of those who don't. If you just stick with the shiny wrapper mentality instead of rethinking brand as a set of values that permeates everything that your organization does, you're going to get in trouble. Here's an example of that:

A brand launches lauding a strong, culturally relevant platform such as the intersection of radical feminism, sex positivity, and breaking the taboo around periods. This company was (and is) run by a woman, employs women, and has used anecdotes about young girls missing school because of their period as its M.O.

So when a company like this is exposed for abusive company culture – from not providing employees more than two weeks of paid maternity leave and resisting tough compensation conversations to name calling – it becomes highly prone to failure. Despite leadership changes and savvy PR navigation, our company in question (Thinx, if you haven't guessed it) has been unable to shake the brand/business inconsistency that is now tied to its name. This is a classic case of 'brand as a shiny wrapper,' and exactly what we're here to help you build against.

The point of purpose: from shiny wrapper to instinct

The evolution of 'brand' as we've described it is nothing new. In fact the 'brand as a shiny wrapper' perspective is (thankfully) fading into the background and many know that we need to drive to purpose that permeates a company, not just the marketing materials, per the example above. But how?

The ultimate goal is a concept that we call 'Brand Instinct.' Brand Instinct is built on four key components (Figure 6.1). It begins with a company knowing its purpose. Purpose is then operationalized through both internal and external behavioral frameworks – the second and third components, respectively – and is ultimately perpetuated through an ongoing stream of purpose-adjacent activity that serves audiences both inside and outside the company.

Brand Instinct is when everyone in a company – from marketing creatives and software engineers to financial wizzes and operational gurus – knows its ethos in their bones. It's the instinctual knowledge of what is 'right' or 'wrong' when executing on behalf of the company and the brand. It's beyond values; it's how an employee makes decisions against those values day in and day out.

THE FOUR COMPONENTS OF BRAND INSTINCT

Purpose: an organization's north-star

Internal Behavioral Frameworks: organizational language, rituals and reward structures that articulate the purpose with consistency and cohesion internally

External Behavioral Frameworks: communications and engagement strategies that drive how the purpose comes to life across channels, where it appears and where it doesn't, and how it acts out in the world

Ongoing Fuel: a steady, honest, proximate stream of stimulus and listening from the culture that a brand lives in and the audiences it serves, quantitatively and qualitatively. This keeps the Frameworks, both internal and external, relevant as culture and audiences shift

---

Figure 6.1 The four components of Brand Instinct

When done right, Brand Instinct creates a workforce that can move quickly and efficiently, and function in ways that are aligned with the overall company ethos, creating incredible consistency for the audiences. And if the company is bold in articulating its purpose, values, and frameworks, the resulting interactions with audiences will be similarly bold, making the brand and company impossible to ignore. When it comes down to it, brands are emotional infrastructures and organizational toolkits that do, at some point, manifest themselves in evocative commercials and eye-catching billboards (and ideally more!) as one part of their articulation – but only after the brand has saturated how a company operates.

In short, Brand Instinct is a practice that aligns brand, business, and purpose to the point where improvements in one mean improvements in the other. A well-built brand, with a strong guiding purpose, will impact how you construct your business – everything from your communications, to your hires and fires, to your innovation pipeline.

The first step is getting to the purpose, which we will focus on from here on out.

Discovering purpose: the nexus of four truths

Purpose is an organization's north star.

It's the organization's reason to exist in the world.

It's the common thought that an organization and brand consistently pivot from.

It's why every person who works for and with an organization shows up to work day in and day out.

It's why every customer continues their relationship with a brand.

It's the relationship that the organization has with the world.

As we set out to find our north star, it's important to first understand the entire context in which a brand and business live. In order to do this, we go back to brand basics to identify four key truths, ensuring that each brand undertaking begins with integrity (Figure 6.2).

Be bold about your investigation. Asking the same questions as everyone else will get you to the same answers as everyone else. Don't shy away from provocation, and always, always keep your business in mind.

And a VERY important pro tip before diving in – when approaching a four quadrant exploration, oftentimes the 'unlock' and energy around the purpose will lean more into one of the quadrants than others. That's normal. In our case studies below, we illustrate, through real client examples, how one quadrant in a complete investigation of all four gave us the magical 'a-ha!' moment that set the purpose, and company, up for boldness.

Company

All company truths sit within its walls, and to build powerful brands, it's important to always build from the inside out. To unearth the core truths that your business

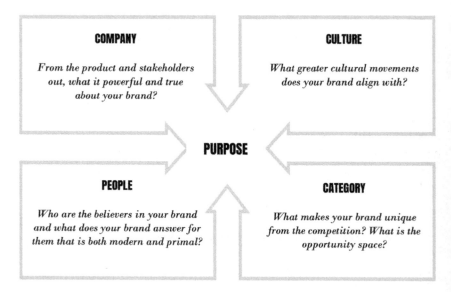

Figure 6.2 Discovering purpose

lives by, deploy Socratic methodologies, extracting information from the people who know your brand best – your employees. Ask questions such as:

- Why was the company founded?
- What was our founder's insurgent mission?
- What problem was it created to solve?
- What is a really good day at your company? What makes it really good?
- If the brand is wildly successful, what change will the world see?
- What is your brand/company's spiritual enemy?

A favorite example here is a company called HER, an LGBTQ+ dating app for women. As a queer woman herself, Robyn Exton, the founder of HER, noticed that lesbian and queer women lacked spaces to connect to each other. From the outside looking in (and to be straight, according to investors), there was a low economic upside of serving a community with lower discretionary spending than most. Because of this, physical spaces like bars were closing down regularly, and online dating apps were not created with queer women in mind. So when Robyn first embarked on the journey of redefining herself, seeking out places to explore her identity and preferences, she repeatedly came up short. She didn't know where to start or how to meet people. Even as dating apps like Tinder and Bumble started including different identities, the app experience wasn't built with queer women in mind. As Robyn got more entrenched in the community, she realized that in the early part of their journeys, many women felt the same.

So she developed an app called HER (previously called Dattch) that was designed to serve the dating needs of this community. She began socializing and pressure-testing the concept with the very women it was meant to serve by attending queer parties in the UK. During this process, it validated her suspicion that while dating was a part of what queer women needed from HER, it wasn't all-encompassing. Women weren't just looking for romantic/sexual partners, they were often also looking for women with more experience who could help guide them. Creating this space became her insurgent mission.

Today, this spirit of connecting and guiding the LGBTQ+ community – exactly what Robyn was looking to find when she first embarked on her journey – is core to the brand, and the business. This was powerfully echoed by HER employees we spoke to. As mentioned, talking to employees at this early stage of discovering purpose is so critical – they know what is true and the lore in the company's founding story, and they already instinctively know when the brand is at its best. We held a 'HER University' with these employees to unearth the existing knowledge of the brand, category, cultural context, and audience. We supplemented this with one on one employee stakeholder interviews to dive into their stories, passions, excitements, and concerns about the company

Harnessing the energies of various stakeholders inside the company's walls, W&W worked with HER to transcend beyond the app and into a true platform for the community – spanning romance, friendship, mentorship, and ultimately even thought-leadership. By creating a purpose that served the emotional needs of the queer women community in a more expansive way, HER has been able to elevate the growing spectrum of queer identity, giving womxn at large a place to feel safe, acknowledged and supported. To bring this to life, HER changed their visual identity from kitschy and sexy, to edgy and inclusive, grew their advocacy base by recruiting womxn directly from the app for their new campaign, and created in-app and in-real-life groups, feeding off the passion of HER's employees, in which the community can learn from each other, truly rising above their dating-app origins to become a social-and community-based platform.

Culture

If you understand the world around your brand, you can envision a world in which your brand plays a powerful role. And that is magical stuff that makes people pay attention and flock to brands and their products. We must always remember that brands live not only within a category landscape, but cultural landscape as well – many brands find their power by leading with a point of view about that culture around them.

Knowing this, ask questions like:

• Which cultural movements does your brand align with?
• Which cultural movement can your brand authentically contribute to?
• Where does it sit on a spectrum of awareness to activism?
• Do you want to be a platform brand for others to use to create?

Bonobos started out as the khaki pant brand that helped men find the perfect butt fit. But its founder, Andy Dunn, had a hunch that Bonobos could stand for much more, that it could be a brand that helped guide men through a new masculinity. His hunch was all about finding the truth in culture and positioning the company in relation to that truth.

W&W worked with Bonobos to dive deep into what is means to be a modern man at a time when the idea of 'man' is being re-examined, especially in light of flourishing feminism. Together, through intense cultural investigation, we learned that while it is a tough, interesting, provocative, powerful time to be a woman, it is a strange and confusing time to be a man. As 'what it means to be a woman' was gaining power, 'what it means to be a man' was becoming increasingly convoluted.

Because of this, a lot of men were ditching the old confines of masculinity and grappling with who to look up to in a world where everything had changed. In the absence of institutions and role models, men were increasingly redefining masculinity on their own terms . . . and it wasn't always positive.

Through uncovering these cultural truths, we found a sweet spot for the Bonobos brand through cultural investigation. Not only could Bonobos help men find their perfect fit of clothes, Bonobos could help guide men as they found their fit in this ever-changing world, standing for an archetype of man that is powerful, positive, and thoroughly modern.

While defining their purpose through the lens of culture helped define the Bonobos brand, leading to work like 'Role Models not Male Models' from their creative agency, CAA, it also informed their product development, helping them stretch into categories that helped serve men in a way that was both modern and comprehensive. By owning this rich cultural space, Bonobos set itself up for a successful acquisition by Walmart in 2017.

People

Notice, we didn't say consumers. The biggest mistake that you can make in thinking about who you want to attract to your business is thinking of them only through the lens of the interaction with your product of category.

You are trying to attract *people*. People are multi-faceted, emotional beings. When investigating your people, honor the context they live in and the experience they bring to bear to your interaction. By going deep in understanding, they just might go deep in interacting with you. But you have to take the first step.

- What is the aspirational mindset your brand is creating for? This is your muse.
- Who is your muse out in the world? What do they really care about? What honestly takes up their mind-space during the day?
- Do they even care about you, your product, your category? Why? Why not?
- What do you answer for them that is deeply human?
- How does your organization truly help serve them?

NOLS is a global wilderness leadership school propelled by a deep love of the backcountry (that would be the great outdoors for you city folks). But pure passion isn't enough and without a clear purpose, their organization had grown tremendously, but faced with a new era, it felt confused: where does the wild fit into a world of screens and smartphones?

We had a major challenge: NOLS is a heritage brand and came with some strong non-negotiables. Heritage brands want to keep their spirit alive, so their stakeholders are looking for a perspective shift that brings light to a truth deeply ingrained in the history of the brand and illuminates it for new audiences.

Working with NOLS brought us to their headquarters in Lander, Wyoming where we immersed ourselves into their wilderness, met with NOLS' large council of stakeholders and shadowed their team of highly skilled instructors as they walked through the 'outdoor classrooms' of nature. More importantly, we began discussing the experiences of NOLS' students. The NOLS experience was undoubtedly transformational – and had been for 50 years – but we needed to get deep with those who had experienced it and translate it for a new generation.

With the NOLS experience as our investigative center of gravity, we did a slew of in-depth interviews to understand the experience from different audience perspectives: from a 65-year-old who had racked up five NOLS courses, to prospective high schoolers who had never been on a trip, to instructors who had taught students with the school for decades. From these insights, we developed a comprehensive muse persona that spoke to the core of the transformational experience, while serving as the heart of the NOLS brand story and purpose. This purpose helped reorganize their offering portfolio, supercharged an engagement and content strategy, and drove a refreshed visual identity and website.

Category

Of course it's important to differentiate from the category. Sometimes, finding that white space against the competition *is* the battle. However, it's also important to push your investigation beyond the obvious category, as opportunities can exist beyond the current purview. When future-proofing brands, think about which other brands and categories you can learn from. It's as much about identifying who you don't want to be (your competition), as who you *do* want to be.

- What are you *really* in the business of?
- Who would your brand hang out with at a party?
- What is fresh and interesting about the category? What is stale and due to be disrupted?
- Where can you transcend the category?

When we met MeUndies, the young and scrappy LA company was riding a successful wave with their irreverent and cheeky brand – a brand that was grounded in creating underwear for both genders. While they enjoyed success, it was time for them to mature their brand to drive their next wave of growth.

After spending time with the crew, we realized that pushing boundaries and doing right by their audience was in their DNA, if not always fully expressed in the brand just yet. We needed to find the entry point to modernize their conversation with their audiences and get them pushing the world forward.

The unlock came through a very simple, but ultimately powerful, category observation: whereas the category clung to and profited from classic gender stereotypes (think the stereotypically sexpot women of Victoria's Secret or the brawny men of Hanes), MeUndies product didn't cleave to these norms. They weren't trying to out-sex women brands or out-dude male brands: instead, they made underwear driven by irreverent prints first and then articulated those prints into specific cuts for both men and women. And their audiences loved them for it.

In a category obsessed with dusty norms, they were about modernity and fun.

We took their inherent category difference and ran with it. Working with the MeUndies team, we guided them to a strategy that was all about embracing new ideas of sexuality and gender, rooted in feeling good, embracing each person's 'me,' and having fun. This shift allowed them to advocate for their audiences in new ways, coming to life via non-traditional models and couples of all shapes, sizes, and colors and supporting influencers who live on the edge of gender redefinition, like Amber Rose and her SlutWalk. They significantly grew their audience with this provocative and decidedly modern brand POV.

From truths to purpose

So, you've dug into your four areas of investigation. Like our friends above, if you've done your job right, you've realized that there's one quadrant in particular where there is a lot of energy. That's natural. Borrow from the other quadrants and then lean into this center of gravity to unearth your purpose.

Your purpose sits at the intersection and culmination of the four truths you surfaced in your investigation. With this ideology set, instinct follows. This is the moment when the brand starts to occupy both a holistic, external world-view and a nuanced, internal point-of-view.

Great. So, how do you get to your purpose? This is where the creative process comes in (Figure 6.3). Because figuring out purpose is a creative exercise, there is no formula or step-by-step instructions for this moment. However, our advice in this part of the process? Play with it. Get everything you know on a wall and try to fit the puzzle pieces together. Free your brain from doubts and limitations and do what you really believe is the right thing.

GET CREATIVE WITH PURPOSE
BY LEANING INTO LOVE, PAIN, AND TENSION

For HER, it was about harking back to the painful truth that queer women didn't have a space in which to connect, romantically and beyond, and pairing that with Robyn's insurgent mission to serve a community that she had grown to love, in a way that no one else had.

For Bonobos, it was about the difficulty of defining and understanding masculinity in a culture filled with stereotypic tropes and dated paradigms, and a desire to bring new role models, and forms of expression to the forefront.

For NOLS, it was about helping a new generation fall in love with the great outdoors, the way the employees had, in the midst of an increasingly digital world where a salt-of-the-earth company could easily get lost.

For MeUndies, it was about standing up and out against gendered and sexualized norms and giving people a radically individualized way to engage with a category that was stuck in its ways, all while having a bit of fun.

Figure 6.3 Get creative with purpose by leaning into love, pain, and tension

A purpose is a simple statement. It is usually quite short. You can surround it with more information later, but this main statement is a rallying cry that is simple, memorable, and motivating.

Get the jargon out of it. Make sure it's evocative. Make sure it lands easily. It should make the people that work there proud and motivated.

A few of our favorites:

- Oscar: Make it Right
- Zappos: Deliver happiness
- Chan Zuckerberg Initiative: A Future for Everyone
- Bacardi: Liberate Soul

Conclusion: so now what?

As we cued up before, purpose represents an organization's north star – why it exists in the world. Purpose elevates you beyond the realm of rigor and into the realm of truth and action. It leaves the 100-page strategy deck that collects dust on a marketing executive's desk in the past, and instead builds brands that stay intrinsically tied to the DNA of the company, informed by the cultural, categorical, and consumer context, while also informing a company's communications, investments, hires, fires, etc.

The most potent and future-proof brands in the world put in the hard work to pinpoint and develop purposes that can drive not just their brand forward, but their entire business forward. But by now we all know that purpose doesn't end with articulation. The success of purpose-driven brands comes with the follow-through.

So what we've described, setting the north star, is just the beginning. In the rest of this book, you will find sage advice on how to build instinctual organizations that in turn drive successful businesses. Our friends and peers will walk through how to build the internal and external frameworks to ensure purpose comes to life, and how to make sure this type of work is impactful and long-lasting.

7 Transforming the organization
Designing for purpose and humanity

Tom Andrews

For more than two decades Tom has helped chief executives lead their organizations through transformation — as a personal advisor and strategist, a leader of client teams, and the President of SYPartners' Organizational Transformation practice. He founded TJALeadership to pursue his interest in integrating leadership strategy into organizational and cultural transformation. Tom has a deep love for leadership development, and has helped design leadership curricula for GE's Management Development Institute at Crotonville and the U.S. Military Academy at West Point. He has spoken at Fortune 100 companies and high-performance organizations such as the U.S. Olympic Committee, on the topics of culture and leadership.

* * *

Organizations operate in an ever more unsettled world – customer preferences change rapidly, competitors emerge suddenly, technology shifts unpredictably. In this context, it's survival of the fittest, and in Darwinian fashion those organizations that are too slow to adapt to new realities go into crisis mode, thrash around a bit, and die. External change has always been an existential threat for companies, but today it's always just around the corner and you see the effect in the lifespan of many companies. In 1964, the average tenure of a company on the S&P 500 was 33 years; by 1990, it was 20 years; it is forecast to shrink to 12 years by 2027.

What is clear is that the greatest brands of today have shown the ability to adapt and transform themselves to stay ahead of change. IBM has remade itself multiple times, from being a medium-sized maker of tabulating equipment and typewriters into a computer industry leader in the 1960s, again in the 1990s as a leader of the e-business revolution, and today the company is navigating a massive transformation to a cloud computing model. Starbucks went from increasing irrelevance and a steady decline in business in 2008 to reinventing itself as a true coffee icon. Planned Parenthood has been attacked for over a century by highly motivated political forces, yet persists, stronger than ever.

How do these organizations do it? And why do they succeed where others fail?

I've dedicated my career to helping leaders answer those questions, motivated, I suspect, by a deep curiosity about the human story that underlies any organizational transformation and particularly the clash of beliefs that must be resolved. My first seven years of life were spent growing up in Beirut, when it was a beautiful, multicultural, polyglot, Mediterranean jewel of a city. Then a civil war took over the country and tore it apart – a clash of beliefs that left bullets in our front door and forced my family to flee to London. My journey since then has involved, more and more, a quest to decode the narrative behind so many events that traumatize us. When I studied languages at Cambridge, it wasn't the languages themselves that I found particularly interesting, but rather the modern and medieval epics and plays with their layers of meaning, only revealed with patient attention. That may seem a long way from business, but in the course of more than 25 years of working with some of the most extraordinary CEOs in the world I have found ever more truth in Shakespeare's observation that "all the world's a stage." Everything in organizations boils down to human nature, the stories we tell ourselves, and the subconscious scripts that are encoded in our minds.

Historian and writer Yuval Noah Harari captured the concept elegantly in his book *Sapiens*: what distinguishes humankind from other species is our ability to use fiction to cooperate in extremely flexible ways with countless numbers of strangers.[1] At its core a human organization is just a group of individual strangers who cooperate with each other on the basis of a fiction: the belief that the organization exists beyond words on a legal document, that it will reward you for your work, and that it does something that other people value. So when you strip away the physical things – the things that we fetishize in business, such as capital, physical space and equipment, 'IP' (Intellectual Property is another concept that exists only in our minds) – we are left with a set of beliefs and ideas around which a group of human beings choose to cooperate.

Purpose and culture

The biggest belief of them all is the 'why' of an organization – its reason to exist beyond profit – or what we might now call its 'purpose.' The belief in the purpose of an organization gives people a reason to belong to that organization over others and to act in ways that are consistent with countless other colleagues even though their job functions might be quite different.

Great organizations start with a deep sense of purpose that is sometimes explicit, sometimes intuitive to the founders. Planned Parenthood started with an explicit belief that women should have control over their own bodies and access to birth control (a radical belief at the time). Emily Weiss started the Millennial beauty brand Glossier with a belief that the beauty industry should be democratized. IBM started with a belief that scientific progress would lead to human progress. These purposes, together with a system of related beliefs, attract people and resources and, as the organization becomes increasingly successful, inform behaviors that become ingrained as fixed patterns and routines.

With increasing success the organization develops a distinctive culture, and certain behaviors and beliefs become routine. Supporting structure (spaces, policies, processes, financing) evolves to promote and institutionalize what works, strengthening the culture.

A strong company culture – think Apple, Nike, Facebook, IBM, the U.S. Military – can be a massive competitive advantage because it cannot be easily copied. But crises happen when these cultures become fixed and insulated from a reality changing around them. As technology changes and as customer needs evolve, a closed culture sticks with its current set of routines and ignores the signals of change. Video giant Blockbuster resisted change while the DVD upstart Netflix kept pivoting to take advantage of new technology. When Blockbuster filed for bankruptcy in 2010 they were $900 million in debt. That same year, Netflix's stock price jumped 219 percent. Now Netflix is ubiquitous and has disrupted TV viewing.

So there is a paradox to success. The more successful a culture has become with its routines, the more likely it is that those routines start to replace the original purpose and beliefs. The more people you hire, the greater distance you create from the 'why' behind what are now established ways and routines, and you end up with mindlessness on a large scale. It doesn't matter how great your purpose, if it has become obscured by routines, and if the reality of your business is diverging further from the internal fiction. An organization that has become insular and forgotten that its purpose must engage with reality, starts to experience decline. It loses customers. The front line gets defensive, mistrust spreads, people start to leave, and the organization gets stuck in a downward spiral. The way out of that spiral is through a journey that reconnects purpose to operational reality.

Howard Schultz faced just such a situation in 2008 when he stepped back in as the CEO of Starbucks. Starbucks had become so routine-focused over time that everything was gradually becoming automated, from the actual coffee making process, to the opening of new stores. The organization's original purpose of creating a 'Third Place' for community between work and home had become lost. And the skill of coffee-making had become lost with it. What was left was just mechanics. With the brand in decline, customers were voting with their feet.

Howard's initial thought was that this was a customer experience issue. But as he dug deeper, he realized it was a cultural one: the founding beliefs about community had been lost in blind assumptions about opening more stores. So, when he set about rescuing Starbucks from decline, he focused on its culture and a renewed commitment to the company's purpose.

Likewise, when asked on a podcast how Netflix could pivot from one technology to another, engineering a radical business model change from DVDs by mail to streaming video content (to, now, original content), CEO Reed Hastings said one word: "Culture." When Lou Gerstner reflected on his turnaround of IBM in the 1990s he famously said, "I came to see, in my time at IBM, that culture isn't just one aspect of the game, *it is the game.*"[2]

Transforming organizations is essentially all about culture change and commitment to a purpose that will act as your 'north star.'

So, how do we do that? How do we recover a sense of purpose and reveal the animating beliefs of a business that will carry it through change? How do we step by step solve the most complex problem any leader will face?

It all starts with design.

Designing transformation

"The best way to predict the future is to design it."

—Buckminster Fuller

Let's start with re-framing your mindset about process.

I believe the best way to approach transformation – a wickedly complex challenge – is to treat it as a design problem that is best solved through a design perspective.

Most business leaders and MBAs (and there are now a *lot* of MBAs in business) have been well trained in business administration. They can figure out what's going on in the market, where they're underperforming, and how to make smart, strategic choices about the future. But they can be woefully underprepared for the psychology of change and the irrationality of human nature. The best leaders of transformation are purpose-driven, emotionally intelligent people who intuitively understand their fellow human beings. They understand that change happens only when you bring people into the process emotionally and wholeheartedly. And they know that what's needed is a creative approach to a problem of huge uncertainty.

This is why design is a powerful method, becoming a competence sought after by corporations such as Facebook, Google, IBM, and even the big management consultancies such as McKinsey and Bain. Design acknowledges the human being in the human system of a culture. It elevates the imagination, necessary when change involves venturing into the unknown. And, perhaps most of all, it concerns itself with *experience* rather than theory – it puts the *form* in trans*form*ation.

Let's unpack the value of design a little.

Good design integrates the human being into the process

Good design is empathetic. In a transformation, that means designing the system of change around the people who must adopt a new set of beliefs and behaviors. When Howard led the transformation of Starbucks, his design choices were always oriented around how partners (the Starbucks term for 'employees') and customers would experience the intended purpose. For example, he replaced the existing espresso machines with lower height versions so that baristas had an unbroken line of sight to customers – he couldn't ask baristas to connect more with customers if the system actually blocked them for doing so. This is what we mean by 'human-centered.'

Good design elevates the imagination

Rather than being a reactionary escape from an existential threat, great transformation means animating a sense of purpose and crafting a shared fiction of a better future. This requires imagination, creativity and the design mindset – an intentionally open-minded comfort with ambiguity and curiosity about what might be possible. The design method (prototyping, visualizations, journey maps, etc.) helps us imagine that future vividly until it becomes achievable. By elevating the imagination, design allows us to proactively conceive 'what can be,' rather than react to external pressures and focus on what has been lost.

Good design is obsessed with making things until you get it right

At its essence, all design is about giving form to intention. The more beautifully and effectively form expresses intention, the better the design. This means design emphasizes constantly testing out an approach to see if it works in real life: it's messy and iterative, and it focuses on *making* things and seeing how they work in practice rather than *thinking* about how things might work in theory.

These principles of design help give full, imaginative form to the intention of a transformation. But now for the twist: transforming an organization is not a single design activity. Transformation unfolds over time, in a series of acts and scenes in between, and requires various meaningful transitions from one scene to another. What you are really doing, when you design a transformation, is thoughtfully creating the scenes of change and the building blocks of a new organization – of a human system that comes into its new form over time.

Transformation in a series of acts

I have come to find the analogy of a play as one of the best ways to think about the roles of various people, and the shifts in context over time. Everyone must play a role, so the question becomes how you script that role and how you design the set to produce the best conditions for change. If you stick with this analogy, then there are a few key roles to start with as you think about designing transformation (Box 7.1).

Box 7.1 The cast of characters

The Chief Executive

In my experience, no organization-wide transformation can succeed without the full and ongoing commitment of the Chief Executive (and my worst experiences have been with CEOs who were half-hearted). They set the vision and the tone, remove roadblocks, and make the difficult decisions necessary to overcome the defense mechanisms that any culture has against a threat to its status quo.

The Chief Transformation Officer

In some cases, particularly a smaller organization, the CEO is also the Chief Transformation Officer – taking charge of change, setting the tempo, operationalizing decisions. In other cases, another highly competent executive plays this role, side-by-side with the CEO. For example, Michelle Gass played the Chief Transformation Officer role by Howard Schultz's side during the transformation of Starbucks 2008–2012. Maryam Banikarim – who also writes in this anthology – played a similar role when CMO of Hyatt, working side by side with Mark Hoplamazian and helping put change into practice.

The Transformation Team

You will need a team of empowered leaders to manage the transformation as a dedicated part of their jobs. With the CEO as sponsor, this team is essentially your A-team of high potential leaders who are not executives (so that they can dedicate the time needed), with a very strong Program Manager. Like any high performance team, it would be limited to 5–7 people and chartered effectively with a clear mission and objectives.

The Executive Team (or Senior Management Team)

In a smaller organization, the Transformation Team might be a subset of the Executive Team, with one or more additional people. The role of the Executive Team is to make the critical decisions that enable momentum, particularly around removing any roadblocks to change.

The Extended Leadership Team

Think of this as the next level of leaders in the organization, who will benefit from being involved early and often in the transformation planning.

The Change Cohorts

The Change Cohorts – affectionately called Tiger Teams by some companies I've worked with – are the teams chartered to execute on the transformation agenda, the blueprint for change. These are the foot soldiers of change, leading on the front lines and reporting frequently to the Transformation Team.

Think of transformation as three major acts that involve a rotating cast of actors (Figure 7.1). If you're designing and leading a transformation, you're scripting and directing. But consider that a lot of the day to day is improv!

	Act 1: Committing	Act 2: Coordinating	Act 3: Consolidating
Scene 1	Seeing everything with fresh perspective	Putting a system in place for coordinating and learning	Incorporating the new narrative in word and deed
Scene 2	Committing wholeheartedly to a shared purpose and vision for change	Engaging the right tribes	Reinforcing change with structures and rewards
Scene 3	Bringing change to the front line through empowered change cohorts	Launching pilots for innovative organizational elements	Disbanding cohorts and replacing out of date cultural elements

Figure 7.1 Transformation, in three acts

Act 1: committing

The idea of purpose-led change is inspiring. Think of any political campaign: the aspiration of change brings hope, vision, momentum, and fervor to any group of people, and the same can be said for an organization. But I suspect that, while inspiration is important, transformation efforts that fail do so because their leaders focus on this upfront motivation and not enough on commitment. Actually making change happen is *hard*: it requires a long-term emotional and financial investment on the part of key people. This kind of commitment, in my experience, happens when someone is fully enrolled in the *why* of change, knows *how* to move through it, and feels fully *accountable* for their role.

To clarify this 'why' and 'how' requires a few distinct scenes:

Scene 1: seeing everything with fresh perspective

Transformation starts by seeing things differently. The status quo can be so fixed in people's minds that no earnest change can begin without shaking up everyone's assumptions, and this phase is all about helping everyone see the future though multiple fresh perspectives.

Scene 2: committing wholeheartedly to a shared purpose and vision

This scene is about integrating and distilling the mix of perspectives shared in Scene 1 into a belief system about the future that is deeply anchored in your organization's purpose: who are we, what do we care about, where do we want to go, and how are we going to get there? Getting people aligned on a shared vision means creating a narrative that everyone can believe in.

Scene 3: bringing change to the front lines through empowered change cohorts

Once leadership has aligned on the narrative, we need to build commitment to purpose-led transformation into the front lines of an organization. This is done through *change cohorts* – or highly motivated groups of individuals who believe in the purpose and have the will and skill to go out and make change happen.

So what does this look like in practice? A pharmaceutical company ('PharmaCo') we worked with was struggling to commit to the transformation that the founder intellectually knew was needed. They had built a business on one big pharmaceutical innovation and had not yet proven that they could produce more from their pipeline. Their employees were increasingly disconnected from the purpose of the organization – "changing the course of human health for the better" – and being poached by other firms. Endless conversations with the CEO's leadership team were not leading to much enrollment.

If you think about the first 'scene' I describe, the team wasn't yet sold on the problem they faced and they needed their assumptions challenged. This is pretty typical. The opening scene of a transformation can often be a busy mess of perspectives and symptomatic complaints. As one executive put it to us, "What you see depends on where you sit," so you get the CEO offering a diagnosis or a vision that can be about perplexing failings in the culture, a CMO arguing that the problem is a lack of investment in marketing, or a line of business managers claiming that the leadership team is out of touch with the frontline. The truth is likely somewhere in between, but the problem is not necessarily getting to the truth – it is getting to a *shared truth*. That requires creating moments for people to come together and view their situation through new perspectives. The role of outside partners is to bring in those perspectives.

At PharmaCo we brought the problem to life, in dramatic fashion, through the lens of patients, employees, and forces at large in the industry. With large-scale visual displays we highlighted the dramatic changes that had happened to the organization and its environment in the previous decade and the current trajectory of innovation. We followed that up with exhibits that each told a story about forces at play in the pharmaceutical sector. We facilitated discussions to explore all the beliefs the executives held about PharmaCo and the future – asking execs to walk quietly from exhibit to exhibit, writing down their reactions. They then had to share their notes in a group forum. The visuals created a shared view of data, and the exercises produced the dialogue to shape a commitment to change. There are many exercises you can do to accomplish the same end, and the point is to make sure that people start to see their situation through new perspectives, to the extent that they can then embrace a new possibility.

At that point, we moved into Scene 2, and began to imagine the future that PharmaCo wanted to create, based on its purpose. Arguably this is the harder part for most leadership teams, which are better trained in critical thinking than creative thinking. Envisioning the future is a creative act that is all about the power of a great story about a future that is both believable and desirable.

That starts with initial beliefs – 'the moral of the story' – that emerge from discussions with leaders and is connected to the purpose. The design task is then to co-create a narrative that illustrates those beliefs and has the tension of a good plot in it. For PharmaCo that tension was in the existential threat of becoming irrelevant, and the harm irrelevance would cause to patients who would otherwise benefit from PharmaCo's technical brilliance.

The narrative can take many forms, and in PharmaCo's case what made sense was a video that animated the story emotionally, brought customers' stories to life, and featured an original musical score that could be shared with all employees and cut through the usual corporate messaging.

PharmaCo's head of HR then set up change cohorts that were regionally based to execute the strategy by region. In most cases organizations execute their change strategy through a series of big moves or initiatives that are led by small teams (the 'tiger teams'). In some cases, regions are so essential to execution that they become the default organizing model.

Act 2: coordinating

Act 2 of transformation is what I like to call the 'messy middle.' You've made all the opening moves and the initial clarity of the start is behind you, but the satisfaction of an ending is out of sight. You're left with all the messiness of an in-between state, both practically and psychologically. This is the most treacherous part of a transformation, where much can go wrong. In some cases I've seen CEOs replaced in the messy middle because they promised results too soon, and when results didn't come fast enough, leaders lost the confidence of their board. At this point the whole organization is essentially back to square one.

Designing this act well means accepting, at some level, the inherent messiness of every moment, while keeping the strategic clarity of your purpose and your intentions in sight. There will be twists and turns. Rather than resist them, design them into your process, and create learning and adjustment mechanisms in each scene . . .

Scene 1: putting a system in place for coordinating and learning from the implementation

This looks like some kind of regular cadence of meetings by a governing body – which should include the CEO, the Transformation Team, the Executive Team, and the Change Cohort team leaders. But these meetings shouldn't just be about the theater of business performance. Their tone must be open and curious, and purpose-driven. And ideally you have a dedicated collaborative space for shared work that always makes visible the progress of each track of work.

Scene 2: engaging the right tribes

Cultures are not monolithic. They tend to decompose into many smaller tribes, like the sales tribe and the marketing tribe. Designing the best way forward in the messy middle of transformation means first fully empathizing with the different tribal needs within a culture and second, prioritizing which tribes will require more attention sooner – either for business reasons, or for cultural ones.

Scene 3: launching pilots for innovative organizational elements

Prototype new elements (i.e., team structures, processes, technologies) before deploying them at scale, and you learn invaluable lessons about what will work before you inflict your ideas on the whole organization – and risk the fallout of a flop.

One of the confounding problems of any organizational transformation is the tension between making speedy progress on multiple fronts, and integrating that progress so you don't end up with a Frankenstein of old approaches and new ones. And add to this the fact that nothing goes as planned.

That's why creating the right system to coordinate and learn from change matters in this act more than anything else. For example, at SYPartners I worked with a major midwestern retailer (call them RetailCo) on their transformation. We launched six teams for six implementation strategies that needed to be reworked multiple times over the three or so years in which they were implementing their transformation. As the CEO remarked, "When we began, we were overconfident in our ability to execute the basics. We had to get those right and it took a lot more time than expected."

Therefore the design job for the opening scene of the messy middle, is to create a system for coordinating activity that is optimized for quickly learning and sharing what works. Mostly, that's a cadence of meetings that are run effectively.

With RetailCo, the CEO governed the process and ran it with unrelenting discipline. Every Monday he held half-day executive sessions to grill the Transformation Team on progress and ensure they were addressing issues right away. They used regular board updates as milestones for monitoring progress and creating interim deadlines for the execution teams to aim for. And they addressed an often overlooked aspect of the system, which is creating *space* for cohorts to come together to do their best work and think out loud constructively.

Ideally that is physical space. Some of my clients have transformed conference rooms into working spaces that they can return to easily, their recent work still on display, without having to fight for precious slots in a shared room. Others have created 'lab' spaces – bringing in new furniture, whiteboards, and other resources that are stimulus for the work they need to do. Physical space goes along with mental space. Cohorts need to be able to meet frequently and at length to be effective. In RetailCo's case, the CEO dedicated a conference room near his office to ongoing planning (a sort of 'war room'), and made use of a retail prototyping store to test out new concepts.

The Transformation Team also accounted for the different cultures within RetailCo – especially the difference between corporate center and store cultures. Given that a primary driver of the transformation was a goal to increase engagement of customers and traffic, it was critical that we effectively engaged the store leaders and field staff first. The team spent a lot of time on the road and in regions, enrolling the various store leaders in the plan and ensuring they could accomplish what was effectively a dramatic shift in the design of the stores and the delivery of a guest experience.

They also successfully used piloting techniques early and often. They carved out different regions to test retail concepts. They launched loyalty concepts with small groups to test the functionality of their app before launching publicly. They used a warehouse to prototype different in-store displays and merchandising approaches for new format stores.

The result of all this discipline and patience was a rare success story in retail – a department store that went from decline to a bright light in retail and a return to growth that continues under a new CEO who had acted as the Chief Transformation Officer along the way.

Act 3: consolidating

The final act resolves the messy middle with definitive moves. The right people have been engaged and you've tested out your assumptions through pilots. You should by now – likely a year or so into the process – have enrolled a critical mass of people, proven you're on the right course, and found momentum. But you're still an organization in transition. In fact, there will probably be a lot of tension between old models and new ones, as people are more awake to the new ones and engaged in moving forward. The design task therefore is to scale what is working and to focus on allocating resources. It's incredibly important in this stage to ensure the purpose of the organization has been fully integrated. Any lack of integrity holds you back.

People's faith at this point depends so much on leadership signals. Culture always carries with it the inertia of its past behavior. Inevitably people revert to the comfort of what was familiar. That's why the distinct scenes of this final act require leaders to signal with absolute clarity that the future is here, and that they haven't 'moved on from the purpose' but are living it in all their actions – and will continue to.

Scene 1: incorporating the new narrative in word and deed

You'll be tired of your narrative of purpose and change long before anyone else is. And consider that everyone, and I mean everyone, is scrutinizing what you say and what you do, especially when they feel uncertain about the future. So as Meg Whitman – CEO of eBay and HP – once said to me, "You have to say what you do, then do it, then say you did it." Rinse and repeat until everyone in the organization can repeat.

Scene 2: reinforcing change with structures and rewards

Make your purpose and new cultural elements both effective and real by putting structure around them and rewarding new behaviors. Beyond obvious policy decisions, this scene is about ritualizing certain practices that have great value to the future and that signal what is meaningful about the new organization. For example, Starbucks executives created a coffee-tasting ritual at executive meetings to remind everyone about the company's purpose to nurture the human spirit one cup of coffee, one cafe, one community at a time.

Scene 3: disbanding cohorts and replacing out of date cultural elements

We humans, as a psychologist friend told me, are "good at hellos and terrible at goodbyes." The same is true for organizational transformation. At some point – and you will know when, because you have been managing your goals, right? – it is time to declare an end to the transformation, at least for this version of the organization. You will be disbanding teams, declaring success, and most important, auditing and shutting down any policies, practices, etc. that are now out of date. And then you get to write your *Harvard Business Review* case study!

The CEO of one of the world's largest consumer packaged goods companies (CPGCo) realized that it was time to fully put into operation a strong new purpose. She and her executive team – together with a smaller transformation team that included their CMO, head of communications, and the president of an organic foods company they acquired – had done the hard work of enrolling 100 leaders in a new vision and strategy. They had managed their way through a challenging roadmap to execution. It was time, she felt, for a conclusive signal of change.

With her Executive Leadership Team she decided upon the complete reorganization of the company into three business units from six, with a primary focus on a new purpose to provide 'real food' that was authentic and delicious in life's everyday moments.

They also realized that to truly reinforce a purpose and culture of real food, they would have to make hard decisions that they had avoided until then: decisions to alter the ingredients of their most profitable products. It was one thing to buy new organic companies to add to their portfolio. It was quite another to meddle with mainstay products. But after a lot of debate, the team under her leadership recognized that they could not truly stand for a meaningful purpose and ask their people to operate with a belief in real food – nor make a promise to all their customers – if any products that they sold undermined that purpose.

So they removed all artificial coloring and flavoring from their products – an unprecedented move given its impact on the bottom line and a history of reliance on a certain color and flavor profile. Next, they went a step further, becoming the first major food company in the United States to voluntarily disclose genetically modified ingredients in their products.

All of this took place in the context of a rigorous communications campaign from the office of the CEO that included interviews on the road, internal rallies with the top hundred leaders, and an annual report that was devoted to the topic of the new purpose and how it was being operationalized and incentivized at the company. The communications team worked overtime.

As the reorganization took hold, and as their product ingredients caught up to their purpose, The CEO went on the road herself to promote the transformation – signalling to all the change that the company had made. Internally, the original teams were disbanded and new ones formed to explore innovation. Since then, CPGCo has continued to evolve and remake itself, but now with a better footing.

The reality is – as one executive told me – "You are never done with transformation. You just get to the next point."

Parting thoughts on best practice

People buy in when they can weigh in

It's important that purpose, vision, and change narratives – while they may be ultimately penned by one person – are orchestrated for co-authorship by key leaders so there is commitment upfront. There's a moment with many brands we've worked with, where a leadership team will actually sign a final copy of their vision narrative, as a symbolic gesture of alignment. For Coach under Victor Luis, it was this intentional act to publicly sign the new vision statement that galvanized executives. For Starbucks it was an unscripted moment when leaders from across Starbucks' ranks came up to shake Howard's hand and sign a statement of purpose.

Enrolling leaders beyond the executives also means co-creating the implementation of strategy with the people best positioned to understand its effects. That means front-line leaders – store managers, sales reps, etc. They are the ones who will be out in the field, deep in the organization, leading specific missions. They must have the leadership space to invent the right approach given the circumstances they encounter.

Never let process trump purpose

A disciplined process is necessary but not sufficient for great transformation. Remember how important that true north of purpose is, and ensure *how* you execute your process is in service of that, rather than mindlessly following a plan. Matt Dixon, a friend and client who runs a high-end athletic performance company, is fond of saying to his pro athletes "You must be an active participant in your plan." I would say the same to executives with a transformation plan. When Jeff Immelt and Beth Comstock led the Imagination Breakthrough process at GE, which successfully transformed cultural traits for innovation, teams were expressly asked not to come with PowerPoint decks. Instead the goal of each meeting was to go through the challenges each team was running into, and use the group's collective brainpower to generate new approaches or remove roadblocks. Leaders had to show up ready to be fully present and on their toes.

Communicate, communicate, communicate

When asked for his leadership lessons about leading Kohl's department stores through their improbable transformation, one that stuck out for Kevin Mansell was how much more he had to communicate than usual, and how important it was to consistently stick to the script. If you listen to every single earnings call in the past five years since Kohl's introduced what it called its 'Greatness Agenda' for revitalizing the store chain, you will find that in every single call Kevin refers to the

Greatness Agenda, anchors all conversation on it, and tells stories rooted in each of the pillars of the agenda.

Lead by doing

Leaders are the example. We emulate them. And if what they do differs from what they say, we emulate the *doing* part, not the *saying* part. If what they do is congruent with what they say, we start to trust the path forward more. If it doesn't, we hesitate. Micro-behaviors – a leader seeking a more collaborative culture who starts to ask for more input in meetings, say – all make a far bigger difference than most of us realize. For better or for worse. One pharma CEO client was concerned his team wasn't engaging enough in leadership meetings. I observed the next one. After kicking off the meeting he handed over to his COO, and then sat back and started checking his Blackberry for emails. Within less than a minute, most of the room followed suit. I had to take the CEO aside after and point out what was happening and he was genuinely surprised!

Of course macro-behaviors can be hugely impactful too. Especially when they are bold, visible, public demonstrations of a leader's intent, such as the moment when Howard Schultz shut down all of Starbucks to retrain baristas. Or when incoming CEO Michelle Gass and Kohl's leadership team announced a breakthrough partnership with Amazon and a new store format. Or when President and CEO of CVS, Larry Merlo, declared they would no longer sell cigarettes as part of its new health-oriented transformation strategy.

Conclusion: a call for mindful leadership

Great leaders of transformation in my experience tend to be very active and purpose-led participants in the journey itself. They are *mindful*. They are present in the change process – attentive to the flow of information between people, curious about what is working and what isn't, discerning blind spots and willing to detach themselves from their own personal biases. They don't mindlessly follow a plan, but instead design and then re-design the conditions that will lead to a better state, based on what they experience.

Beth Comstock, who recently ended a long career at General Electric as vice chair after seeing the company through several transformations, is particularly adamant about how critical it is to get out and see for yourself how things are going: "Yes you can read a lot. People can give you reports. But I firmly believe that at some point, you have to go see for yourself."

That looks like a lot of listening, a lot of walking the halls, a lot of speaking to employees at all levels, and a lot of getting out and talking to customers and partners to gut check your assumptions. It looks like a dedication to creating the right conditions for change to occur – to accepting your role as a 'designer of transformation' even if you wouldn't use those words. And it looks like a willingness to continuously test your own assumptions as a leader, as the reality of change unfolds in all its unpredictability and its fundamental *human-ness*.

It might take a year. It might take five. But it's worth really leaning into this journey, because there is no more profound opportunity to forge leadership, for yourself and for your leadership team, than to face the uncertainty of change and lead through it, scene by scene.

8 Putting values into action

Delivering on purpose by establishing, embedding, enacting, and expressing your values

Alexandra Dimiziani

Alexandra's international life and lattice career reflect her belief that necessity might be the mother of invention, but diversity is its father. She cut her career teeth in luxury brand advertising in New York City, then leaped to the non-profit sector, marketing subsidized health products and services to the most vulnerable populations in Central Africa. Alex went on to lead global creative strategy and direction on The Coca-Cola Company's health and wellness portfolio and Corporate Social Responsibility effort, and then ran marketing communications across all of the company's Western European initiatives. In 2014, a little-known brand in Europe offered her the opportunity to help disrupt the way we travel and change our experience of the world for the better. As Airbnb's first European Marketing Director, Alex built out a highly diverse and high-performing team, drove a rapid rate of growth in brand awareness and love, and won the company accolades in region and around the globe in the areas of creativity, effectiveness, and purpose. In 2016, she moved into Airbnb's Global Marketing Director role and over to the Bay Area. After a nearly four-year long masterclass in purpose and values, in mid-2018, Alexandra co-founded TwentyFirstCenturyBrand, a consultancy that partners with founders and CEOs of the world's most innovative companies to realize transformational growth through brand and marketing excellence. But Alex is no slave to the CV. In between professional stints, she has backpacked the world (most recently, through Central America with her husband and two small children), written a book, and obtained a master's degree in investigative journalism.

★ ★ ★

If a tree falls in the forest and no one is there to hear it, does it make a sound? The same question could be posed of purpose and the answer would be similar. In the instance of a falling tree, the air would still vibrate but without an ear to receive the waves, there is no sound. In the instance of purpose, a company can profess it, but if its stakeholders, internal and external, do not experience it, then it does not exist.

Purpose, as previously covered in this book, is an organization's reason for being, or its 'why.' Values are the 'how.' In the most cliché terms, values guide the 'walk' to the purpose 'talk.' As the phrase suggests, values are about action. They manifest in the countless, daily deeds that a company's constituents, communities, and consumers experience, thereby propelling its purpose into existence.

Values govern the behavior of individuals in an organization, and the *collective* workforce, thereby defining a culture driven to realize the purpose. But it's not just employees who are expected to adhere to them. The organization is accountable to enact them, too. If, for example, transparency is at the crux of a core value, then the company will do its part by keeping the workforce wholly abreast of direction, decisions, finances, successes, and failures, and fire employees who hide mistakes, misrepresent truths, or engage in office politics – regardless of their seniority. What's good for the goose should be good for the gander, because when it comes to values, they apply to *every* agent in the organization *equally*.

The behaviors of the business in the marketplace must also be values-led. We have all known people who vociferously voice their principles. When their actions do not back up their beliefs, our reactions may vary from eyerolls to cries of hypocrisy, but our takeaway is the same – they are not who they say they are. Hence the axiom, 'Actions speak louder than words,' and it is as true for brands as it is for ex's. When purpose drives the behaviors of a business, the brand is seen to live up to its promise, building trust and love, that will set it apart from competitors and help it weather reputational storms.

Essentially, values are the 'operating system' – producing a unified and unique culture and delivering a strong and differentiated brand – that put the purpose 'belief system' into practice. Given how foundational values are to the health of the business and, ultimately, its performance, they have grown in priority for inspiring and aspiring twenty-first century companies. Importantly, though, for values to yield the desired outcome, the process needs to be inside-out, *in that order*. Organizations must be intentional in establishing, embedding, and enacting the values, and *then* they can express those values to the world.

Establishing the values

The first stage in the values lifecycle is identifying and communicating them. Ideally, this would occur with an initial articulation of an organization's purpose, demonstrating intent to act on it from the onset. If not then, some catalytic event, like a merger, or another palpable point of inflection should provide the impetus. But make no mistake, values are not strategies that shift with company priorities. For values to create and preserve the culture and a competitive brand advantage, they must endure. It is therefore critical to take the time to deliberate, and have the courage to be deliberate, in the development of the values statements.

Define distinctive values

Thankfully, those days when companies' walls were papered in generic values posters – rowers illustrating 'teamwork,' a happy family portraying 'customer satisfaction,' finely woven fabrics depicting 'quality' – are fading from memory. Leaders of today's iconic brands recognize that the real value of values lay in their distinction.

As we've seen previously in this book, purpose is ideally born from an existing organizational, brand or product truth. When Airbnb's two initial founders, Brian Chesky and Joe Gebbia, were unable to make rent in San Francisco back in 2007, they threw together a makeshift website, blew up three airbeds, toasted a few Pop Tarts, and hosted their first guests. But they soon realized they were onto something bigger. Rather than the typical tourist traps, they, being local residents, were able to show visitors an authentic version of San Francisco, and the two groups of people who had been strangers just days prior became friends. The platform, the founders realized, could enable travelers to experience a place like a local, and forge bonds between hosts and guests, increasing understanding and acceptance across people of varied backgrounds. Over time, and in the course of conversations with avid members of the Airbnb community, it became apparent that the brand's purpose is to help "create a world where anyone can belong anywhere."

Like purpose, core values should also reflect an existing truth. They should not represent a *volte face* leadership wants to see in the behavior of its least effective employees, or convey the consensus of the entire employee base. Values should reflect how the most effective employees already act on a good day. Often, though by no means exclusively, values will describe the behaviors of the founders in the nascent stages of the organization, and can serve to sustain the high-energy, high performance culture of the early days (referred to by consulting firm Bain as "the Founder's Mentality® culture").[1]

"Be a Cereal Entrepreneur" is an Airbnb value, and a reference to the enterprising ends to which the Airbnb founders went in order to stay afloat in the early days. In the year following that first Airbnb stay, the founders, now including a third, Nate Blecharczyk, had among them racked up a $40,000 debt. During the 2008 U.S. Presidential elections, they designed, packaged, and sold cereal they named 'Obama O's' and 'Cap'n McCain's,' glue-gunning every single box by hand. With a fistful of burns, they were able to continue funding the Airbnb platform until they landed outside investment. As you would expect, this value guides the company's continued entrepreneurial behavior, encouraging a culture of original thinking and resourcefulness.

Design for positive impact

If values are to shape a productive culture, they must induce positive behaviors. 'Be a Host' is an Airbnb value that drives behaviors designed to engender a sense of belonging, like 'caring for others,' 'encouraging others to participate to their fullest,' 'listening,' and 'communicating openly.' A good host also ensures that 'expectations are set clearly,' so that everyone understands the contribution asked of them and how it advances the broader goal. The result is an employee base clear and focused on those behaviors that foster the purpose, and a workforce whose individuals experience the very kind of belonging they seek to bring to the world at large.

Uber is a topical example of a company whose values bred a counter-productive culture. 'Toe-stepping,' 'Always Be Hustlin',' and 'Principled Confrontation' were just a few of the company's original values. While they were distinct and a reflection of founder Travis Kalanick, they were also easily used to justify bad behavior. Rather than steer the company toward positive conduct, the values fathered Uber's infamous 'bro culture' that spawned one reputation scandal after another.

In 2015, the *New York Times* ran a piece entitled, 'What Uber Can Learn From Airbnb's Global Expansion.'[2] It highlighted the real-world impact of the two organizations' starkly contrasting values, as demonstrated in their early approaches to engaging with local governments. "Since it began in 2009, Uber has entered city after city, in Europe and elsewhere, with a largely catch-me-if-you-can attitude," the article states. This behavior is anything but surprising; it was practically *prescribed* by Uber's values. The result was that Uber's "aggressive attitude put it at odds with regulators in many cities that are crucial to the company's global ambitions."[3] On the other hand, Airbnb "tilted toward courting local politicians in many of its most popular markets," and while it "has not gone unscathed by regulators . . . by and large, Airbnb's approach has been to work with regulators, not against them."[4] The value of 'Be a Host' played a pivotal role in the course the company chose to follow.

Dara Khosrowshahi, who succeeded Travis as Uber CEO, came into the organization under intense pressure to change the culture and the brand's reputation. Among his first tasks, he revised the values, including far friendlier ones like "We build globally, we live locally," 'We celebrate differences,' and 'We do the right thing,' which seek to redress many of the negative behaviors previously exhibited by the company.[5] Stakeholders the world over are now waiting, spoon in hand, salivating at the prospect of some value proof in Uber's action pudding.

Build guardrails (not straightjackets)

For values to provide guidance, their expression must include specificity. If an organization relies on headline statements only, it may leave open too wide a field of individual interpretation. A unified culture will remain elusive and the experience of the brand will grow incoherent.

The Airbnb value, "Champion the Mission" (in this case, mission and purpose were used interchangeably), includes specific behaviors sought, some of which include, 'prioritizes work that advances the mission' and 'builds with the long-term in mind.' These short phrases carry heavy weight because in a corporate world where quarterly results can bear outsized influence on a company's actions, this behavioral expectation recognizes the distant horizon over which Airbnb's north star twinkles.

However, each behavior can, and should, be evidenced in a wide variety of actions. The way any given employee chooses to enact the values will be based on preference and life experience. It is thus an expression of individuality. The onus is on the organization to ensure a common understanding of behavioral expectations in order to create a cohesive culture, but to stop short of dictating the actions those behaviors should elicit, in order to foment a diverse workforce.

Make them memorable

The very point of values is for them to guide behavior in the spur of the many moments that happen everyday in which decisions are taken, until those behaviors become instinctive. So, for values to be useful, they must be memorable. When Khosrowshahi took over from Kalanick as Uber CEO, he shortened the list of values from a frightful fourteen to eight. In Airbnb's early days, the organization had six values, but in recent years, reduced them to four.

While there is no magic number, long lists of values can be paralyzing rather than galvanizing. When an issue arises, and immediate response is required, employees might wonder which of the many values they should apply, and in which order of priority. People may apply values opportunistically, pointing to those that justify their desired course of action and passing over others that challenge their direction.

The implicit message in a values laundry list is that no behavior is wrong. The real opportunity is in explicitly defining the few *right* behaviors that everyone is expected to exhibit, all of the time, to create a culture that will drive the organization toward its vision.

Embedding the values

For values to take hold, they must be cultivated across the organization. *Colere*, the Latin root of 'cultivate,' means 'to tend.' Gardening is an apt metaphor for the process of embedding the values. If your goal is a prolific garden, you don't throw seeds into one corner, then expect plants to organically flourish across the land in the months that follow. You gingerly plant them throughout the garden, checking on them frequently as they take root, sprout, and grow. If there is an infestation, you protect the plants and nurture them back to health. If you discover that one plant is harming the health of the others, you pull it out and remove it from the garden.

For stakeholders to experience the values all of the time, they need to be integrated into all facets of the organization, across every process, policy, and practice. The idea of embedding exhaustively can seem . . . well, *exhausting*, but when values are deeply embedded, organizations grow infinitely more efficient. With purpose providing direction, and core values defining behaviors, all company resources point in the same direction, compounding the contribution of each. The workplace becomes friendlier and more collaborative. Decision-making can be decentralized, enabling a more agile operating model to emerge, as individuals and teams are better equipped to respond to volatility. This not only improves speed-to-market, it also creates a workplace far more compatible with the devolution of power demanded by today's workforce, accelerating the shift from the 'directive' management mode of days past and facilitating the 'empowered network' of the future.

Remember that values are expectations for behavior, and undertaking behavior change is a formidable ambition. Like matter, people resist any change to their position or state of motion. In order to be great enough to overcome inertia, the force must be coordinated and consistent. Embedding the values, therefore, requires vigilant effort, a multi-disciplinary plan with timelines and targets, cross-functional owners and teams, ongoing stakeholder engagement and frequent measurement.

Put on your jersey – it's another team sport

We've seen purpose referred to as a team sport previously in this book. The same is true for the values initiative – it needs a manager, captain, and champions who work together and with the wider squad to cascade the values in a top-down manner and ignite a bottom-up movement. Founders or the CEO instigate the initiative and unveil the values, signaling the importance of the effort. They must also personally enact them, visibly hold everyone accountable for exhibiting them, and audibly call out successes and failures. Otherwise, the values will appear vacuous and trust in the leader will be tainted.

The 'captain,' if not the CEO or founders, should be appointed by and have total alignment with them, and be a leader in their own right. The appropriate individual and their team will already possess strong cross-functional alliances they can leverage as they appoint and motivate department heads and other leads to embed the values broadly across their teams and profoundly into their processes and practices.

'Champions' should be appointed across the organization's geographic footprint and levels of seniority. These are employees who innately demonstrate the values and are natural influencers among the ranks. Whether through modeling the behaviors or in a more structured capacity, they play a vital role in encouraging adoption of the values throughout the workforce and prompting positive peer pressure for continued momentum over time.

Share the values, ad nauseum

Lest there be any question, cultivating values does *not* happen in one all hands meeting. The values should be promoted at every opportunity. As values are experienced only if they are enacted consistently, they should form the basis for continuous conversation. Presentations might inform a congregation, but conversations help people internalize information, and remind them of their individual obligation to uphold the values.

The values should also be illuminated in landmark company stories, like the founding, or the turnaround, or the expansion, and elucidated in the everyday stories from employees, the community, and customers. As anyone in marketing will tell you, stories are a powerful way to make information meaningful, motivating, and memorable, so they should be habitually shared across the organization.

Airbnb fastidiously collects, curates, and circulates such stories. One highlighted a Parisian employee's epitomization of "Champion the Mission" when he welcomed a Syrian refugee he had met on the street into his home, taught him French, and helped him get on his feet. Another told the tale of a guest-turned-embodiment of 'Be a Host.' The guest, a licensed pilot, took his aviophobic host for a flight, helping her confront and overcome a lifelong fear. Stories that highlight the values in action (or, inaction, in the case of negative examples for which the company was seeking a solution) were told in routine project meetings, bi-weekly company-wide gatherings, quarterly financial updates, and beyond. This makes some feel queasy, and appeals to others as cultish, but core values that are woven into the fabric of company mythology make for a cohesive culture.

Measure progress as a matter of course

Just as with other projects, the organization should establish the 'look of success' for the values initiative and systematically measure progress against it. Where there are triumphs, they should be trumpeted. Where there are failings, they must be examined, addressed, and announced publicly, otherwise unexpected weeds can take hold, take over, and damage the wellbeing of the whole garden.

Regular pulse surveys reveal employees' experience of the values in the workplace, and help the company understand the source of successes, which can be replicated, and deficits, which can be corrected. Partner and customers' experience of the values should also be measured frequently. This can be done through a variety of methods, like satisfaction surveys, online forums, or more in-depth interviews.

Measuring employee progress in adopting and enacting the values should become a fundamental part of the performance management process. At Airbnb, how employees accomplish their work carries just as much weight as what work, and the standard to which that work, was accomplished. But feedback need not await an annual or semi-annual loop; the more frequently values hits and misses are recognized or rectified, the sooner the behaviors become intrinsic.

Values are a valuable recruitment tool

Performance management is, of course, only one part of the employee process, whereas core values should be embedded into its entirety, from a candidate's first interaction even before interviewing, to the moment they join the LinkedIn alumni group. Given its ability to rapidly impact company culture, recruitment is also worth further exposition here.

In early 2014, I received a message that made my heart soar. Would I be interested in discussing the role of European Marketing Director for Airbnb, I was asked. A million times, yes, I answered. Cookie-cutter travel accommodations have always made me feel like a cow in a herd of cattle subtly being sent to the slaughterhouse of sameness. Airbnb satisfied my preference for local homes, and removed the need to endlessly trawl through homeowners' individual sites and listings across the internet, so I joined the community back in 2011, as a relatively early user.

But it was more than product fit or platform ease that lit me up on first contact; it was the perfect match between the principles with which the company so evidently operated and those that were so inherently my own. As such, I invested everything in making it work, and I negotiated less. A company with strong values has an efficient leg up − it attracts like-minded people, improving the chances for a positive employee and organizational outcome, and often, at a lower cost.

Core values also provide the organization with an effective means to screen for the most relevant talent, thereby preserving the organization's hard-won culture. At Airbnb, candidates are, of course, evaluated on their functional expertise, but select employees also determine candidates' culture fit. The goal is to hire those people predisposed to the desired behaviors, who are more likely to contribute to the culture right from the start. No degree of professional competence trumps core values. If candidates don't already demonstrate them, they simply are not hired.

Importantly, Airbnb's core values interviewers are trained to recognize the difference between *personality* and *values*. This distinction is paramount, because personality reflects our inherent patterns of thinking and feeling, while values involve judgement, reflecting what we choose to do. When characteristics and core values are confounded, employing people who are a culture fit can easily slide down a slippery slope to 'identity recruitment.' The result can be a homogenized workforce with a startling lack of diversity and dangerous group-think.

Deployed judiciously, however, recruiting against core values can create a workplace where people feel ideologically in-step with one another, resulting in numerous gains in productivity, both in 'soft' and 'hard' terms. When members of a team have aligned principles, differences − in personality, points of view, and more − are easier to overcome and can become a catalyst for creativity. When an organization's values mirror that of the individual, employees are liberated to be their true selves, sidestepping one of the greatest stresses in life, according to psychologists − that of pretending to be something we are not. Employees are happier and more fulfilled, as their energy can be expended on a higher quality and quantity of work, rather than squandered on second-guessing their congruity with the crowd. All of this makes for a better employee experience, and reduces turnover and the associated drain on company resources.

Enacting the values

People evaluate brands for what they do, not what they say they are. This really isn't any different to how we assess people. If you and I were to meet at a party, and I told you that my lifelong purpose was to inject a bleak world with more humor, you might initially be intrigued. If, over the course of our interactions that evening, I elicited anything from a chuckle to a belly laugh, my proclaimed purpose would become real for you, as you personally experienced it. With my words backed by action, I would gain your trust and stand out from the other guests who may have reduced you to tears with tedious small talk. If, on the other hand, I did not get even a giggle, you'd be disappointed. You might even deride me as dishonest. Likewise, if a company does not consistently enact the values, inside their walls and 'in the wild,' it will lose credibility among the workforce and the public, and fail to build a strong, differentiated brand in the marketplace.

What happens on the inside matters on the outside

In Kin&Co's 2018 report, 'How To Avoid F###king Up Purpose,' research showed that almost half of workers say their company does not act in line with its purpose and values, and this perceived hypocrisy makes them want to leave their company.[6] Sixty-eight percent said talking purpose but not living it would have a negative impact on their work, causing distrust in leaders and reduced productivity.[7] While this is bad news, it gets worse, because employee grumblings no longer stop at the water cooler.

Warren Buffett once noted, "It takes 20 years to build a reputation and five minutes to ruin it," and never is that more true than in our digitally-connected era.[8] An employee whose experience of the core values is anything less than the promise can take to community apps like Blind, where they are able to anonymously spill the sordid beans, and the press is all too happy to regurgitate them. Customers care, too. Kin&Co reported that 63 percent would not buy from a company that didn't treat their employees well and 61 percent would not buy from a company they felt was hypocritical.[9]

Companies do not have the luxury of focusing exclusively on the external enactment of the values to reap the purpose rewards. The actions they take on the inside inevitably leak out, and the result can be, and often is, a corporate reputation crisis.

What happens on the outside is seen as an inside matter

The supply chain has been the source of a great many corporate misfires. For years, Nike enamored people by rooting for the potential in all of us. But by 1997, the company became symbolic of sweatshop labor, as their subcontracted factories exploited children, and employees were subject to cruel conditions and nominal pay. The purpose they had heralded so loudly suddenly sounded hollow.

The company's initial response was that they did not own the factories and consequently could not control what happened in them. But core values need to be applied to the selection of any kind of partner, from payroll to production to customer service. People are often not aware, or simply do not care, that there is another company behind the scenes. When we choose to work for a company, or buy a company's product or service, we vote for that brand. We expect the company to retain responsibility for the enactment of its values across every part of every process that culminates in the ballot we cast. Any discrepancy will be discovered and the deviant behavior of one will tarnish trust in the other.

Values are often the best course to correct a crisis

While the source of so many reputation scandals today is a failure to enact the values thoroughly, the good news is that values can also help steer an organization through, and out, of crisis. By taking swift action that puts the walk back into the talk, a company can emerge relatively unscathed and, in some cases, stronger.

In 2016, a Harvard Business School study uncovered that across a sample of five U.S. cities, requests from Airbnb guests with distinctively African-American names were 16 percent less likely to be accepted by hosts relative to identical guests with distinctively white names. In swift order, the empirical evidence came to light on social media, particularly via the #AirbnbWhileBlack hashtag. The company was stunned. How could a behavior so antithetical to its values exist within its host community? And what could the organization do to address it?

The response started with a return to the values. In accordance with "Embrace the Adventure," which calls for 'owning and learning from mistakes,' Airbnb executives admitted that they had not created the platform with racism in mind, and, likely, that had something to do with it being started by three white guys. If the company was going to "Champion the Mission" out in the world, they declared, it needed to start by ensuring everyone belonged within its workforce. Managers underwent unconscious bias training, new guidelines regarding under-represented minorities in the candidate pool were put in place, relationships with more universities historically serving minorities were forged, and an executive mandate conveying the priority of diversity over recruitment speed was issued. The organization also extended this drive for diversity to its supplier strategy.

Furthermore, former United States Attorney General, Eric Holder, was hired to help craft a new anti-discrimination policy, and a bespoke team of engineers and product managers was created to experiment with all aspects of the platform – from identity elements like name and photograph to the algorithm – with the objective of fighting bias.

In November of 2016, reflecting the "Be a Host" behaviors of 'communicating openly' and 'setting clear expectations,' Airbnb rolled out the Community

Commitment, requiring every Airbnb user, old and new, to agree to "treat everyone in the Airbnb community – regardless of their race, religion, national origin, ethnicity, disability, sex, gender identity, sexual orientation, or age – with respect, and without judgment or bias" or else be removed from the platform. And it wasn't a stunt. In one of several instances, Airbnb removed users associated with the August 2017 white nationalist rally in Charlottesville, North Carolina.

You will know you're acting on purpose when it inflicts pain

Values force hard decisions and provocative action. But if you are not adhering to principles when those principles are hardest to implement, then they don't exist at all. In the face of a great societal ill like racism, it sounds crass, but the inescapable truth is that Airbnb made tough trade-offs and left some things on the table many companies would not agree to. Engineering and product resources were diverted from activities that could have had an instant impact on business. New steps were introduced on the site risking user drop-off. Hosts and guests were removed for not agreeing or adhering to the values, potentially shrinking supply and dragging demand.

These choices can result in notable losses, and while Airbnb did not experience such setbacks, no one could have predicted the outcome before making the difficult decisions. Because the company acted in a manner congruent with its values, and valued long-term purpose over immediate profit, the organization, and the brand, came out stronger.

Expressing the values

As someone who has spent the majority of her career in marketing, it may seem strange that I am getting to the marketing bit only now. But purpose, core values, culture – these are all organizational issues, not marketing ideas. They simply have no place in a company's external messaging if they have not been first enacted and experienced. That said, purpose and values can, and indeed should, extend to an organization's consumer-facing marketing; it is right that a company communicates what can be expected from it. However there are a few key tenets by which a brand must abide in order to do so with integrity.

Continuity of values

Why can Coca-Cola take on the U.S. immigration issue in an ad and be largely lauded, while Pepsi takes on police-brutality protests and is largely lambasted? Putting aside the quality of execution, it is mainly because one rang true to long-held company values and the other rang hollow.

Coca-Cola has a history of championing unity. This was clear back in the late 1960s when, following the Detroit race riots and assassination of Dr. Martin Luther King, Jr., the company took bold moves for the times with their ad, 'Boys on a Bench.' Black and white teens sat shoulder-to-shoulder, on a segregation bench, enjoying a Coke. It was evident in the famous 'Hilltop' ad ('I'd like to teach the world to sing') during the divisive climate surrounding the Vietnam War. It is a value that is communicated through the company's repeated sponsorship of global events like the Olympics and the World Cup. By the time 'America the Beautiful' aired, during the 2014 and 2017 Super Bowls, it demonstrated an enduring brand ideal.

On the other hand, in April 2017, Pepsi aired an ad in which Kendall Jenner uses the beverage to overcome tension between protesters and police. The timing – when protests against the killings of black people by police were in full swing and filling our newsfeeds – made the move appear manipulative, because the ad was not a demonstration of an enduring brand ideal, but rather a fleeting advertising idea. The public perceived the ploy, and the backlash forced Pepsi to issue an apology for its tone-deaf ad and pull it immediately.

Enlightened self-interest

In the 'Pepsi Jenner' example, the role of the brand was implausible, and to many, offensive. Accompanying an image of her father being pushed back by police officers during a protest, Dr. Martin Luther King's daughter, Bernice, sarcastically tweeted, "If only Daddy would have known about the power of #Pepsi."

But the issue is greater than a conceivable product role in marketing executions. In the case of any for-profit organization, it behooves the brand to have 'enlightened self-interest' in driving the constructive cultural or social change. Airbnb can sincerely make a play for its purpose because when you travel – and you live in someone's home, discover their neighborhood gems, learn from craftsmen, essentially, connect to the local community – you leave that place feeling a sense of belonging. There is also a clear interest for Airbnb to promote belonging beyond an altruistic one. The more people feel confident that they can belong in more places, the more likely they are to travel, thereby growing the company's future audience.

While businesses increasingly operate with more than money in mind, financial health is still a fundamental business imperative. A purpose that does not also serve a company's long-term profit prospective is less likely to procure broad stakeholder support, endure over time, and be credible.

Act first, talk later

For Airbnb, belonging is about principles, not politics. So when, in January of 2017, President Trump issued the travel ban, the company's values forced a prompt response. The organization committed $4 million to the International Rescue Committee (IRC) to support displaced populations, and to provide housing to a minimum of 100,000 refugees over the ensuing five years. The company also enabled donations on its site for the IRC, the International Refugee Assistance Project, and The National Immigration Law Center, pledging to match them to the tune of $100,000 per organization.

In rapid succession, Airbnb founders Brian, Joe, and Nate agreed to buy as-of-yet-unsold airtime during the 2017 Super Bowl. In true "Cereal Entrepreneur" style, they locked themselves away in an editing suite to revise a film, mainly featuring Airbnb employees, that had first been used to bring the Community Commitment to life a few months prior. In under 24 hours, and destined for the year's biggest advertising stage just days later, they birthed the #WeAccept ad:

> We believe . . .
> No matter who you are,
> Where you're from,
> Who you love,
> Or who you worship,
> We all belong.
> The world is more beautiful,
> The more you accept.

The film, which excluded brand mention, was crafted to suit the objective, which was not one of brand preference or conversation. Employees and the core community were proud of the brand's stance, and the film and social activation did generate mentions across media, punching well above its investment weight. But the primary imperative from the start was to drive *participation* in the company's *actions*, by mobilizing the community and consumers to open their homes to refugees in need, or make a much-needed donation.

Make love and alienate people

If beliefs morph to please people, they are not principles, they are pawns. As mentioned before, being true to values forces trade-offs, and this can boil down to reach versus intensity of brand appeal. Airbnb's perspective, a point-of-view I have long shared, is that "it is better to have a hundred people love you than a million people sort of like you."

If a brand stands for nothing in particular, it won't be differentiated, as no distinguishable difference will exist. No one will revile it, but it will never be more than palatable to most. If a brand stands for something specific, the business must embrace that not everyone will stand with it. A brand's purpose grows distinct when values consistently determine its actions. For those not aligned to the ideology, the purpose will be disagreeable and they will recoil from the brand. This is a bitter pill for many companies to swallow, but the flipside is this – when a brand stays true to its principles, the people who stand with it, don't just like it. They *love* it. They become loyal users and advocates, spreading positive word-of-mouth throughout their network, the best marketing a brand can't buy.

This sentiment is neatly packaged in another phrase that echoes through the Airbnb halls, one that reminds employees, when hard choices are being made, that it's ok to leave something, or some*one*, on the table. Simply, but eloquently stated, "Love drives growth. (Not the other way around)."

Conclusion

When I speak on purpose and point to Airbnb examples, I often receive the riposte, "That's great for a company established with purpose at it heart . . . but what about the rest of us?"

The fact is that for any organization, acting on purpose is a delicate balance of nature and nurture, and involves trial and error. Airbnb's purpose was in the nature of the organization at the outset, yes. But, as it experienced rapid growth, had its purpose not been persistently nurtured through the values effort, it would not be admired as the mission-driven brand it is today.

In the case of companies not born with it in their DNA, purpose can be nurtured. The process involves looking inward at the people and the products and reaching deep into the organization's past. It entails looking outward, at category and competitive trends, and cultural tensions. And it necessitates looking onward, at what the organization aspires to be one day and the legacy it longs to leave. The purpose can then be ingrained into the organization's nature, and be experienced by the world at large, through the continual cultivation of the values, from the company's core on out.

The initiative requires time and tenacity. But the rewards reaped – a distinct culture and differentiated brand that perpetually act on purpose – can be great, driving transformative financial value for the business, and transformative social value for the communities in and for which it conducts its business.

9 Activating living experiences

Building brand relevance by putting purpose to work

Jorge Aguilar

Jorge Aguilar is a partner in Prophet's San Francisco office. With experience on both the consulting and industry sides of branding and marketing, Jorge combines strategy and creativity to transform organizations and drive profitable growth. He has partnered with brands such as Samsung, Sony, Marriott, PepsiCo, and Lyft to address their most pressing issues across North America, South America, and Asia. He earned his M.B.A. from Dartmouth's Tuck School of Business, and his undergraduate degree from the Instituto Tecnológico Autónomo de México.

★ ★ ★

For all the reasons already discussed in this book, purpose has gained a great reputation as a powerful tool for re-imagining brands and businesses. But when it comes to building the future, there is one consistent truth: it is easier to think and talk about it than to make it real. It is easier to talk about a future that affects others than a future that requires one to think or act differently. It is just human nature. And this applies to purpose as well. For most companies, while purpose has become part of the everyday business language, there is little to show for it.

Often, companies get it wrong because they think simply having a purpose is the point. They work hard to define that purpose and spend resources communicating it to employees and customers. But the real objective is different. The objective is to become relentlessly relevant in the lives of customers. Why? Because becoming relevant results in extreme loyalty, a tendency to ignore competition, and a commitment to advocate the brand to others. Think about brands like Tesla that have created categories of one in highly competitive markets.

My point is simple: while everybody's talking about purpose, very few understand and unleash its transformative power. And those that do? They're using purpose to continuously find ways to delight and engage. These brands become relevant and indispensable. And as a result, they grow faster than competition.

Take for example, T-Mobile. When rival AT&T called off its bid for T-Mobile in 2011, the struggling business was stuck in fourth place in a category that was both fiercely competitive and utterly despised. But T-Mobile noticed an opportunity in what some might have seen as a dire situation: they saw that consumers were primed for an industry-wide revolt. Wireless carriers were ripping them off at every possible turn and cluttered the experience with fine print and poor customer experiences. The company reoriented itself to solve this problem. They had discovered their purpose: to be the 'Un-carrier,' committed to treating customers right.

Guided by this north star, T-Mobile become the champion of simplicity, fairness, and value in a category that was known for anything but. Instead of just creating a new advertising campaign to launch the Un-Carrier, it decided to make a big move. It put an end to the two-year contract – a business model that had dominated the category for years. And T-Mobile did not stop there. The company became a crusader for better experiences, introducing a steady stream of experience enrichments, each reinforcing this new purpose and adding more benefits.

Over the years, it has continued moving away from a yearly product launch mindset to ongoing innovation. That has included unlimited data, more lines, more music, and most recently, more TV. It's engaged people more frequently and with greater authenticity, creating deeper, more meaningful connections, and delivering ongoing inspiration, even when people are not in the moment of purchase. These experiences resulted in significant value: T-Mobile has become the fastest growing wireless company in the nation and has more than tripled its market capitalization since launching the Un-Carrier strategy.

So let's break this down. What was it that T-Mobile got right, and how did they use purpose to help turn their business around?

First, T-Mobile established shared values with customers. Their brand not only expressed what they stand for, but also spoke to the underserved needs of the customers they serve. They built the 'Un-carrier' purpose on the value they share with customers and were not distracted by competitive activity – in fact, it was going directly against competitor activity and instead being consumer obsessed that provided this major unlock. How brands build communities around shared values will be further explored in the next chapter.

Second, purpose helped them power their transformation from the inside out. Relevance will only happen when an organization lives the purpose day in and day out. As we've already seen in previous chapters of this book, this happens when the culture and the internal capabilities are in line with the requirements to deliver the purpose, and when employees are highly engaged in doing so. Changing a company's culture means challenging everything: its symbols, stories, rituals, and beliefs. And it needs to begin at the highest levels. In T-Mobile's case, its CEO continues to be the Un-carrier's biggest cheerleader, wearing the brand's trademark pink T-shirt for every video appearance as he advocates for fairer, simpler experiences.

What we will dive into in this chapter is the third thing T-Mobile got right: launching a rolling thunder of living experiences. T-Mobile continuously launched products, services, and experiences to embed themselves in the context of people's lives, beyond the moment of purchase. And it used a strong purpose to guide the development and activation of these experiences.

Getting living experiences right is absolutely critical to delivering on purpose. It is how you activate purpose, and the thing that takes purpose from an academic concept to something that changes outcomes, drives growth, and creates financial value.

Living experiences: what are they?

In the past, an 'exciting' pop-up store would have been enough to make people pay attention to a brand. But the reality is that we live in a new world. We are now always on, always connected, and expect the world to revolve around us. In this new reality, people have increasingly higher expectations about brands they work with and trust. This new world raises the bar for experiences. It is no longer enough to do big experiences hoping that they will resonate with everyone, everywhere.

Experiences must be living. As technology continues to improve and get adopted by consumers, the opportunity to create experiences is endless. Experiences take many forms including new products, services, revenue models, as well as unique partnerships and promotions. With this in mind there are five requirements for living experiences to be effective today and into the future.

They are *hypersonalized*. Experiences are driven by human empathy and designed to feel made 'for me.' As a father of three young kids, one of my favorite examples is Disney's Magic Band. It tracks everything Disney guests need for a smooth vacation – it opens hotel rooms, links to credit cards, and serves as a fast-pass for rides and attractions. Not only is it empathy-driven, based on the understanding that eliminating small hassles will make Disney vacations more magical, but it's also individual – down to enabling cast members to call kids by their favorite nickname. Magic Bands have made our holidays even more special as a family.

They are *intelligent*. Experiences enable brands to not only be in learning mode all the time, but also use this knowledge to inform how they think, act, and engage with others. My favorite example is Netflix as it makes specific product recommendations, based on my unique searching and viewing history. It's a feature we've all become so used to that we might miss its stunning accuracy: Netflix says an astonishing 80 percent of all watched content stems from its algorithmic recommendations. What human – even your significant other – could boast that kind of batting average? This is becoming increasingly important as people get wiser about the value exchange between the data they share with brands and the experiences they get in return.

They are *contextual*. Through experiences, brands shift how they feel and look according to the environment in which they operate. This reflects the same pattern we see in people, where they adjust their behavior based on context. We don't tend to act the same when we are in a business meeting and when we are on vacation, yet we are still true to ourselves (hopefully!). My favorite example here is YouTube Kids, which behaves differently and offers different content for kids. Living experiences use that to their advantage to only serve contextually appropriate content.

And finally, they are *engaged*. Brands need to deliver an ongoing stream of experiences, but they can't barrage people. Infused with a digital pulse, they sense when to turn off and on, so they can engage customers in conversations and experiences at the moment when they add the most value. One of my favorite examples is Amazon's Alexa – which makes it fun and natural for people to strike up conversations with Amazon – about everything from the weather to household purchases.

I'm often asked for examples of brands that excel at every single aspect of living experiences. Spotify always comes to mind. Besides its ability to know my musical moods and cravings even before I do, it learns all the time, constantly improving its suggestions – and my musical universe. I especially love its contextual savvy, with a playlist engine providing different songs for time of day, like commuting, or mood. I like that it learns from mistakes, such as killing off the running feature that sucked the life out of phone batteries. And I admire how it stays with me everywhere, with the Uber partnership following me from home to phone to my ride. Spotify is a relentlessly relevant brand for me, given the experiences it provides in my life.

But in reality, delivering living experiences is no easy feat. That's why partnerships have become a core part of building brands. And again, this requires a different approach to partnerships. Why? Historically, organizations tend to focus their partnerships on driving financial value. This is a blind spot as partnerships can and should work harder for them. Some partnerships are great for building the brand, others for driving financial value. Brand-driven deals help shape perceptions and increase the ability to extend into peoples' lives beyond the traditional scope. And increasingly, partnerships are helping brands acquire and make the most of data for marketing and customer experience purposes. Although the best partnerships hit on one of these elements, organizations need to approach partnerships from a portfolio perspective. There is rarely a silver bullet when it comes to partnerships.

Again, T-Mobile provides a compelling example. Besides its partnership with Netflix to provide free subscriptions to customers, it's teamed up with FreeMove to help businesses with global calls. And it's working with FourBlock and Columbia University to create MOOCs (massive open online courses) aimed at the U.S. military community. T-Mobile could not continue to deliver on its purpose over time without creating partnerships that extend its reach and capabilities.

How to build living experiences

There are stark differences between brands that are set up to offer living experiences and those that are not. At the core, brands need to have a purpose that creates shared values with their customers. But delivering on purpose means companies need to think and act differently. And while digitally native companies are in the best position to do this, established companies can, too, but it requires a different lens to run the business and make decisions. I have observed companies make five very clear pivots to shift from static to living experiences and become relentlessly relevant with customers:

1. (Truly) solve for the customer

Traditionally, brands spend large amounts of time and resources gathering 'Voice of the Customer' research and (slowly) translating learnings into products. A common lens is looking at category growth to understand where consumers spent their money to then inform future innovation activity and investments. This process can take months – often planning a year or more ahead of a particular season. By the time a product is ready, there is so much time and money invested, it must be sold, resulting in brands forcing products down consumers' throats.

In this new world, however, living experiences require continuously analyzing inputs, such as eyeballs and traffic, to proactively develop and test products, services, and experiences. The process results in a stream of innovations that respond to current needs in close to real time. To offer living experiences, brands are increasing the variety of data they use, accelerating the frequency of looking at leading indicator data to inform decisions, and really backing away from investments that no longer serve customers.

2. Celebrate speed over perfection

Traditionally, brands like to make a splash with every launch. They spend heavily on media, activation, and promotion and then starve these products of resources as they go after the new shiny thing.

Living experiences require shying away from big splashes and embracing ongoing micro-launches, placing small bets along the way. This shift places less emphasis on profitability and more on relevance – with a willingness to take a hit on short-term gains to get it just right. Brands are focusing on relevance instead of short-term profitability (or at least achieving a better balance of both), engaging customers in pre-launch, from early testing to sampling, and investing on an ongoing basis.

3. Make learning central to the culture

Traditionally, brands prefer home runs to singles, and employees want to work on the highest visibility initiatives to boost their careers. Living experiences require seeing 'failure' as learning, and learning equals success. They understand that decisions generate data to learn from and, as a result, create teams that are biased for action. These teams are empowered to invest or pull the plug on initiatives.

To offer living experiences, brands are redefining values to celebrate action and in-market learning, removing friction from the innovation process, and using metrics that support innovation on longer term time frames with progress checkpoints.

4. Make process a means to an end (not an end in itself)

Traditionally, brands often follow a buttoned-down, well-established process to manage operational and capital investments. These processes are usually protected and inward focused, limiting the flexibility for brands to correct themselves when they go off course or play outside their traditional sandbox.

Living experiences require seeing processes as a high-level set of mechanisms that flex with business conditions. For example, Amazon's package-delivery process tends to be 95 percent automated, but the ultimate execution is up to an empowered individual with the tools necessary to monitor and take control of the process at any minute to keep it on track. Individuals have the authority to continuously modify the process and approve a set of actions to get to successful outcomes. To offer living experiences, brands are adding flexibility and more options to processes, using new technologies – such as AI – to continuously improve, as well as empowering participants to tweak the process for better outcomes.

5. Give employees the chance to say 'Yes'

Traditionally, it's typical to find organizations where many people can say 'No' but very few people can say 'Yes' to pushing innovation forward. Employees often complain of the length of time and amount of effort required to make big decisions.

Living experiences, however, require designing mechanics to empower employees to make decisions. Amazon is famous for 'one-way' and 'two-way' door decisions. One-way door decisions are those that are not reversible and thus will always get more scrutiny. Two-way door decisions (and most are when thought through) are delegated to the business general manager and can move ahead rapidly. To offer living experiences, brands are clearly defining the few 'one-way' decisions that require additional scrutiny and push 'two-way' door decisions down as deep as possible into the organization, breaking large teams into small pods of highly skilled staff to become faster, and re-aligning recruiting and talent development based on an empowered, ambiguous culture rather than functional fit.

Conclusion

I am a believer in the future, in the opportunities it represents. In this context, purpose has become an over-publicized and under leveraged tool to realize those opportunities. If purpose is to become a useful value-creating tool, leadership teams must embrace it to transform their organizations and create living experiences that make their brands relentlessly relevant with customers around the world. And that will lead to uncommon – and more profitable – growth.

10 Building community
Revolutionizing the way we manage brands

Thomas Ordahl

Thomas Ordahl is chief strategy officer of Landor, responsible for managing the global strategy practice across Landor's 26 offices as well as leading brand development for a broad spectrum of clients. He has over 20 years of experience building powerful and agile brands for prominent organizations. Thomas writes, comments, and speaks frequently on strategic branding. He has authored articles for publications that include Admap, Forbes, and The Economist. He has been interviewed and featured on NBC's Today show, CNBC's Power Lunch, MarketPlace radio, and NPR, as well as The New York Times, the Financial Times, Fortune Magazine, and The Washington Post. Thomas regularly lectures at business schools such as New York University's Stern School of Business and presents at conferences for organizations such as The Economist, the Conference Board, Columbia Business School's BRITE Conference, and the American Management Association.

* * *

In 2017 Landor conducted a study analyzing what makes brands successful in today's marketplace.[1] We found that the key factor differentiating top-performing brands is what we came to call the Agility Paradox – the seeming contradiction that the most successful brands have the ability to remain both true to their organizational purpose while adapting to a rapidly evolving environment.

It's widely accepted that in today's fast-moving, highly competitive marketplace organizations must embrace a greater degree of risk, tolerate more failure, and cede control. But what is perhaps less obvious, is that today's marketplace also demands that organizations have a deep and broadly held understanding of their purpose. So how, then, do we *manage* this paradox? How do we balance remaining true to who we are while evolving with the marketplace?

The industry standard term is *brand governance*. It sounds so foreboding and severe, smacking of rules and regulations, policies and procedures. Yet the phrase is not altogether inaccurate. It used to be that the role of brand governance was to ensure that brands were presented consistently, that guidelines were properly executed, and that the rules were followed.

That role is now changing dramatically.

We've spent the last few years examining the intersection of agile brands and brand governance. We interviewed more than 20 Fortune 500 companies, identified best practices, and spoke with industry insiders to better understand the challenges facing brand governance today.

We then assembled a panel of senior executives from leading global brands, many of whom you will hear from in this chapter. Our goal: to establish a new model of brand governance – one as resilient and flexible as the brands it serves.

Brand management has traditionally been occupied with constructing rigid edifices – polished logos, perfected environments, and carefully scripted experiences. But in today's complex, fast-moving marketplace, the concept of control is a fallacy. Michael Kolleth, director of corporate advertising and branding at Dow Chemical Company, comments: "In today's environment, companies have less direct control over their brands than they did 20 years ago. They have to be okay with other people influencing their brands and managing within a more complex ecosystem."

The brand leaders we spoke with overwhelmingly agree: standard brand governance practices are no longer effective (See Box 10.1).

Box 10.1 Five challenges facing brand governance today

1. **Brand has never been more important – or more marginalized**
   - Organizations lack understanding about what brand does and how it should be used.
   - Brand leaders aren't included early on in brand and business decisions.
2. **The brand team are perceived as 'brand cops'**
   - Brand managers are placed in the role of reactive monitors rather than proactive leaders.
   - Brand leaders are not treated as part of the corporate strategy team.
3. **The traditional brand toolkit no longer fits its intended purpose**
   - Adherence to guidelines doesn't guarantee being on-brand.
   - Command-and-control tactics make brands rigid, inefficient, and unrelatable.
4. **The focus is on *what* instead of *why***
   - Brand leaders are overly focused on 'what to do with the assets' rather than the *why* behind the brand.
5. **There is little room to experiment or take risks**
   - All decisions are treated as having equal weight.
   - Brand is inflexible, unable to tolerate small inconsistencies.

"Brands are not static, but highly dynamic. They live and breathe."
—Client panelist

Brands today are shaped by innumerable people across multiple channels and experiences. These groups include employees, partners, agencies, and a wider set of third-party influencers and superfans. They are not passive audiences to be governed, but active participants to be nurtured.

To address this new reality, we need to let go of outdated assumptions. We need a new playbook.

The Brand Community Model

Communities are the linchpin of our new approach to brand governance. If brands must adapt continuously to remain vital, then we must encourage the involvement of those who know them best and care most about them.

Harnessed effectively, communities can be product developers, market makers, help desks, content creators, problem solvers, and more. They are the force that enables an agile brand to grow and flex according to circumstance.

What does it mean to manage brand through community?

"Learning to let go has been key to our success."
—Amy Hogan, Executive Director, Consumer Brand Strategy,
Blue Cross Blue Shield Association

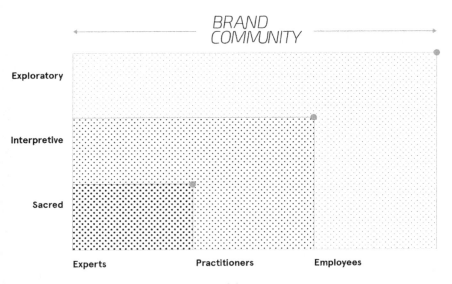

Figure 10.1 The brand community model

To start, it requires challenging two of our most basic assumptions and relinquishing some of our most sacrosanct practices.

The first assumption to debunk: treating all audiences the same. In the past, brand books, guidelines, and training materials were created with the expectation that they would serve everyone equally well. With so many people influencing a brand today, a more nuanced approach is called for.

Second, we must do away with the practice of treating all brand expressions as equally important. Some expressions define the very essence of a brand. Others do not. Prioritization is imperative.

The following framework illustrates how audiences and brand expressions come together to bring a brand to life.

Three levels of communities

Brand leaders need to know how to identify and speak to the multiple audiences within their organizations, providing the right tools and guidance for each. Broadly, we see three levels of communities that play a major role in shaping a brand.

1. Experts

The expert community includes leadership, brand and marketing teams, and agency partners. Experts understand the *why* behind everything the brand does. Their job is to set strategy and define the future of the brand, which requires extensive knowledge of business goals and brand assets. Critical decisions – those that could fundamentally alter the brand – should be made by this community.

2. Practitioners

The second group is made up of the people who implement a brand in the marketplace. They have strong knowledge of the *why* of the brand, but at a more general level than experts. Practitioners include product developers and client managers – and also external brand ambassadors and influencers.

Giving these players a voice in brand governance would have been unthinkable ten years ago. But their impact is huge, and they can be powerful advocates when properly engaged. Allegra Rich, senior director of brand identity at Comcast, notes that "providing permission to explore the brand within certain boundaries is key to fostering innovation."

3. Employees

Employees, the third community, represent the brand on the front lines of consumer interaction. While every employee may not require access to the full range of brand assets and technical guidelines, they must be able to speak for the brand, make quick decisions, and react appropriately to customer requests.

April Britt, director of global brand at FedEx, says, "People within the organization are our advocates. It is fundamental that we help everyone understand what is sacred to our brand – who we are and what we stand for."

Three levels of brand expressions

Just as communities can be identified according to role, brand expressions can be categorized by priority. They fall into three main groups.

1. *The sacred*

These are the elements – verbal, visual, behavioral, experiential – that fundamentally define a brand, making it what it is. They are inviolable. And what's sacred for one brand may not be for another.

For the Salvation Army it could be the sound of the ringing bell and the red kettle. For Singapore Airlines it's the scent of warm towels. Taking away or altering these expressions detracts from the essence of the brand.

2. *The interpretive*

For brands to be agile and responsive, there must also be room for interpretation. The elements that fall into this second group can be adapted based on context, market, or geography.

The five rays at the top of IBM's Smarter Planet logo are sacred and remain constant. But the central icon underneath – the interpretive element – can take on almost any form, from raindrops and flowers to snowflakes and apples, as long as it's contextually relevant.

Google invites interpretation through its Google Doodles, improvisations on its basic wordmark. Most are created by Google staffers, but fans are also invited to submit design ideas commemorating people or events. Google selects the best Doodles to appear on its homepage throughout the year.

3. *The exploratory*

Other aspects of a brand can be opened up for even more creativity and risk. These exploratory expressions may be freely adapted or altered, provided employees use good judgment in representing the brand's values. Opening the door to experimentation can result in unexpected and inspired ideas.

Becky Folds, managing director of consumer brand strategy at Blue Cross Blue Shield Association, explains, "It's about energizing fellow employees to have a common vision for a brand while also understanding that there are 36 or 37 different ways to get there."

Take Disneyland's water art. It was a park custodian who first drew water cartoons of Disney figures on the ground for visitors to enjoy; now the practice is encouraged among all staff. One park worker reflected, "At first I was doing it because it was more fun than cleaning, but then I realized how much guests really liked it. I cried on my last day working because I drew Minnie Mouse for a little girl who hugged me to say thank you because she didn't speak English."

Putting the brand community model to work

Identifying the various communities and expressions of a brand is just the beginning. Success comes from mobilizing the communities and giving them a shared sense of purpose and responsibility.

Here are five actions brand leaders should take to develop strong communities.

1. Prioritize and delegate

Brand leaders must prioritize the most important decisions and expressions, while delegating others. This allows them to focus on major issues and emphasize strategy over tactics.

Amazon founder and CEO Jeff Bezos explains that there are some decisions, like choosing a name or navigating an IPO, which a company cannot easily reverse. Other choices are less significant. A social media message or blog entry, for example, can be altered even after posting. These reversible decisions don't need to be as closely supervised.

> "We prioritize key strategic initiatives that support critical aspects of the long-range financial plan for the company."
> —Allegra Rich, Senior Director, Brand Identity, Comcast

An organization's expert community should handle any irreversible brand decisions – the choices that require deep understanding of positioning and strategy. Experts should also control the brand's sacred expressions, as alterations to these have larger business implications.

Changeable decisions can be delegated to practitioners and employees. These communities have enough understanding of brand values to make informed choices as long as guidance is provided. In this way brands can create appropriate spaces to take risks and test new ideas.

Ritz-Carlton empowers its practitioner and employee communities to make hands-on, day-to-day decisions. Through its WOW initiative, every staff member is allotted $2,000 per day to offer guests the best possible experience. Ritz-Carlton's experts trust its practitioners and employees to understand what is on- and off-brand and act accordingly.

2. Require agency collaboration

A great idea can come from anyone, at any level of an organization, at any time. The same is true of agency partners, from creative teams to media agencies to digital groups, who can cross-pollinate each other's thinking.

Collaboration at this level will be a new and possibly uncomfortable concept for many agencies. One tactic to encourage such teamwork is to set aside a budget specifically for this purpose.

Procter & Gamble makes a point of organizing all-team, all-agency work sessions prior to the launch of new initiatives to ensure that everyone's opinions and questions get heard. The resulting campaigns and ideas tend to be stronger and more holistic, representing multiple viewpoints.

3. Shift from what to why

Shifting the brand conversation from *what* (what assets to use, what the guidelines say) to *why* (why we use assets in specific ways, why the brand holds its core beliefs) enables deeper understanding of how the brand functions. Armed with this knowledge, employees are better equipped to make decisions without detailed guidance from management. This creates a feeling of ownership and gets employees personally invested in the company's success.

> "I believe in a new brand management model that embraces openness and prioritizes the understanding of the why behind the brand."
> —Rich Narasaki, Director, Global Brand and Design, GE

REI's statement of guiding principles emphasizes its values of "fresh air, taking care of our land and communities, and – oh yeah – getting good deals on great gear." Last year, REI walked the talk with #OptOutside, closing its stores on Black Friday to encourage its workforce and customers alike to get outdoors.

4. Broaden the brand team

Specific missions and incentives can create a stronger connection to the brand. This tactic is particularly helpful in bringing untapped ideas from practitioners and employees to the attention of the expert community.

Researchers at Carnegie Mellon and Stanford University, in their effort to fight disease, needed a new approach to mapping ribonucleic acid (RNA). Searching for fresh ideas, they developed an online game, EteRNA, and invited the public to play. Some 40,000 participants took up the challenge, with spectacular results: Today, 99 percent of the solutions proposed by this ad hoc community produce more stable molecules than those generated by computers.

5. Embed the brand

Employee engagement doesn't have to be oversimplified and boring. When done properly, it can be a masterful way to help staff internalize the *why* behind a brand and encourage on-brand behavior.

To help new hires get up to speed on its wide range of menu choices, Domino's turned the pizza-making process into interactive, digital learning modules. This ensures that new employees, no matter their role, know exactly what Domino's offers and what it stands for.

Warby Parker, a retailer specializing in eyeglasses, solicits weekly feedback from staff. Employees report on their accomplishments, rate how happy they are, and submit their innovation proposals, big or small. This enables management to respond quickly to ideas and concerns. Even better, it keeps everyone in sync with the brand and focused on its future.

Conclusion: it takes a community

The Brand Community Model, far from undermining brands, is a dynamic strategy for making them stronger and more viable. If we can rethink assumptions and learn to cede control while at the same time remaining clear and steadfast to our purpose, the implications are exciting and complex. For brand leaders in particular, this approach demands a willingness to change and a focus on:

- *Rallying everyone* – employees and external partners – to play a role in bringing the brand to life
- *Prioritizing decisions* and brand expressions
- *Fostering flexibility* and intuition

Unnerving and uncharted as it may be, managing by community is the path of the future – and the surest way for purposeful and yet adaptive brands to hold their competitive edge in a constantly shifting marketplace.

11 Using those strengths for greater good
A social impact journey and toolkit

Corrie Conrad

At Sephora, Corrie has led the design, launch, and growth of Sephora Stands with key initiatives to support women entrepreneurs, people at transition points in their lives, employees in need, and the planet. Additionally, she oversees inclusion programs to promote diversity and belonging. Corrie believes that one of the biggest opportunities for positive global impact comes from companies intentionally and strategically using their strengths for greater good. Prior to Sephora, Corrie was at Google for eight years where she led program management for an engineering team and ran a number of programs for Google.org. She's also lived and worked in Rwanda with the Clinton Foundation HIV/AIDS Initiative. She was a Morehead-Cain Scholar at UNC-Chapel Hill and earned her MPA from Princeton University.

★ ★ ★

In college, I remember being annoyed when people interpreted my International Studies major to mean International Business. "No," I'd explain. "It's not about making money. It's about helping people." I actually cringe a bit now writing that, but that's how I felt at the time. Maybe things often start black and white until life experience reveals the infinite possibilities of blending and the beauty of gray.

I started my career in the non-profit and philanthropic sector. I led a grass-roots non-profit in college that sent 12-year-olds to secondary school in Zimbabwe. After graduate school, my first job was working with the Clinton Foundation in Rwanda to help the government get kids access to the HIV medications they needed. If you'd told me when I lived in Rwanda that my next job would be at Google, I'm sure I wouldn't have believed you. And if you'd told me that I'd leave Google after eight years – during which I'd worked my way into the engineering department (no small feat without an engineering degree) – to go to Sephora, the world's leading prestige beauty retailer, I probably would've said "Huh?" But that's exactly what I did. And here's why.

In the early years of my career I got to see the incredibly important, meaningful work that the non-profit sector does. But consider this: according to the National Philanthropic Trust, the top 10 United States philanthropic foundations by 2017 assets have endowments totaling over $127 billion.[1] If five percent of that is spent a year, the legal requirement for a private foundation, that's about $6.3 billion per year going to charitable work. Compare that to the 2017 Fortune Global list of the top 10 companies by revenue, which totals over $2.7 trillion.[2] If these companies were to allocate just half of one percent to social impact, that would equal over $13.5 billion a year – more than double that back-of-the-envelope calculation on the required annual giving of the top philanthropies.

Given the incredible potential of corporate social impact work, I've spent the last 12 plus years of my career in the private sector helping companies identify and use their unique strengths for greater good in the world. That might include philanthropic giving, but often the real opportunity for strategic impact is more likely to come from a company authentically doing what only they can do to make the world a better place.

So, you want to build an intentional and authentic social impact program within a purpose-led company? I hope the tools and stories I share in this chapter may help you to do exactly that. But first, let's get clear on what I mean by social impact.

What's in a name?

To me it matters less what a do-good department is called and more what a do-good department does. There's too much that needs to be done in this world for us to be divided among ourselves over what we call it. That said, Corporate Social Responsibility (CSR) is the moniker traditionally used to describe the do-good work of a company. More often than not, this takes the form of some kind of philanthropy, or giving money (and possibly volunteer time and company products) away to charitable causes to make a positive difference in the world. At best, corporate charitable giving might resemble the work of private philanthropic foundations – like the Bill and Melinda Gates Foundation for example – should a company decide to set up and staff a separate corporate philanthropic foundation themselves. More often, however, companies simply aren't set up to be as intentional and strategic in their giving as a philanthropic foundation might be – where there are teams of people with expertise in grant-making, coalition building, measurement tracking, and evaluation. Lacking this expertise, CSR efforts might talk about how much money or how many products they gave away, or how many hours they volunteered with how many non-profits, but they may not be able to tell you what that giving actually accomplished in terms of impact.

In addition to philanthropy (giving money, time, and product), CSR can sometimes include sustainability programs. Of course, it might include more, but in my experience, more established companies with a history of community-focus use the term CSR to mean charitable giving.

The concept of 'Shared Value,' coined by Mark R. Kramer and Michael E. Porter in 2006, along with the B-Corp movement, have started to shake up the CSR space, strongly influencing a newer wave of thinking about the relationship between corporations and society. The premise of this new wave is one echoed throughout this book – that values and value go hand in hand, and that companies can connect how they make money with how they contribute to the world.

Reflecting this movement, newer companies are using the term 'social impact' to describe their do-good work. With social impact, the focus is intentionally on generating impact by *using the strengths of the company for greater good* (Figure 11.1). Beyond charitable giving, corporate social impact efforts orient toward actual outcomes and the impact of the work, and recognize that doing good is good for business, too.

Part of the beauty of purpose-led brands making sustainable impact is precisely that companies make money. They have business models. They have revenue and resources they can allocate to do good. At Google, this meant we could do work like Google Flu Trends, using aggregated and anonymous search data for disease surveillance in near real-time. Bringing epidemiologists together with computer scientists resulted in breakthrough work that Google was uniquely positioned to deliver. Over years of working on amazing projects like this, I got to learn about and experiment with what interested me the most: how to use a company's unique strengths in an authentic way to meet needs in the places it operates, to inspire its employees, and to build love and loyalty among its customers. It's ultimately this blending of purpose and profit where I've found my passion.

Enter Sephora.

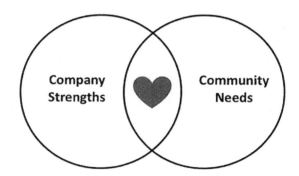

Figure 11.1 Where strengths meet needs = unique social impact

Getting started: place and purpose

Sephora wanted to grow their purpose-led programming and offered me a blank slate to create new social impact programs. To me that sounded fun. I also had the inside scoop from my sister who had worked in two of Sephora's retail locations. She loved working for Sephora. The team dynamic in-store and values-driven culture made a real impression on her and she felt like this role would have real impact across the company. CEO buy-in? Check. Good company culture? Check. Needless to say, I took the job.

So where to start when tasked to re-frame and re-build a social impact program or build one from scratch?

First things first, it's critical to figure out where social impact programs will live within the organization. I've seen the social impact function sit in a variety of different places, and as with most things, each function it could report to has pluses and minuses. Though CEO buy-in is critical, reporting directly to the CEO is not always ideal. Relying on the CEO to fully represent and advocate for social impact programs may prove challenging since CEOs also play a facilitator role among the executive committee. Reporting to human resources has the positive of tying directly to employee experience, a key part of any corporate social impact program, but may be less connected to the customer experience or operations of the company – two key areas you're also going to want your program to engage. Similarly, reporting to marketing often has the positive of customer-facing campaigns and outreach, but may lack the employee and operations connections you need. It can also run the risk being perceived as a marketing tactic instead of as an integrated and authentic social impact program the company is trying to build. You can help set the program up for success by thinking about structure and identifying your executive committee champions early on. Does one department hold more weight than the others? Focus on building a relationship there. At Google, that was engineering. If engineering was on board, resources would follow.

Probably more important than 'what function' is the 'to whom.' A key takeaway here is that if you're the one leading the social impact effort, you're going to want champions on the executive committee. If you're in a position to be on the executive committee, fantastic. If not, it can still work and be highly impactful, you'll just need to make sure that your executive committee representative is a strong advocate, and ideally someone you're reporting to directly. So who is this right person? Do they believe in being a purpose-led company? How will they advocate for social impact? How have they championed other initiatives from their teams? Are they open to thinking beyond traditional monetary donations and embracing creative ways to use the company's unique strengths for greater good in the world? What resources will they provide (budget and headcount)? How do others that report to them like working for them? What type of manager are they? Think about these things and ask questions. Ultimately, the people you work with most closely will have a huge impact on your experience.

In addition to knowing from the outset where social impact lives within the organization, who you report to, and who your advocates are, it's important for someone building a social impact program to understand a company's purpose. Purpose is a company's north star, the 'why' a company does what it does, not the what or the how. The social impact programs should align to that purpose and reflect the how and the what.

From her time in store, my sister shared with me the following story of helping a client who was uncomfortably browsing red lipsticks. "I asked her how I could help, and she shared with me that she'd never worn red lipstick, but her grandmother always did. She said she was headed to her grandma's funeral and wanted to wear red lipstick in honor of her." It was a moment when lipstick was so much more than just lipstick. "That's my why," my sister shared – that personal, human moment, helping someone try something new in honor of someone she loved.

During my first year at Sephora, our leadership team kicked off a focused effort to put words around our company's purpose, and through many internal interviews and much listening, we heard stories like my sister's over and over – stories of our people helping clients define their own beauty, of human connection and celebration, and of inspiring fearlessness. Ultimately, Sephora's talented editorial team captured the company's purpose best with the following:

At Sephora, we believe beauty is for each person to define and ours to celebrate. Together, we support and encourage bold choices in beauty – and in life. Our purpose is to inspire fearlessness.

Whether it's rocking a bold red lip when you've never done so before, or trying a new fragrance before you head to a job interview, or learning to draw eyebrows after cancer treatment, there are thousands of stories where Sephora's employees are encouraging and inspiring fearlessness in our clients every day.

The effort to codify Sephora's purpose happened in parallel with much of my initial work to craft Sephora's social impact approach and strategy. I found that really helpful, as a defined purpose provided the north star towards which we could also orient our social impact programs.

Armed with the knowledge of place and purpose, I was ready to start the work of building the program.

Crafting a social impact strategy

I like to say I spent my first three months at Sephora as an anthropologist. My ethnography and fieldwork training from that International Studies major have proved useful time and again in my career. During those first 90 days I interviewed over 100 colleagues across various parts of the business, at headquarters and in stores. I observed, held focus groups, asked lots of questions, and tried to listen well.

I was new to beauty and retail and, while providing its own challenges, it probably helped me more than I realized. Beyond wanting to discover the unique strengths of the company, I didn't have an agenda going in of what I was trying to build. I was trying to learn who we were and where Sephora excelled. What were Sephora's strengths?

In every interview, focus group, or session I held I'd ask the same question: in one word, what is Sephora to you? I then plotted all those one-word data points in a word graphic. The more times a word was mentioned, the larger it would be in the graphic. This made it easier to see the dominant themes and to cluster words and concepts together that were similar. It also provided a clear visual I could share to reflect back all the input I'd received. Clear clusters emerged around women, beauty, home, innovation, and empowerment to name a few. These could easily be seen as differentiators and as strengths. I'd come from tech where women were less than 20 percent of employees, whereas at Sephora women made up more than 80 percent of the workforce – and that percentage went even higher when looking at our customer base. It's a company of amazing women leaders serving incredible women clients.

Sephora's a beauty company – uniquely positioned with strengths in color cosmetics, fragrance, skincare, haircare, wellness and accessories, and a history of being disruptive in this industry. When Sephora got its start in the U.S. in the late 90's cosmetics were still behind glass cases in department stores and salespeople were paid commission for selling specific brands. Sephora innovated and said, come play with the product, try it. No more glass cases. Beauty Advisors, Sephora's in-store employees, were paid to help the client find what would best fit her needs from across the whole assortment, rather than commission for pushing a particular brand. Additionally, the well-known brands at the time weren't as interested or able to launch with Sephora. Some had pre-existing contracts with other retailers that didn't allow it, others weren't yet sold on the new business model Sephora proposed. Sephora's merchants and buyers weren't discouraged. Instead, they went and found new brands that weren't yet discovered and helped those founders build their businesses. There was a history of supporting entrepreneurs and innovation at the heart of Sephora's start in the Americas. I loved learning that.

A final theme I'll comment on here is the concept of 'home.' I was not expecting for so many people to answer that for them, Sephora was 'home' or 'family' or 'team.' I was touched by this. Though Sephora's the only retail company I've worked for, I dare say this sense of community is unique. Others with more retail experience than me agree. There was something very special about the sense of camaraderie and family in our stores and across our company. I began to ponder how we might tap into that in some way.

Having identified strengths in 'women,' 'beauty entrepreneurship,' and 'home,' I then facilitated brainstorms around these topics. What are the needs in the communities where Sephora has stores? Where and how might our unique strengths meet these needs?

Sephora has three core brand behaviors: teach, inspire, and play. How might these align with the other strengths identified to meet needs in our communities?

Sephora offers free beauty classes in store to teach new make-up and skincare tips – how might we make use of that existing infrastructure and expertise for greater good? I pulled data on the top selling beauty brands and discovered that the majority of those at that time were led or founded by men. Women were underrepresented, even in beauty leadership, among top brands. How might we address that? What could we do to improve gender equality, as a company with so many women as employees and clients? These were the questions I asked as I began to move from gathering information and listening to crafting a strategy.

If the first three months were me as an anthropologist, the next three were me as consultant. The skills I honed synthesizing content, creating decks, and presenting while at Google.org under the leadership of a former McKinsey partner came in very handy during that time.

Announced publicly in January of 2016, Sephora Stands became our social impact umbrella to support the beauty of fearlessness. With the help and input of colleagues, we identified what became an initial three key initiatives that used Sephora's strengths for greater good: Classes for Confidence, Accelerate, and the Together Fund. Classes for Confidence would offer beauty classes for people in transition. Accelerate would build an ecosystem of support for women entrepreneurs in beauty. And the Together Fund would provide financial support to members of the Sephora employee family during emergencies and disasters, with all employee donations receiving a 100 percent match by Sephora. These programs would build on the strengths and core brand behaviors that surfaced during that listening time (teaching, inspiring, creating a sense of 'home' and 'family') while also speaking to our larger brand purpose platform: whether going for a job interview, starting a woman-owned beauty company or facing a personal emergency or hardship – all potentially scary and daunting things – Sephora Stands would use Sephora's unique strengths for greater good in our communities and for our people, to inspire fearlessness.

With this shell of a plan, and executive committee buy-in, we were ready to bring the program to life. To do this, I needed cross-functional guidance and ownership – until the end of that first year, when I hired my first two team members, I was still a team of one. Enter the 'task force' concept. For both Classes for Confidence and Accelerate, I created and managed task force teams with six to ten people from the relevant departments to shape and define what these programs would become.

Classes for Confidence: the importance of a pilot

To bring to life the process we followed when building each of the programs under the Sephora Stands umbrella, I want to home in on one. Classes for Confidence would use our existing in-store class infrastructure (Sephora already provided free in-store classes) to provide a special 90 minute class tailored to the needs of people in transition.

We decided to start with a focus on work-force entry and re-entry. We could easily tweak existing class curriculum to teach a natural, professional look that would be perfect for job interviews. Research had shown that the make-up a woman does or doesn't wear in a job interview was correlated with the outcome. According to the study, too much make-up didn't help. Neither did wearing no make-up. There's a natural, professional make-up look that did help, and we could teach that – in fact this opportunity uniquely played to Sephora's strengths. This was the part of the workforce entry journey Sephora could help with, and could potentially include a product donation opportunity to participants, as well. We just needed local partners that were taking a holistic approach to help with the rest of the workforce entry journey – things like resume writing, wardrobe provision, and interview skills.

Was this a good idea? How could we find out? I subscribed to the test and iterate approach to program development, or, as product development was often described at Google, 'launch early and often.' If you wait until things are perfect, you'll never start, and there is so much to be learned by doing and learning and tweaking and doing better next time.

So, we piloted. We held our first Classes for Confidence pilot at a Sephora store in Houston in July of 2015 with a local non-profit partner that helped women find jobs. They provided holistic support covering interview preparation, resume writing, and wardrobe. We offered the piece we were good at: teaching a make-up look that was on point for job interviews.

That first pilot class was followed by about ten others in diverse locations. We learned a ton. I went in-person for that very first class and took one of my two summer interns with me (I've had incredible interns – they were key to the early progress). Turnout was great and our Sephora employees were so inspired and motivated. It meant a lot that they were being paid for their time to give of their skills in support of their community. (That's right. This was not a volunteer program. We were building this into the paid time for our people.) So in addition to the use of Sephora's store and the special private class event we were hosting for that non-profit partner, we were paying our employees to run it and providing a free gift to those class participants that attended.

When one participant brought her child, we learned we'd need to give guidance about that. We learned that many participants relied on public transit to get to the class and that transit options would need to be a consideration to ensure access. We hadn't even thought of these things before that first pilot class. The pilots gave us the initial data needed to iterate and make Classes for Confidence a company-wide program that launched in spring of 2016.

Two and a half years later, 80 percent of Sephora stores in the United States have participated in Classes for Confidence and we've held our 1,000th class reaching a total of over 10,000 people, 83 percent of whom report feeling confident after attending a class. We've added two new curricula: 'Brave Beauty in the Face of Cancer' and 'Bold Beauty for the Transgender Community.' Each was developed with guidance and input from our own employees with relevant personal journeys, and we've directly partnered with over 500 non-profit organizations in our communities through these classes. We've also inspired global Sephora interest, with Classes for Confidence rolling out in Canada and parts of Southern Europe, so far. Here are quotes from two Sephora Stands' Classes for Confidence participants:

> "I have to say that every time I tell someone about the Brave Beauty class I well up! It was one of the most inspirational mornings I have experienced. I've seen some of the women since that class and they are still raving about their experience . . . they loved being in the Sephora store and for a while they could take their mind off of their cancer. I am just in awe."
> —Darla K. Watanabe, BSN, RN, PHN, Director,
> Supportive Care Programs, Stanford Health Care Cancer Center

> "One of our clients who attended a Class for Confidence also participated in a hiring event at our office two weeks later. She shared with her Case Manager how she did her make-up just the way she was taught during the Sephora class. She felt confident and ready to participate in the job interviews, and was hired on the spot later that day by one of our employment partners! It appears that your Classes for Confidence had the exact impact we all hoped they would."
> —Brandon Cosby, Director of Development, OAR Fairfax

Measure. Measure. Measure.

At the very start of this chapter I mentioned that a key difference between CSR and social impact in my mind is that social impact has a strong instinct toward measured impact outcomes. If you're going to build an impact program, you have to think through how you're going to measure that impact very early on.

I spent a decent amount of time thinking about and studying measurement, including concepts like program 'monitoring and evaluation' and 'theory of change' in graduate school. But it was while working at Google that I was introduced to a logic model called 'Outcome Mapping,' a concept presented by the Canadian International Development Research Centre (IDRC).[3] Outcome Mapping is a tool for tracking and evaluating the outcomes of a program. Originally, it was developed to measure research outcomes, where outcomes are defined as behavior change. It's a systems-thinking approach that recognizes any program as part of an interconnected web of relationships. It can be used for planning, monitoring, and evaluation.

Inputs	Activities	Outputs	Outcomes	Impact
What it takes to make your program go.	The things you do.	The things you measure from the things you do.	The "so what?". The change your program actually achieved.	Even bigger "so what?". The ultimate impact that positive change will achieve.

Figure 11.2 Outcome mapping for Sephora Stands, overview

I've adapted this model a lot throughout my career and found it very helpful when thinking through measurement metrics for the Sephora Stands programs. Though I've definitely made it my own (and the original authors might cringe at my simplification of it), I'm sharing what it roughly looks like in case you'll find it helpful, too: Here's an example of what this looked like for Classes for Confidence:

Inputs	Activities	Outputs	Outcomes	Impact
Employee time to run classes	Train class facilitators	# facilitators trained		
	Provide classes	# classes provided		
Payroll dollars to pay employees	Outreach to local partners and communities	# people attended classes		
Store space		# stores participated		
(Often inputs are time, money, venue)		# local partners involved		
		# employees participated		

Figure 11.3 Outcome mapping for Sephora Stands, Classes for Confidence example

Notice that you can have responses for those first three columns without actually being able to show whether your program is working – whether it's actually achieving the positive impact you intend. This happens all the time. Outputs are easy to measure and to talk about. I did it earlier in this chapter. We've held over 1,000 classes reaching over 10,000 people. I'm proud of that reach, but if we stopped there? I hope you'd be asking 'so what?' At Sephora, we want to increase confidence. We want to inspire fearlessness. Are we doing that? How do we measure that?

Inputs	Activities	Outputs	Outcomes	Impact
Employee time to run classes	Train class facilitators	# facilitators trained	Changes in positive emotions (like confidence) and negative emotions among class participants	Jobs found by Classes for Confidence participants
Payroll dollars to pay employees	Provide classes	# classes provided		Effect on love and loyalty towards Sephora both for participants and employees
Store space	Outreach to local partners and communities	# people attended classes	Effect on employee pride in company	
(Often inputs are time, money, venue)		# stores participated		
		# local partners involved		
		# employees participated		

Figure 11.4 Outcome mapping for Sephora Stands, getting to the 'so what?' of Classes for Confidence

This is a simple outline of the things the Classes for Confidence task force identified to track. We felt pretty good about the outcomes as at least a starting point. Impact is often elusive to truly measure because there are so many variables that can influence the ultimate impact you're hoping to achieve. We hoped over time to be able to gather data that might prove telling. To measure outcomes we focused on self-reporting through surveys. One survey was for the class participants and the other for the employees that helped. Each has been tweaked a bit over time and was developed with guidance from Sephora's market research insights and analytics team.

The surveys include questions that help measure social metrics like increases in confidence and happiness. And they also include some of the same questions you'd find on a survey after attending one of Sephora's regular (non Classes for Confidence) classes, like how often the respondent visits a Sephora store and whether they received the level of assistance they needed in the class. They include *both* social metrics and business-relevant metrics. This is important, and potentially uncomfortable for some people who prefer to keep their do-good work completely separate from their business strengths. Being clear on primary motivation can help.

At Sephora our primary motivation for Sephora Stands social impact work is that it's the right thing to do. As a purpose-led company we seek to use our strengths for greater good in our world, to inspire fearlessness. In addition, it turns out that doing good is also good for business. So, of course, my team is tracking those metrics, too.

Sephora started its main classes program as a business initiative to attract clients. The classes are free, and a chance to introduce clients in a fun, hands-on environment to products they hopefully will want to purchase. From a business perspective, those classes work when they yield happy new clients who purchase products. With Classes for Confidence we were taking that existing class infrastructure and asking how it might be used for greater good. The effectiveness of Classes for Confidence isn't measured by products sold, or number of new clients that purchase. And yet, if class participants want to purchase, of course they may, and we are tracking whether they are new to Sephora.

What we're seeing is this. Classes for Confidence attract many people to Sephora who have never been in the store before and previously thought it wasn't for them – over half of Classes for Confidence participants are new to Sephora. This is a business win. The data shows that our stores which hold more Classes for Confidence also have lower class facilitator turn. Retaining class facilitators is another important business goal. And our employees who participate in Classes for Confidence are experiencing and reporting extreme pride in the company.

If we find Classes for Confidence wind up attracting more participants that become new clients of Sephora who actually end up purchasing more than those in other classes, while also influencing retention of key employees, who knows? Maybe over time the whole class business strategy would move toward holding more Classes for Confidence.

Sound easy? It's not.

Patience. Something I've never been very good at. As this book is coming out, I've been at Sephora for four years. We have real results and we have real stories from lives touched and changed. I wish everyone knew about Sephora Stands, but most people don't yet. It takes time.

A few months ago some colleagues in marketing came to me and shared they'd done some focus groups and learned that those they interviewed really wanted to know more about Sephora Stands. My marketing colleagues shared, "They said, if you're doing all that good stuff, why aren't you talking about it?" It was an 'aha' moment. Focus group members said learning about Sephora Stands made them more likely to shop at Sephora in the future. Marketing is seeing an opportunity to say more about Sephora Stands, and we're ready.

Recently, one of our executive team members asked me to prepare a presentation about our do-good work that he could use and present. After presenting it at a local Rotary meeting at the invitation of his friend, he scheduled time with me to share his experience. He was blown away by the positive reaction they'd had to his presentation. "I get it now," he said.

To me, these 'aha' moments by my colleagues are huge wins. I can talk and talk and talk about the topic, but the power of social impact is best experienced personally. I often think about holding Sephora Stands programs with open hands, about sharing the ownership and building up champions that begin to think with the lens toward greater good from where they sit.

My team does a lot, but there's only so much we can do. Part of our job is to create opportunities to share the experience, so others can see first-hand the impact of Sephora Stands and the benefits of using Sephora's strengths for greater good, and be provided a chance to help us think of new ways to do so in the future.

Lest you think this all sounds so simple, straightforward, and easy (ah the beauty of summarizing the highlights for a book chapter!), let me assure you that it wasn't. It was hard. I stumbled through that first year trying to learn a new industry and business and keep things moving forward. I stepped on toes I didn't mean to step on and needed to humbly apologize more than once. Also, on a personal note, I joined Sephora shortly after finishing my maternity leave from Google. I was a first-time mom of a six-month-old trying to blaze a new trail in a well-established company. Thankfully, Sephora is full of kick-ass working moms and I was pleasantly surprised by the support and camaraderie I experienced professionally on that front. Personally, it was still hard.

Looking back there are things I would've done differently, key partners I would've met with much sooner. It's hard to drive toward action and bring everyone along. It's hard to build programs that require the buy-in of many different departments. It's hard to educate toward an impact model that blends the business strengths of a company with the do-good mission. Some people are still more comfortable with charity being clearly charity.

Not that any new undertaking is easy, but I can see the attractiveness of running social impact as an island – specifically if it means more independent decision-making and budget. And yet, what amazing opportunities would be missed. In my experience, the ability for unique impact with depth and scale comes precisely from using the strengths of companies for greater good. That is where the transformative power of business lies. Imagine what we could do if every business used its strengths for greater good. Imagine the world we could create. It isn't easy, but it is worth it. Join us.

III

Case studies on practicing purpose

12 VF Corporation
The journey of becoming a purpose-led portfolio

Haley Rushing and Letitia Webster

With Simon Mainwaring, Nicole Resch, and Ranjani Iyengar

Haley Rushing is the Chief Purposologist and Co-Founder of The Purpose Institute. The Purpose Institute is dedicated exclusively to helping organizations discover and bring to life the core purpose at the heart of the organization and the core values that animate the culture. She co-authored the bestselling book entitled: It's Not What You Sell, It's What You Stand For: Why Every Extraordinary Business is Driven by Purpose *and is a contributing author to* The Conscious Capitalism Field Guide: Tools for Transforming your Organization. *Her years working alongside leaders from Southwest Airlines, Whole Foods Market, Walmart, GE, and John Deere have fueled her passion and commitment for helping organizations on their journey to becoming purpose-driven.*

Letitia Webster is Global Vice President, Sustainability & Responsibility at VF Corporation. As leader of VF's Sustainability & Responsibility program, Letitia Webster is the visionary behind the transition of sustainability into a value driver for VF encapsulated in its recently launched strategy, Made for Change. She's also leading VF's journey to become purpose-led, with the recent launch of their new first ever enterprise-wide purpose. This effort includes working with the brand portfolio to support their purpose efforts and to develop the business strategy that embeds and activates the purpose across the regions, functions, and brands. Her leadership in the field of sustainability and corporate responsibility and her passion for being purpose-led has made her a true champion of using business as a force for good in the world.

★ ★ ★

In January 2017, CEO Steve Rendle, along with the VP of Global Corporate Sustainability Letitia Webster and the Senior Leadership Team, committed VF to becoming a company that would drive positive change across the globe – an orientation that would bring critical relevance to the business and the brands in the VF portfolio. They aspired to be both performance-driven *and* purpose-led.

Making good on this commitment meant they would have to not only re-tool their own organization (what they make, how they make it, and how they market their brands to the world), but also challenge the entire apparel and footwear industry. They would have to re-imagine their role in the world and leverage their unique relationship with employees and consumers to work together to better our shared future.

Changing the very core of any company is no small commitment, but this is particularly true for a heritage portfolio company like VF. Founded in 1899, VF is a $12 billion apparel, footwear, and accessories powerhouse. A global leader with more than 20 brands – including *The North Face®, Vans®, Timberland®, JanSport®, Dickies®, Icebreaker®, Smartwool®*, and many more – VF operates in over 170 countries with over 70,000 associates (what VF calls its employees). Despite an impressive century-long track record of success, when Rendle stepped into the business as CEO it was clear that the world VF had come of age in was radically different from the marketplace the company was now facing. A changing retail landscape, increasing apparel competition, changing consumer lifestyles, a rise in conscious consumption, and the imminent consequences of climate change all made it abundantly clear that business as usual was no longer an option.

So in January of 2017, VF embarked on a purpose discovery journey, tapping into the collective wisdom of the organization to find a higher purpose that would enable them to successfully navigate the new world with passion, clarity, determination, and a sense of urgency. The team partnered with The Purpose Institute and Chief Purposologist, Haley Rushing, as their guide. This is the story of that journey – from the discovery of purpose, to launching it within the organization, to putting it to work for the business.

Discovering purpose

So, where to begin?

Aristotle said, "Where your talents and the needs of the world intersect, therein lies your calling."

With the wisdom of these ancient words in mind, we set out on our journey to discover the authentic purpose at the heart of VF by taking stock of three fundamental elements (Figure 12.1):

1. The *Strengths* of VF: What does VF have the wherewithal to do? Where does VF's potential for greatness reside?
2. The *Passions* of associates: What motivates the people that make up the heart and soul of VF? What do they care deeply about? What do they find meaningful about their work?
3. Areas of *Meaningful Impact*: What problems does VF believe it's equipped to solve? What difference do the people of VF aspire to make in the world?

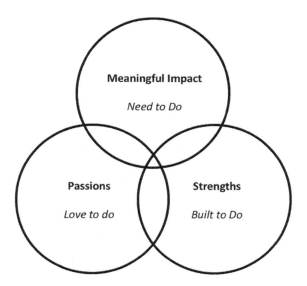

Figure 12.1 The Purpose Venn Diagram

Taking stock

For purpose work to be meaningful and successful, buy-in and engagement from the top is essential. So we began our journey with one-on-one, in-depth interviews with VF's leadership to understand how they thought about the organization's strengths, passions, and potential for meaningful impact. Once we had a good sense of what the leaders believed was possible for the enterprise, we reached out to collect input from over a thousand highly engaged associates throughout the VF portfolio. A final phase then explored the 'needs of the world' that VF could potentially serve. We engaged external stakeholders (in this case, apparel industry experts, NGO's, supply chain partners, retail partners, lifestyle and trends experts, lifestyle enthusiasts and customers, and socially responsible investors) who painted a vivid picture of the problems needing to be addressed in the apparel category and society at large – and the potential role that VF could play in helping solve these problems.

After this exploration was complete, we meticulously crafted three viable purpose statements that captured distinct opportunities that emerged. With these options in hand, we set off to explore them with associates around the globe. We conducted almost two dozen focus groups with approximately 250 people in Asia, the United States, and Europe, and from these conversations we learned what was and wasn't working with the potential purpose statements.

For a global company, this work is essential to ensure that a statement translates well around the world. But for all companies, this socialization also provides an important opportunity to ensure that a potential purpose is ambitious enough to grab the hearts and minds of the people who will be asked to champion it going forward. Deep dialogue was generated around each statement exploring the expectations and hopes for what it might do for the culture, the business, society, and the planet at large. We found that many of the statements that were developed early on, while accurate and true, did little more than reinforce the current state of the business and elicited comments like, "I'm not sure what I would do differently based on that purpose." We received a clear mandate for a purpose that would give people something that connected with their own personal ambitions for working in the service of something they believed in, something that mattered deeply, and something that would force everyone to think differently about the business.

All of this groundwork is essential for arriving at a purpose that will be understood, embraced, and championed by the organization – particularly an organization as complex and diverse as VF. People are much more likely to embrace and champion a purpose that they themselves help to create.

This process of being leader-led and grassroots-fed allowed us to uncover our strengths, passions, and meaningful impact – and ultimately to find the purpose that connected them all (Figure 12.2).

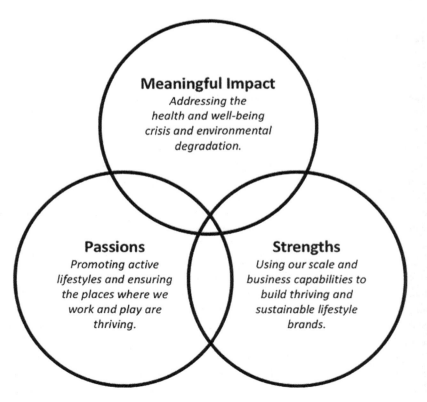

Figure 12.2 VF's Purpose Venn Diagram

Strengths: what can VF be the best in the world at?

"Using our scale and business capabilities to build thriving and sustainable lifestyle brands."

As one of the world's largest apparel and footwear companies with iconic brands, VF has the unique ability to energize people into action and change the rules of engagement for the apparel industry. Almost all stakeholders felt strongly that VF could use its outsized global scale and resources to drive positive impact in ways that smaller players simply can't accomplish on their own.

Passions: what are the people of VF passionate about?

"Promoting active lifestyles and ensuring the places where we work and play are thriving."

The VF portfolio of brands support active lifestyles, whether that's climbing a mountain, skating a ramp, enabling creative self-expression, pursuing adventures, or working with your hands. It's really about pursuing the things you care deeply about and being passionate about your life. It's about never being satisfied as a bystander and leaning into life with our whole selves – emotionally, physically, socially, and spiritually. There was a wellspring of enthusiasm for not just selling lifestyle products but actually powering movements that encourage and support people to live vibrant, fulfilling, active lifestyles.

There was also a passion for ensuring that those active lifestyles are pursued in a *sustainable* way. Sustainable isn't just about being 'green.' It takes on a much larger definition. It's about protecting the natural environment to ensure a stable climate, clean air and water, and abundant resources so that our workers, associates, consumers, and communities around the world have the opportunity to live vibrant and healthy lives for the long-term. Sustainability to us is also about protecting the environments and places that we outfit our consumers to explore, that many of the active lifestyles we promote depend upon, and then helping people get out there and enjoy them.

Meaningful impact: where can VF make the most impact?

"Addressing the health and well-being crisis and environmental degradation."

One of the biggest threats facing a portfolio of active lifestyle brands is the rise of sedentary lifestyles around the world. As people spend more time behind screens engaging in virtual worlds, we're witnessing a precipitous decline in participation in real-world lifestyle activities that are known to positively impact physical, social, and emotional wellbeing. As a result, we're seeing a rise in obesity, lifestyle-related chronic illnesses, depression, and loneliness around the world.

As a portfolio of lifestyle brands, this trend means that VF can no longer take for granted the demand for their products. VF has to move beyond just selling great products to inspiring and enabling people to pursue active, fulfilling lifestyles that the portfolio brands fuel and support. It is also abundantly clear that the negative impact of the industry on the environment is unsustainable and the workers' lives in the supply chain can be continually improved. Because of VF's scale, VF can make decisions and take actions that have significant influence and impact on people and the planet. This was seen not only as an opportunity, but as a responsibility for VF as a leader in the apparel industry.

Taken together, then, these insights informed and inspired an authentic and meaningful purpose for VF:

> "We power movements of sustainable and active lifestyles for the betterment of people and our planet."

The extent to which every word in that sentence was debated relentlessly and explored exhaustively cannot be overstated. In the end, a nutrient-rich statement that captured the depth of meaning the organization was looking for was born.

We = One VF: corporate, supply chain partners, each brand in the portfolio, and all 70,000 associates around the globe are in this together.

Power = We will use our scale and influence to power the change we aspire to make.

Movements = We are no longer just brand-builders, we're movement-makers; creating the catalytic conditions for sustainable and active lifestyles to take root and take off.

Sustainable = The long-term health and viability of people and communities and their ability to thrive on this planet in a sustained way.

Active Lifestyles = Active pursuit of the lifestyles at the heart of each of our brands.

Betterment of People and our Planet = Our ultimate 'why' – the aspiration to use our business and our brands as ways to better the lives of the people we serve and the planet we live on.

While the purpose statement was finalized in the summer of 2017, priming the organization for the eventual purpose launch had already begun. What follows is the roadmap we used to prepare for launch.

Roadmap for the launch

Starting the conversation

Even just starting the conversation on purpose can start to shift the energy in the organization.

While the purpose discovery process was still underway in spring of 2017, the new CEO and his executive team met with VF's top 300 global leaders across the organization for the first time at the annual Global Leadership Conference. The meeting signaled an intended shift in energy, priorities, and leadership style. And it also started a discussion among the wider leadership on what it meant to be a purpose-led organization.

The meeting was designed to be an immersive experience for the leaders to explore the power and possibility in several emerging purpose territories that had been unearthed through the purpose discovery process. We were testing each for its power to elicit the strongest emotional connection and for its ability to serve as a guide for strategic choices facing leaders. VF partnered with Ranjani Iyengar, Managing Director, Bridge-Partnership and a team of Bridge facilitators to help the group consider questions like, 'What difference can purpose make to VF's associates, customers, partners, and the communities it is a part of?' and 'How might a potential purpose territory influence our go-to-market strategy?'

To shift the conversation from the purely analytical we brought in the voices of different stakeholders to speak about their experience of VF. For example, there are millions of factory workers in the apparel supply chain whose lives could be positively impacted by the standards set by apparel companies like VF. A day-in-the-life video of factory workers in a cut-and-sew plant in Bangalore, India served as a wake-up call for leaders to consciously consider the impact of their business practices on lives far removed from their own. Another powerful wake up call was hearing from the Millennial generation that worked at VF and the causes they cared about. Inspired and moved by the possibility of making lives better for the thousands at VF, the leaders created a vision of the future they hoped to realize – a montage of all the individual hopes and dreams of the leaders involved in shaping the next stage of VF's future.

The result of this meeting was the formation of 300 leaders who were inspired, informed, and engaged in the journey to create a purpose-led VF.

Creating a Purpose Council and Purpose Ambassadors

To enroll leaders in further driving the conversation on purpose, we created a Purpose Council. The Council was designed to solicit feedback from VF associates that could help to further refine and vet the emerging purpose territories and begin exploring the implications for how purpose might transform the business. About 60 leaders from the Senior Leadership Meeting signed up to form the Purpose Council. They became the official 'Purpose Ambassadors' during formulation, testing, and launch of the purpose. They were supported and coached on how to conduct and facilitate focus groups, allowing them to capture data free of their own biases and judgements. Through the Council, leaders started to own the purpose and change journey within the organization from very early on in the process. This meant that when the purpose was finalized in the summer of

2017, these leaders were primed and ready to play key roles in helping to prepare for the official launch.

Developing a purpose-aligned portfolio

One of the first things the Purpose Ambassadors realized was that VF's *enterprise* purpose had little chance if it did not align with the individual *brands* within the portfolio. Brand leaders needed to see how their brand would (or could) align with VF's purpose. So, with a newly minted purpose statement, we began working on purpose-alignment across the portfolio in the fall.

For some brands, like *Vans®* and *The North Face®*, the alignment was clear. In many ways, these purpose-led, performance-driven brands played a major role in providing key insights during VF's purpose discovery journey that helped the VF purpose take shape. They had already made the shift from world-class brand-builders to active life-style movement-makers; *Vans®* in the world of creative self-expression and *The North Face®* in equipping and inspiring people to get outdoors. Other brands, like *Timber-land®*, and *JanSport®*, had existing purpose statements in place but that they needed to refine and evolve to be more fully aligned with the new VF purpose.

The workwear division at VF (*Red Kap®, Dickies®, Timberland Pro®, Kodiak®, Walls®, Bulwark FR®, and Horace Small®*) eagerly embraced the opportunity to develop purpose statements that aligned with the VF purpose. The makers, workers, and doers of the world lead some of the most active lifestyles on the planet and they rely on their workwear to get the job done. Great workwear brands are purposefully designed to outfit active lifestyles on the job in a way that will ensure those active lifestyles are sustainable (e.g., the worker is safe, or comfortable, or able to perform well). In many ways, workwear had the potential to become an incredible proof point to the new VF purpose. A series of purpose-discovery workshops were done with each brand in the workwear portfolio – some facilitated by VF associates who had been trained in purpose discovery facilitation and others facilitated with help from The Purpose Institute. After several months of work, a purpose was articulated for each of the workwear brands and for the workwear division overall – and all were 100 percent aligned with the new VF purpose. This process of pulling purpose from the enterprise level through the division level is still ongoing. But getting it right is critical to embedding purpose.

Preparing for an enterprise-wide purpose launch

After a year of testing, shaping, and refining the purpose, we were ready to launch the final statement to the organization at the Global Leadership Conference in May 2018 – the same forum where we had started the purpose conversation just a year before. The Ambassadors were ready to go. And brand purpose statements throughout the portfolio were largely aligned with the soon-to-be-unveiled enterprise purpose.

The goal for the launch was simple but profound – to inspire and engage the entire enterprise to become a truly purpose-led organization. Simon Mainwaring, CEO of We First Branding, and his team led the charge to create the key communication assets essential to a successful internal launch.

As with any important announcement, VF teased the release of its purpose statement with a series of webinars, desk drops, and messaging that hinted at the importance of what was to be announced. The event itself began with Rendle delivering a highly personal speech on the importance of purpose to his personal life, to the brands, and to VF as a whole. This was accompanied by a purpose manifesto video that articulated exactly what VF meant by its purpose statement and the powerful collaborative role that its brands could play to bring it to life. This was followed by an animated 'Bringing our Purpose to Life' roadmap video that outlined the various forms of support that VF would provide to help each of the brands become movements in their own right – from training, to activities, to tools, and to partners. Thousands of VF associates across the world also received a purpose handbook that outlined in detail what VF's purpose statement was, what it meant, and the various ways that VF associates could bring this purpose to life in their professional roles.

All these efforts were unified through a singular visual ID system, style guide, and purpose logo designed specifically for the purpose launch to help bring all the independent efforts together in one visually seamless and aligned effort. Campaign assets including digital templates, posters, stickers, wallscapes, elevator wraps, and floor graphics installed at VF's global headquarters and regional hubs further socialized VF's purpose work internally while showcasing its commitment to the endeavor for the long-term.

VF also understood that it's one thing to want to become a movement and another to realize that ambition at a head and heart level with each and every member of their brand teams. To that end, two specific types of experiences were designed for the launch event to help brand leaders identify what movements they wanted to lead and how to execute them.

The first experience was a movement immersion room in which leading movement makers (unrelated to VF and/or the footwear and apparel industry) shared their personal experiences in building movements, whether the focus was ocean clean-up, diversity and inclusion, or solving the manufacturing skills gap. Large mural walls accompanied each immersion room showing participants statistics and quotes from research and international stakeholders that could inspire brand movements and, on the strength of their experiences, participants were to write their personal visions for the brand movements on walls that became emotional artifacts for each brand.

The second experience was designed to be more of a roll-up-your-sleeves and begin identifying the building-blocks of a purpose-led movement by brand, in which brand leaders from different functional roles and regions around the globe got to brainstorm what their brand movement might be and the most powerful ways to bring it to life. Critical to the success of this event was the collaborative nature of the experience for brand leaders. This was consciously built into the agenda and format of the event culminating in a powerful moment in which representatives of all VF brands took to the stage with rally signs that called out the movements they had committed to. That moment was both exciting for the brands and symbolic of VF's intent to become a movement of movements. This then built to an awards ceremony where individuals and brands were recognized for their contribution to the company's growth and impact. The collaborative experience of the Global Leadership Conference left attendees aligned and inspired to drive business growth, with heart-felt purpose as their guide.

Uniting personal and organizational purpose to amplify impact

VF and its leadership understood early on that developing and launching an inspiring corporate purpose was just the first step in becoming purpose-led, performance-driven, and value creating. Beyond discovering the business' purpose, a second step was to help every associate gain clarity around their own *personal* purpose – and to link this personal purpose to the organizational one. To facilitate this linking, VF invited each one of its 70,000 associates to form a personal connection to *powering movements of sustainable and active lifestyles for the betterment of people and our planet.* VF partnered with Imperative to map out a three-part, *individual* purpose discovery plan.

Part one was to prepare the VF executive team to share how they themselves connected with the VF purpose. Rendle and his senior leadership team started by taking the Imperative Purpose Profile which surfaced their personal purpose based on their preferred scale of impact, values, and unique approach to leading in their work. With this combined set of insights, each member of the executive team developed a 'personal purpose story' to share at the Global Leadership Conference. This executive storytelling, led by Steve Rendle, Letitia Webster, and Jeremy Moon (founder of *Icebreaker®*) started to destigmatize the notion of personal purpose in the workplace. And beyond that, it signaled – to the entire global leadership team – VF's commitment to creating a safe space for people to share their stories and placing purpose at the center of the new employee value proposition.

Following the executive purpose stories, Rendle made a public commitment to all associates that they too would have the opportunity to discover their own sources of fulfillment and create an authentic connection to the VF purpose. To kick off that process, each member of the global leadership team was invited to take the Purpose Assessment. Then, during a 90-minute Personal Purpose Workshop at the GLC, every leader participated in a one-hour, guided conversation with a partner to begin to explore the role their purpose drivers had played in their fulfillment at work. These conversations concluded with a thought exercise about how their individual purpose drivers might serve the VF purpose in the future.

Part three in the journey will be to bring personal purpose to all VF associates around the world. To do this, VF is creating an Individual Purpose Discovery Portal.

Recognizing that purpose is deeply personal, the portal offers associates many different opportunities to engage in their own purpose activation, from independent experiences like the Purpose Assessment to group conversations and webinars. The goal is to provide associates with insights into what they find most fulfilling, and then explore how to bring that to life in service of the VF corporate purpose.

Putting purpose to work

In strategy

There has been a considerable investment of time spent exploring the relationship between the new purpose and the business strategy, which had been established prior to the purpose initiative. Workshops were designed to explore how the purpose might be used to shape the strategy to fulfill the promise of the purpose. For example, in the age of Amazon, Alibaba, and online shopping, 'reinventing retail' is a strategic imperative for VF. The new purpose inspired leaders to explore how retail might be re-imagined as a potential hub for each brand movement.

They brainstormed how to evolve the retail model from product-driven, largely transactional environments to lifestyle-driven, experiential environments designed to inspire and equip lifestyle enthusiasts to pursue the activity at the heart of each brand. This is just one example of how purpose can be used to inform strategic imperatives that are essential for a viable business in today's competitive landscape.

In marketing

When brands have a clear and compelling purpose, marketing can become a powerful force for bringing the purpose to life. At *Vans®*, for example, their purpose is "to enable creative expression – and inspire youth culture – by celebrating and encouraging the Off the Wall attitude that comes from expressing your true self." While the *Vans®* brand was born out of the active lifestyle of skating, it's much more than just skating. It's the attitude embodied in the phrase 'off-the-wall' – a term originally used by skaters to literally describe going off the wall in a drained swimming pool that has now evolved to describe a state of mind or way of being.

Vans® celebrates and enables creative self-expression in those who chose to accept the call to embrace their unique individuality and express themselves to the world – through sport, music, art, or other aspects of youth culture. Just one example of how they've activated their purpose in marketing is through the creation of House of Vans locations across the country. These venues feature places to skate, art installations, free concerts, and opportunities to customize your *Vans®*. *Vans®* is committed to sponsoring sporting events and music events that give people an opportunity to participate and celebrate in the music and arts culture.

Like *Vans®*, other brands in the VF portfolio are now moving beyond table-stakes *brand-building* to life-enhancing, *movement-making*. They're putting their purpose to work by asking how they can use their marketing spend to actually power a movement inspired by the active lifestyle and/or sustainable practices at the heart of their brand. This shift has unleashed a new wave of creativity and unearthed a new realm of meaning for marketers at VF.

In corporate sustainability

Another major initiative that was underway during the purpose journey was the development of VF's global sustainability and responsibility strategy known as 'Made for Change.' In many ways, the work that Letitia Webster and her team was already doing to embed sustainability throughout the business informed, in no small regard, key aspects of the purpose; and as the purpose began to take shape, it too informed the development of the sustainability strategy.

The key elements of Made for Change also served as powerful proof points to the promise of the purpose – stating very clearly what VF was committed to doing to power sustainable and active lifestyles for the betterment of people and planet, specifically:

1. We will pursue *Circular Business Models* such as branded rental and re-commerce business strategies, and emphasize products that are designed to have a second life. This will help to reduce the amount of raw materials we take from the earth to make our products while also enabling us to create new revenue opportunities.
2. We will use our global *Scale for Good* to lessen our impact on resources such as water and cotton and consistently lower our greenhouse gas emissions. Most importantly, we will continue to take actions that focus on the one million workers across our global supply chain to ensure they are working in safe factories and have access to programs that provide clean water, health and nutrition, childcare, and education.
3. VF and our brands will become *Movement Makers*, uniting to serve as a catalyst for global movements that help more people live active lifestyles and access sustainable and responsibly-sourced products. We will support these efforts with strategic investments, targeted advocacy, philanthropic gifts, and collaboration with public and private sector partners.

The key point here is to begin the process of actually using the purpose to inform and shape the activities of the business. Purpose really begins to come to life when it is used as a lens through which decisions are made, strategies are formed, and actions are prioritized. The sooner you begin the hard work of putting purpose to work inside an organization, the sooner it will begin to take root in a truly meaningful way that actually drives the business and creates meaningful impact.

The journey continues

Far from an end, what's been described in this chapter is just the beginning of a new future for VF, its brands, and associates. The through line between personal purpose, company purpose, industry leadership, and cultural impact began at the Global Leadership Conference in 2018 and is now beginning to inform every aspect of decision-making at VF.

The results it hopes to achieve will take hard work and consistent effort over time. Nevertheless, the commitment to purpose has already deepened the humanity of VF, refreshed its brands, and re-energized associates around the globe who are working together *to power movements of sustainable and active lifestyles for the betterment of people and our planet.*

13 Diageo's Ugly Distilling Company
Distilled with purpose

Ila Byrne and Ryan Hunter

Ila Byrne is Ideation Director for Diageo North America with a special focus on holistic innovation for new-to-world and existing trademarks. A traditional brand and innovation strategist by training, a non-traditional corporate entrepreneur by practice. With 15 years of innovation expertise both agency and client side, across global brands and categories, Ila has a unique role as Ideation Director for Diageo where she leads the creation of disruptive consumer-led solutions that challenge the status quo. Fusing a passion for cultural, consumer, and category insights with real world business context, Ila seeks to push brands, categories, or consumer experiences forward enhancing value for all. Some of the other innovations Ila led include Ketel One Botanical Vodka, Cascade Blonde American Whiskey, Baileys Almande Dairy Free Liqueur, Baileys Strawberries & Cream Liqueur, and Crown Royal Texas Mesquite Whiskey.

Ryan Hunter is currently CMO at Binske. Prior to this role, he was a Senior Innovation Manager at Diageo North America, developing products for both new to world brands and existing trademarks. During his time at Diageo, he also led Whiskey Innovation for Diageo Europe and has more than 15 years of experience in marketing and innovation. He has a particular passion for turning great ideas into real brands, and some other innovations Ryan led include I.W. Harper Whiskey, Naked Turtle Rum, and Huxley Whiskey.

★ ★ ★

Writing the concept for Ugly took two hours, but bringing the concept to market took over two years:

> "Every day, 1 in every 3 pieces of farm-fresh produce gets wasted just because of the way it looks. That's more than six billion pounds of produce wasted each year due to cosmetic imperfections and logistic inefficiencies. Now that's really disgusting.
>
> At The UGLY Distilling Co. we see things differently. We believe the best ingredients come from how produce tastes and not just how it looks. In fact, greater flavor and character can come from the ugliest-looking fruit because

they have not been mass manufactured to fit strict, unnatural shape or color specifications.

We are proud to be one of the first American spirits companies distilling imperfect-looking fruit into perfectly pure, fruit vodka. Our goal is to distill spirits with a purpose and to reduce waste to make this planet even more beautiful for generations to come. Love fruit, hate waste, drink UGLY."

The Ugly idea was simple and intuitive. Let's turn the unconscionable excess of the food system into a compelling, purposeful consumer proposition. Let's distill misshapen, odd-looking but otherwise perfectly good fruit into vodka – a spirit that unlike others can be made from just about anything.

Though the idea came quickly, it was informed by our deep understanding of the alcohol category, of our consumers, and of culture. At Diageo the role of ideation is to fuse cultural, consumer, and business insights to create ideas that will resonate with the marketplace and above all sell. We were convinced that the Ugly idea was not just a nice thing to do, but something that could yield viable business results. The idea of an American vodka distilled from imperfect farm-fresh fruit felt like it could really upend the status quo that had defined the vodka category for decades. Quality in this category to date has largely focused on the number of times the vodka liquid is distilled and filtered; we wanted to shift that paradigm and focus on the ingredients to demonstrate that our ugly but fresh fruit ingredients could make an equally delicious vodka. Our focus on where our vodka comes from and how it's made could drive a conversation around ingredients and process transparency – a conversation that is largely owned by whiskey and the craft movement.

Beyond challenging category norms around the vodka liquid, we also wanted to challenge what a modern alcohol brand is. We knew consumers were seeking real connection, transparency, and something to believe in. Eighty-one percent of Millennials expect companies to make a public commitment to good corporate citizenship and they reward those that do – 66 percent of global Millennials are more likely to purchase from brands who do good, and 73 percent are willing to pay a little extra for sustainable offerings. Good is the new cool, and consumers want to 'vote with their dollars' for brands that champion the change they want to see. With the Ugly idea, we saw an amazing opportunity to bring purpose into a category that can sometimes seem superficial and to create a modern alcohol brand built on substance and defined by purpose.

So that was basically the pitch – what if we could create a brand that makes a real difference for our consumers and our planet? "Beautiful vodka distilled from ugly, unloved fruit." We took our pitch to our then CMO of Diageo North America and he gave us the green light on the spot. But he also cautioned us "to do it right or not at all." This unique combination of freedom and direction was exactly what we needed. To make Ugly the right way meant challenging everything we knew about making alcohol, but his support also meant we never settled. We built purpose into our business idea from day one and it quickly became the guiding force for everything we did. This is the story of how we built Ugly and what we learned along the way.

Doing it right: understanding the problem and identifying what we can do about it

From some simple upfront research, we knew that the food waste issue was a massive and growing one. The statistics are jarring. More fruit and vegetables (52 percent of all that's produced) are wasted and end up in a landfill rather than eaten in the U.S. – that's enough wasted fresh food to fill 730 stadiums each year. But why the food system – which starts at the farm and ends at the consumer – produces so much waste was something we needed to better understand.

Over the course of two years, we spoke to dozens of experts in this space – from academics, chef personalities, industry veterans, bartenders, and government officials to farmers, packers, truckers, campaigners, and consumers – who helped us dig behind these statistics. We learned that the food waste problem persists for a number of reasons, with perhaps the biggest one being the laws of supply and demand. We, as consumers, are so accustomed to eating (and drinking) whatever we want whenever we want that food's seasonality has lost its importance. Fueled by years of marketing, we demand perfect, ripe produce year-round and grocery stores meet our demand, keeping mountains of fresh fruits and vegetables on display for us to pick from. Consumers often don't know they can eat 'imperfect' produce until exposed to education around this. Because of our unrealistic and unyielding cosmetic standards when picking our produce (let's be honest, we all reach for the most ripe and unblemished options), it is often cheaper for farmers to plough over their 'imperfect' produce than to pick it. Fundamentally we learned that industrialized farming has no infrastructure in place to deal with the excess produce that does not fit standard specifications. And until very recently there was no demand for 'non standard' produce either. This is slowly starting to change and new supply chains are being created to address imperfect produce.

The issue of wasted food also has framing challenges. People hear 'food waste' and assume its food that's not fit to eat when in fact it's perfectly tasty and nutritious. Another framing challenge we faced was that people tend to think 'ugly' produce means misshapen fruits and vegetables. This is in part true, but there are also many other kinds of cosmetic 'imperfections' – from blemishes and slight bruises to color and size – that lead to so much food wasted along the supply chain. The food waste issue is also wrapped up in the larger concept of sustainability, and we needed to figure out how to position ourselves within that conversation. Though we are certainly leaning into the great shifts we've seen in consumers' awareness and positive response to more sustainable practices, we decided to really focus our concept on the food waste space to ensure the clarity of our message would break through.

We were aware that wasting so much good, fresh food has moral, environmental, and practical dimensions but not quite its magnitude. At a moral level, wasting so much food points not just to flagrant excess and overconsumption, but to the precariousness with which we treat food culturally when 40 million Americans are food insecure. With so many hungry in our country, it's unconscionable that we are wasting so much food. At an environmental level, the food waste that ends up in landfills produces a lot of methane which is a greenhouse gas – more powerful than $CO2$ – that heats up the earth's atmosphere. When we waste food we also a waste huge amounts of groundwater and freshwater resources used to grow the crop. At a practical level, the excess of wasted food comes at a hefty cost. Uneaten food accounts for $22 billion lost each year (equivalent to just over one percent of the United States' total GDP!) and on top of that, efforts to fight hunger cost $167 billion. Wasted food is, at its core, a social justice problem, an environmental problem, and a business efficiency problem. It's this multi-dimensionality that, as one leader in the space told us, makes the wasted food issue a "genie that cannot be put back in the bottle." In other words, a change in how we think about food and a revolution of food systems to tackle waste are bound to happen in America.

And the movement is growing. In popular culture, celebrity chefs like Tom Colicchio built awareness for the wasted food issue through documentaries and other media programming. The issue has also been spotlighted by mainstream media heavyweights like Netflix – whose award-winning *Ugly Delicious* original features chef David Chang showing audiences that tasty meals can come from ugly ingredients – and like John Oliver, whose segment highlighting this issue on the popular *Last Week Tonight* has nearly ten million views and counting. In the culinary scene, imperfect produce is also a rising trend, with the likes of chef Dan Barber, who launched a pop up restaurant called WasteED in New York, hoping to show that 'ugly' food is still delicious. Big retailers have also thrown their weight behind the issue: Whole Foods and Walmart both sell 'imperfect produce,' and Trader Joe's and Kroger, in addition to stocking imperfect produce, each have commitments to long-term programs to combat waste in their companies and communities. We also see a whole host of newer companies cropping up, from Full Harvest and Imperfect Produce to Misfit Juice, that have successfully commercialized the trend by turning wasted foods into consumer products.

Though a number of players are raising awareness for and creating solutions to the inefficiencies and excess of the food system, we still have a long way to go. The challenge with the wasted food problem in America is that it is a systemic one, entrenched in business procedure, government policy, and consumer mindsets. Systemic problems require systemic solutions, and with an issue like this there will be – and must be – many players taking different approaches and tackling different aspects of the larger issue.

In order to 'do Ugly right' the challenge was to carve out a meaningful role for our brand to play within the wasted food movement. From our research, we were able to boil down a few major priorities that we had to get right as we went off to create our purposeful proposition. First, at the product level we learned that we needed to make sure we tapped into the right place in the food supply chain to find our vodka's ugly ingredients; there are many amazing players working to make use of wasted food and our role must be to collaborate with these efforts for greater impact and not (even accidentally) co-opt them. Second, we learned that at a consumer-facing brand level, the biggest value we could bring was to help continue the effort to elevate the conversation around food waste and make it mainstream. And finally, at an activation level, we learned that our role was to stand alongside impassioned people and organizations and meaningfully contribute with these Ugly friends at the frontline.

In short, as a big company, we learned that we should be thinking about how we can meaningfully use our unique efficiency and scale expertise – whether in supply chains or mass-marketing – to add real value to the efforts of activists leading this movement.

Finding our Ugly truth

Brand, especially in the alcohol space, is hugely important. Purchase decisions in the category are largely driven by emotional reasons, meaning people tend to choose a brand based on how it makes them look or feel. Brands become 'identity badges' of sorts, publicly reflecting a consumer's values. The job of the marketing function is to make sure that we know our consumers and evolve our brands so that they continue to reflect their identities and aspirations.

Ugly required a slightly different approach. Ugly was built more like a founder brand in that it was conceived at its very beginning with purpose. From the start we had a few guiding principles that we knew to be true. We knew that we were a values-driven, sustainable business that would offer a great-tasting, fantastic-looking product at a fair price. We knew that we needed to bring new levels of transparency around sourcing and manufacturing to the category and that we wanted to make 'eco-siderate' choices whenever possible. We knew that we were never going to be perfect, but that we had to be honest. This honesty also meant knowing our limitations. We're a vodka brand at the end of the day and we can't take ourselves too seriously or be too righteous about what we're up to. We therefore knew that even though we had a bigger reason to exist, we nonetheless needed to approach the world in a fun, thoughtful, and witty way. We also knew that we were directly challenging the sometimes superficial world of spirits by delivering better vodka made in a better way that is good for consumers' cocktails and for the planet. To this end we knew that we wanted to avoid the trend-focused pursuits of many alcohol brands and commit to being part of the food waste movement for the long-haul.

In order to be authentic, our brand would have to be anchored in these beliefs. But we also knew from our research that the value our brand could bring to the wasted food issue was to help bring the message of the movement to the mainstream. We therefore set out to co-create our brand with consumers to figure out, first, how we could make the food waste issue relevant to their everyday lives.

Though our ambition was to eventually be a national brand we started by speaking with people who are very tapped into the movement and already make lifestyle and purchasing decisions to participate in a good food and beverage system – to make sure we didn't alienate these important stakeholders in the food waste movement. We were delighted to learn that the brand manifestation for these folks did not matter so much. The sentiment we heard over and over again was that the product and the business model speak for themselves, and we didn't need to prove our credibility to this group. They believed in the purity and simplicity of the idea. This was a huge blessing and let us focus our efforts on building a purpose-led brand that spoke to mainstream consumers.

To build this brand we spoke to many mainstream Millennial drinkers and one of the biggest insights was that they, too, saw our proposition first and foremost as 'smart' – often even before 'cool' or 'good.' Time and time again we got feedback that they thought the business model of taking wasted foods and turning them into vodka brilliantly capitalized on a market inefficiency while making the food system sustainable. It was exciting for them to see a big business applying its size and scale in a smart way, for both their business and for the food system. This was a big unlock for us. As a company we were putting in the hard work of doing something good, and consumers could participate by simply making a small purchase decision at the bar or liquor store and feel good about their brand choice.

Armed with our guiding principles and with these consumer insights, it was time to focus our brand purpose – the core truth of our business, and the north star that would guide all of our business decisions. Trying to capture a brand purpose like ours in language is an imprecise exercise that will always fall somewhat short. But this exercise is also a necessary one since it channels energy and aligns direction for various partners and agencies along the journey. For the time being our guiding purpose is: "The Ugly Distilling Co. exists to make it fun for people to do good."

Building a purposeful product

Much of Diageo's success in the alcohol space comes from its distillation and supply chain expertise. Years of perfecting this process has made the company one of the most established, effective, and efficient distillers of alcohol products in the world. But making the Ugly product challenged much of what we know about distilling.

When it came time to make the actual vodka, we knew we wanted to create a new product based on an old world idea of turning excess into an essential ingredient. Distilling alcohol from excess produce is not a new idea. In fact, it's one of the oldest American methods of distillation: to make the most of surplus ripe apples, our ancestors distilled them into a brandy that they could not just drink themselves, but could easily store, move, and sell during winter months when crops were sparse. Our vodka was inspired by this practice of our American forefathers, but in order to achieve it we had to explore new ways of distilling and producing alcohol that are not by nature the most efficient. Despite these complications, we were firm in our belief that our purpose-led approach would lead us to a better quality and more interesting tasting vodka, and to a more enduring solution to wasted food that is kinder to the planet.

So, we set out to build our custom supply chain. This was our first major product challenge and we worked with our agency partners, Upstart Innovation, to identify how to build an optimized supply chain. Now we, the masters of efficiency, were intentionally dealing with the inefficiencies of the food system. This meant that rather than relying on the well-trodden path for sourcing high quality wheat or corn (the typical ingredients for vodka), we had to study the food system, figure out the right place for us to source our ugly ingredients, and solve the logistical nightmare of capturing the fruit for distillation. We began by interviewing people at all levels of the fresh fruit supply chain. Speaking with dozens of farmers, restauranteurs, juice suppliers, bartenders, academics, grocery retailers and more, we quickly learned that food gets wasted at all levels within the production cycle, from farm fields to packing houses, from the produce section in our local stores to the refrigerators in our kitchens.

From this research we were able to hone in on two potential areas to focus our efforts. The first area was the retail and distribution phase of the food system since a large majority of produce is wasted here comparatively. But we quickly ruled this option out because most anti-hunger initiatives source from here and we did not want to reduce the supply for their important efforts. We therefore narrowed in on the second area ripe for rescuing our ugly ingredients in the quantities we needed: the post-harvest phase. It's in this early phase of the food system where the supermodels are sorted from the ugly ducklings. While farms send the perfect, good-looking ones on to central facilities for processing and packing, the ugly ducklings experience a different fate: thousands of misshapen or bruised watermelons lie rotting in fields, tankers of 'ugly' peaches are churned into animal feed, and piles upon piles of 'imperfect' plums are destined for landfills. Importantly, there were few players sourcing ugly fruits and vegetables from this phase. Scale and logistics are really needed to make collecting produce at this phase efficient, and until demand increases things will stay that way. As momentum builds and consumers are better educated on the extent of food waste and the quality of products that can be made from them (juices, jams, chutneys, spreads, distilled spirits) demand for ugly produce and products sourced from this phase will hopefully increase.

After figuring out where within the food system we would gather our ingredients, we then faced our second major challenge: with all of these wasted fruits and veggies at the post-harvest phase, which would be our star ingredient? We had to consider two key criteria, sugar content and fruit availability. When distilling spirits, sugar content (or Brix) is critical. High sugar content leads to a more efficient distillation and a higher yield of the end product, vodka. In most cases, fruit has a higher sugar content than vegetables, so we figured a fruit was probably our best option. In speaking with agricultural waste experts we learned that stone fruits such as peaches and plums are more likely to be categorized as ugly as they are more delicate and have a shorter shelf life than other high sugar fruits, such as apples. There is also a glut of these fruits at peak harvest time because there is a poor secondary market for them. This excess in supply, high Brix content, and tendency to be 'ugly' meant we had found our star ingredients.

Even after deciding upon and obtaining the right fruit, translating this fresh, ugly produce into juice and distilling it into a vodka that meets our stringent quality requirements was much harder than imagined. This was our third major product challenge. Natural farm-fresh fruit, albeit funny looking, is significantly harder to work with than mass produced highly efficient GMO-corn, which tends to be the base of many vodkas. The nuances of this task were outside the scope of Diageo's expertise, and so we needed a juice supplier partner with connections to local farmers and a distiller who was comfortable working with non-traditional production processes. We found our partners in a family-owned California-based juicer with deep ties to the Central Valley farming community; and an independent Idaho distillery with a strong focus on sustainability. These partners shared our brand values and complemented our capabilities.

And with that, The Ugly Distilling Co. will become the first ultra-premium American vodka distilled entirely from excess, unwanted fruit. Everything was decided upon with purpose in mind: our ingredients are ugly fruits sourced from American family farms, juiced by a family-owned juicer, and distilled by a sustainable distillery in Idaho. And of course the vodka itself is incredibly smooth and delicious!

Being Ugly

We had our purpose and we had our product. The next step was to figure out how to bring this brand to life. What would the brand look and feel like? How would we act in the world?

We started with a very important brand symbol: the packaging. Ultimately, we needed a structure that would enable us to stand out on the shelf as a different kind of vodka and a different kind of brand from our competitors. While others still focus on different images of status, we wanted to signal a departure from this old world of spirit – both in terms of how we are thinking about the modern brand and in terms of how we make our alcohol. Likewise, we wanted the pack to effectively juxtapose our ugly, unwanted fruit ingredients with a gorgeous bottle, one that would look equally at home in Whole Foods, at a farm-to-table restaurant, or at a rooftop party.

To get exceptional design work we took a non-traditional, slower approach. We pitched the work to six agencies with a wide range of design backgrounds (most of whom had limited prior experiences working with Diageo). We gave each agency the same creative brief and the same short series of 'interview questions' exploring their experience, passions, and ideas regarding eco-considerate design and our Ugly vodka proposition. We eventually selected an agency with experience designing for impact an sustainability. At the time of going to print, we had agreed on a uniquely beautiful bottle inspired by our ugly fruit with the opportunity to re-define the idea of ugly, making something unwanted something to actually be desired. We worked for months to get to a final beautiful bottle design (Figure 13.1) that brought this premise to life. The bottle is meant to evoke the organic, natural bulbous shape and texture of fruit. The copy on the bottle is also fun and personality-filled, telling the story of the brand while also educating the consumer on wasted food.

Figure 13.1 The Ugly bottle, version 1.0

Beyond the bottle, we also needed a visual and verbal identity that would bring to life our purposeful proposition. The brand's identity is built on four attributes:

1. Timeless – always cool, but never trendy, perpetually modern for the consumer who puts real thought into the choices they make.
2. Imperfect – naturally flawed, candid, and beautiful in its imperfection, because being ugly can be a good thing.
3. Cheeky – smart, but not overly clever. Composition that attracts a playful smile, because at the end of the day, vodka is about fun.
4. Bold – strong, clean and minimal, striking in its own right. Premium, with no need for gimmicks.

Drawing on these attributes, the Ugly logo is powerful, disruptive, and iconic in its simplicity (Figure 13.2). It is purest expression of the brand story and reflects the open honesty in this proposition. The logo icon of the 'U' is simple, modern, and represents a revolution born from ugly fruit. Our choice of typeface is a reflection of our personality: bold and confident, yet cheeky and approachable. To communicate a premium look and feel we have used the simplest and most minimal palette: black and white with a vibrant, optimistic pop of green – a direct salutation to mother nature and our vision for a better, happier planet.

Bringing our purpose-led brand to life also required figuring out what is traditionally called an 'activation' strategy, or the ways we are going to show up in consumers' worlds. True to our brand purpose, we knew that we wanted to put the wasted food issue on more people's radar, but we also didn't want to co-opt or trivialize the

Figure 13.2 The Ugly logo

issue. We wanted our activations to be less about us and our image, and more about meaningfully contributing to the movement alongside our partners in purpose. We hoped to bring mainstream buy-in to the movement, to build relationships with grassroots players, and to act rather than talk. In short, we wanted to bring people together to experience food and beverage the imperfect way. We worked with the team at TRIPTK to figure out how we could strategically build cultural traction in order to meaningfully elevate and progress the wasted food conversation. We worked together to strategize how we could bring people into the brand, the process, and the community – a very different approach from other alcohol brands that act as a 'mirror,' reflecting consumers' aspirations. From grassroots activists to consumers to smaller brands working to tackle food waste, we wanted to bring all of these partners in purpose together to experience food and beverage the imperfect way.

To that end, our activation platform of Ugly Dinners will bring together consumers, retailers, bartenders, sustainability experts, and enthusiastic supporters of the wasted food movement together over fun 'farm-to-glass' experiences to draw attention to the U.S. wasted food epidemic while sharing beautiful dishes from waste ingredients and delicious cocktails made with Ugly vodka. Our aspiration is to create a 'Bored Of Waste' of our ugly friends to champion the issue of wasted food because only together can we truly impact change. Taking the movement to consumers, our bar programming will include zero waste cocktails, education on sustainability practices and beautiful cocktails made from ugly vodka and ugly juices.

This is just the beginning!

Conclusion: what we learned the Ugly way

As this book is coming out, Ugly is preparing to launch in the Summer of 2019. We have ambitious plans for its future, but everything we do will continue to be purpose-led; we are still committed to "doing it right or not at all." As we navigate into the future of Ugly, we're taking with us a few lessons we've learned along the way.

Purpose requires investing in and learning to be entrepreneurial

At Diageo we are constantly inspired by the innovative forefathers who created our industry: Arthur Guinness, Charles Tanqueray, John Walker, Don Julio González-Frausto Estrada, Tom Bulleit, and the Nolet Family. By adopting their pioneering spirit and embracing the original methods of distillation we were able to make a truly authentic yet modern spirit for a new generation of drinkers. Learning to 'invent the wheel' differently meant things could sometimes be slower and more clunky than we were used to, but it also meant that we could create something entirely new, and bring learnings back to Diageo to create a more positive future for our category and our planet.

We may not be perfect, but we must be honest

We are part of the largest alcohol drinks company in the world and with that comes certain external skepticisms when getting into the purposeful entrepreneurial space. To pre-empt these, we have no choice but to be transparent. We are a business and we may not be perfect, but we must, and will be, honest. Creating a transparent supply chain is our bold way of opening up our process to consumers.

Compromises are going to happen, but never compromise on purpose

Challenging a status quo designed to maximize efficiencies, profitability and minimize risk is not just a bold move, it is also expensive, labor-intensive, time consuming, and very risky. But disruptive ideas should aim to challenge everything and when reality sets in there will inevitably be compromises. The filter for making these decisions is purpose: we never compromised on our purpose and vision.

Purpose is lived, not written

Whether writing the business plan, articulating the brand vision, or briefing agencies, we had to articulate our 'purpose' for The Ugly Distilling Co. This process is a must to make things happen, but purpose is so much bigger than we could ever capture in words or a single statement. When creating a new brand, the brand purpose really synthesizes the feeling, instinct, and an intention of the idea's creators, a vision for how that brand will act when it emerges into the real retail and cultural world. Choosing the exact words can be painstaking and will evolve, but agreeing on an aligned sentiment can suffice in setting out the brand's intentions. Brand purpose becomes a way to direct the brand as it grows and a lens for making decisions and choosing partners along the brand journey.

The power of passion

You know you've hit on a strong idea when people's genuine enthusiasm is what propels the idea forward. We were given the go ahead to pursue a truly disruptive idea that challenged the very core of how we traditionally distill. As more and more people were exposed to this idea from internal stakeholders, to bartenders, consumers and experts in the sustainability space, their support and enthusiasm emboldened our belief in it. We learned to never underestimate the power of human passion to offset challenging operational and financial barriers to success.

We're not the hero. We're an ally

It would be arrogant, incredible, and irresponsible to ever think we could be the hero in the story of wasted food, but we can certainly be an ally, a champion, and an advocate. The wasted food and sustainability movements will continue to be disruptive forces influencing consumer choice and innovation for decades to come; in fact there may be a time in the near future where all goods must be made sustainably. As part of that narrative we can be early adopters who successfully translated an excess resource into an essential ingredient and who turned a supply chain inefficiency into a viable business model. But most importantly to us, we could use our brand and our not insignificant influence as Diageo, as a platform to educate consumers that the end result – smooth, super-premium vodka distilled from American farm-fresh, ugly fruit – is just as good, if not better, than many of the best-selling vodkas currently available. Hopefully this brand goes a little way toward helping us all think twice about our choices and consider that 'ugly' produce may indeed taste just as good as the perfect ones, we just have to look beneath the surface.

14 Thorn and Wolff Olins
Bringing clarity to non-profit purpose

Sam Liebeskind and Sarah Potts

Sam Liebeskind is a Senior Strategist at Gin Lane. Prior to this role, he was a Strategy Director at Wolff Olins. He's passionate about designing and building brands that are both desirable and good, and is particularly interested in moments where cutting-edge science and technology meet mainstream media and culture. Over the last few years, he's worked with technology companies and fast-growing startups including Google, Microsoft, Grubhub, and Thorn.

Sarah Potts is the head of Marketing and Communications at Thorn. In this role she led Thorn through the brand process, collaborating closely with the Wolff Olins team. Sarah's passionate about communicating hard truths in inspirational ways. Inspired by the world's toughest problems, her favorite moments are when her work can bring the brightest minds from diverse backgrounds to act on behalf of others. Recently she's been leveraging her skills to scale organizations, non-profits, marketing agencies, and robotics startups alike.

★ ★ ★

Launched in 2012 by Ashton Kutcher and Demi Moore, Thorn is a non-profit dedicated to stopping the sexual abuse of children. The organization focuses on the role technology plays in facilitating child sexual abuse and drives technology innovation by leveraging its knowledge and data to create powerful products that change the child safety landscape. Current products include applications that help law enforcement officers identify and recover victims of child pornography and child sex trafficking much faster than previous methods. Supporting this mission is a deep network of partnerships with non-profits, law enforcement agencies, governments, and leading tech companies like Google, Uber, Facebook, Amazon, Salesforce, Microsoft, IAC – and the list goes on.

Though child pornography was on the decline in the 1980's, the rise of the Internet has driven a radical resurgence: since 2004, there's been over a 5,000 percent increase in files reported of child sexual abuse material (commonly known as child pornography), and these reports represent countless child victims. Abusers are emboldened by the anonymity of the dark web and are doing what everyone does online; building communities, and sharing content. Also fueled by the Internet's connective power and anonymity, child sex trafficking in the United States relies heavily on online escort advertising environments. To date Thorn's technology has helped identify over 30,000 victims, and there's a lot more to be done.

This oral-history-style case study explores the work Wolff Olins and Thorn did together, bringing some of the best minds in branding to bear on the question of how to articulate the organization's critical work in a way that could rally partners in purpose.

Why now?

JULIE CORDUA (CEO @ THORN): The sexual abuse of children is not a new issue, but the rise of the Internet has completely changed the dynamics of child sexual abuse. In 2016, with our five year anniversary approaching – and on the heels of our Co-Founder Ashton Kutcher's viral Senate testimony that brought these issues to many people for the first time – it was time to prepare the organization for our next growth phase.

ASHTON KUTCHER (CO-FOUNDER @ THORN): Once I started to gain some level of fame, I was constantly being asked to lend my name to this or that. And I was wondering, is there a single cause that I can really get behind? One night, I saw a Dateline special about sex trafficking in Cambodia.

Those Cambodian kids were seven, eight, nine years old. I started asking around, and people said to me, "Oh, no, it's happening right here in Los Angeles." I began to do my own investigating. And then I learned that in the U.S., approximately 70 percent of child sex trafficking occurs online. I knew a lot more about the Internet, it was something I had experience with, where I knew a lot of folks who could help. That was the inspiration for Thorn. Because of this amazing team we have been able to build those relationships, bringing together folks who would never be in the same room normally. Google, Microsoft, AWS, Facebook, and so many more partnerships have supported our growth and invested in our products – it's incredible. I frequently say, this is my favorite startup.

JULIE CORDUA (THORN): Our work to date had been mostly behind closed doors, keeping a low profile as we built what we knew needed to be built. In our first two years we had helped find 18,000 victims, and been a part of over 21,000 human trafficking cases. But we weren't speaking about our work on a national stage. Now we had the opportunity to speak on a new level, and we needed a brand refresh to help us achieve our next round of goals. We needed a stronger voice, a clear articulation of the purpose that has always been at our center, and a welcoming brand that would allow for people and companies to align themselves with a vision for what the world could look like if we succeeded in our work.

SARAH POTTS (MARKETING @ THORN): We were at this amazing inflection point. In Thorn's first five years we had become a home base for incredible people, including some of the best engineers in the world, we had built products and programs that were radically improving law enforcement's ability to identify and recover victims, and had a community of leading tech companies invested in pushing the work forward. The work is heavy, but our team has a really warm-hearted, practical, can-do culture, and we needed a way to capture what was working internally, and refine it so we could share it widely.

SARAH GARDNER (DIRECTOR OF DEVELOPMENT @ THORN): Based on conversations with potential donors and volunteers, we knew the main barrier for many people was that they weren't sure if they could sustain a personal connection to the cause. It's a huge decision for someone to decide: this is the cause I want to support. It's deeply reflective of their priorities for world change, and personal fulfillment. Two of our biggest challenges are, first, child sexual abuse is a problem that's not super visible. We can't take our donors on a trip to a village with a new well, or speak directly with people who have received life-saving medical interventions. Two, thinking about children being sexually abused is extremely difficult. To commit to years of engagement is even harder.

JULIE CORDUA (THORN): To make as big of an impact as possible, we needed to find a better way to crystalize our purpose, engage partners, and create hope for the future we were trying to build. So we called Wolff Olins.

BRIAN BOYLAN (CHAIRMAN @ WOLFF OLINS): Wolff Olins exists to help ambitious leaders design radically better organizations. For over 50 years we've been helping to create and build some of the most powerful and purposeful brands in the world. We're an optimistic, idealistic bunch who believe that the best organizations are both desirable and good.

Approaching the opportunity

SAM WILSON (GLOBAL PRINCIPAL @ WOLFF OLINS): In this project, Thorn had less of a challenge and more of an opportunity. The more we learned, the more we saw they had great momentum. They were doing all sorts of extraordinary work, had a line out the door of amazing technology talent, and lots of really big plans. It wasn't like anything was broken. It was more a question of: how could we take this amazing organization with the tiniest team, and make them go boom?

MILA LINARES (SENIOR STRATEGY DIRECTOR @ WOLFF OLINS): We tend to work with organizations at a point of inflection. Over the years, we've been creative partners to both leading businesses like Google, PwC, and GE and amazing non-profits like (RED), Amnesty International, and Macmillan.

SAM LIEBESKIND (STRATEGY DIRECTOR @ WOLFF OLINS): Regardless of their structure, scale, or industry, these organizations tend to share an ambition to define and act on a more clear sense of purpose. At Wolff Olins, we believe every organization should be able to explain, in really simple and human terms, why are they doing what they're doing? The best purpose statements are big and true, and when done right, they can become a solid foundation for all kinds of decisions that get made later on.

CYNTHIA PRATOMO (CREATIVE DIRECTOR @ WOLFF OLINS): When Thorn reached out to us, I was incredibly excited. It was my first month at Wolff Olins and I'd just walked into this amazing project. I thought: this is literally why I joined this place. I was excited because I felt like in [Thorn CEO] Julie, we had a really brave partner who already trusted Wolff Olins because she'd worked with us in the past on Product (RED). And on top of that, the whole Thorn team seemed awesome and ambitious.

SAM LIEBESKIND (WOLFF OLINS): I remember thinking Thorn's partnership model of working with big technology companies and others was really unique. Our team talked a lot about how tech companies, with such enormous impact on the world, have a responsibility to make things better when they can. Here was an example of it really happening, and a chance to help push it even further.

ANKUR NAIK (PROGRAM MANAGER @ WOLFF OLINS): We really believed in their cause so we made the financials work. We knew we wanted to do the project in a highly collaborative way, and approached it like we would with any of our other tech company clients: a tight team and a scrappy, share-often style.

MILA LINARES (WOLFF OLINS): So, keeping things collaborative, the first thing we did together was have a discussion to understand the breadth of the Thorn leadership team's ambition for the organization. Child sexual abuse is a systemic problem with so many interconnected issues. There were so many things they could be doing, but where did their hearts lie? We needed to learn which part of their culture and their vision needed to be honed in on, and brought front and center.

SAM LIEBESKIND (WOLFF OLINS): To start to answer these questions, we talked to Julie, Ashton, board member Ernie Allen, and other senior leaders and advisors. Pretty quickly, it became clear that they wanted to maintain their laser-focus on stopping child sexual abuse – and they wanted to keep the emphasis on technology as the tool they would use to do it. While Thorn had given us free rein to imagine this as a re-brand or a brand refresh, these insights helped us decide we weren't looking for a purpose pivot, but an upgrade.

Finding the purpose

SARAH POTTS (THORN): Early on, we held a workshop with both the Wolff Olins and Thorn full teams – all 15 of us! – in San Francisco. This in-person moment was important to the process. We're a passionate group, with almost everyone managing external relationships and holding responsibility for key organizational goals. This candid dialogue gave everyone at Thorn a chance to share our stories, and challenges upfront. This honesty allowed the Wolff Olins team to hear the uncut version of our vision and purpose for the organization. This transparency was key to the whole process.

CYNTHIA PRATOMO (WOLFF OLINS): Hearing the individual team members talk about their goals and ambition in person felt different from the way Thorn was being written about and shared externally. So much of the language and passion in that conversation drove the thinking and work we did later on.

ANKUR NAIK (WOLFF OLINS): The Thorn team really knew what they were doing and where they wanted to go – and remember, they were already really successful as an organization – so this project became less about us inventing this grand ambition for them, more about us taking their ambition, pushing it a little bit further in ways we knew could be really effective based on our experience, and packaging it up in a way that would aid their future growth.

MILA LINARES (WOLFF OLINS): Together, we identified three things that needed to happen for Thorn to become the kind of organization they envisioned:

1. *A more clear story and vision for the future*: Thorn had always been very purpose-led, but people found it complicated to explain the organization to potential recruits, partners, and donors. We wanted to shift the way they thought about themselves, and in turn, how the world thought about them.

2. *A more uplifting expression*: From the outside, Thorn felt dark, making it difficult for donors and volunteers to engage with it for the long-term. We all felt the look and feel of the brand needed to shift.

3. *More compelling experiences*: Thorn needed to make itself and its work more tangible for more people in order to build stronger, deeper relationships.

Research, strategy, and crafting a story

SAM LIEBESKIND (WOLFF OLINS): With a clear business ambition and priorities nailed down, we set out to build a foundation for the brand – a set of ideas that would inspire the story, identity, and experiences Thorn would create. We're generally looking to answer two questions at this point: What's special about them, and what does the world really need?

MILA LINARES (WOLFF OLINS): In about two weeks, we had something like 20 different conversations with team members, donors, and most crucially, law enforcement. The officers we spoke with – people who are really on the front lines, day in and day out, really helped to set the tone. These guys had an incredible balance of compassion and bite – something we also saw in the people at Thorn. What we heard was both tragic, and inspiring.

LIZ BENSON (STRATEGY @ WOLFF OLINS): Back at the office, and working in parallel, we did a bunch of our own research to dive into their world. We started by looking at other organizations fighting against child sexual exploitation to understand the landscape and the role that Thorn was playing, and could play in the future.

SAM LIEBESKIND (WOLFF OLINS): Thorn's technology angle is super unique – not just in the fight against child sexual abuse, but in the non-profit world in general. As far as we could tell, no one else was trying to fundamentally fight problems and change systems by combining the principles of a technology company with the mission of a non-profit in the way Thorn was. We knew this was definitely something to build on.

With these insights as our foundation, we started to define their spirit and write out a story to frame Thorn's ambition in a way that would inspire their audiences and lead to action. As we saw it, that story would answer, as simply as possible, why does Thorn exist?

We'd been seeing Thorn articulate their purpose in a couple of different ways: "*Eliminate child sexual abuse material from the Internet*," for example, and "*Driving tech innovation to fight child sexual exploitation*." Neither was wrong, but after a couple of conversations, we concluded that both felt impersonal and dark. What Thorn was really trying to do was bigger, and different. For one, the team really cared about people – but this wasn't coming through in their story as strongly as it needed to.

As a group, we talked about this idea of 'adding characters to the story.' We thought, instead of a focus on 'eliminating *abuse material*' – an abstract concept that's faceless, limiting, even though technically correct for their field – the story should be about 'defending *children,*' something everyone could relate to and get behind. The second big shift in the storytelling approach was thinking bigger about the 'battlefield.' While Thorn's approach was digital-first and almost all of their work at the time was focused on the Internet, their big ambition was really about using advanced technologies to stop this abuse from happening, period.

MILA LINARES (WOLFF OLINS): While we were thinking about what the story needed to say, we were also thinking about how the story – and the brand overall – should feel. We worked a great deal on understanding and defining Thorn's personality. [Wolff Olins' chairman] Brian Boylan really challenged us to find values that were not only reflective of who Thorn was at present, but also about who they needed to become in order to succeed in the future. This was a key turning point in the project. Ultimately, we captured the spirit of 'Thorn on their best day' in five words: unstoppable, compassionate, nimble, humble, and fearless. This foundation of principles ended up being something we came back to again and again – for both the story and the visual expression. When building a brand, I think capturing a 'spirit' is as important as articulating a 'purpose.'

SAM LIEBESKIND (WOLFF OLINS): Our story needed to consider many sensitivities, and our language needed to be precise. We had to find this perfect balance between on the one hand using natural, everyday language that would resonate with potential donors and volunteers, and on the other, being technically accurate in a way that would resonate with insiders like law enforcement officers. So for example, should Thorn talk about 'child pornography' (a term most of the public is familiar with) or 'child sexual abuse material' (a more technical term preferred by academics and the law enforcement community)? This took some time, and some back and forth. Another example: when we floated the idea of talking about protecting children from 'predators,' the Thorn team hated it. It didn't feel true to them, and they felt it would be counterproductive. They didn't see themselves as these aggressive hunters – that wasn't their mindset. They were focused a great deal on deterrence, not going on crazy witch hunts.

SAM WILSON (WOLFF OLINS): We've found, particularly with our work with (RED), the way to get people excited and engaged in a subject that's not necessarily pertinent to them is to create desire and align everyone's interest around something positive and beautiful and new, rather than dark and ominous. Everyone knows the world is a tough place, a lot is broken. But people are generally optimistic – you'll be compelling if you can tap into that desire to be a part of the solution. Purpose-led brands work best when they balance urgency with aspiration.

JULIE CORDUA (THORN): Ultimately, the optimistic and visionary approach felt right for us. It was true to the spirit of the people at Thorn. We're all incredibly hopeful about the impact and opportunity of our work.

MILA LINARES (WOLFF OLINS): This shift from the dark reality to the positive opportunity was huge. Instead of dwelling on the depths of the problem as it exists today, Thorn would inspire people to join their cause by painting a picture of the world they were trying to create. In other words: showing what happens when kids don't have to worry about being abused.

SAM LIEBESKIND (WOLFF OLINS): With all of this in mind, we articulated a way for Thorn to talk about what they were doing that was both pointed and broad enough for them to continue to grow: "We build technology to defend children from sexual abuse."

Thorn would focus their energies on keeping children safe in the broadest sense – not just on eliminating sexual abuse material from the Internet. This became the initial core of their new story.

MILA LINARES (WOLFF OLINS): While the initial purpose statement was very functional and clear for audiences, we also felt we needed something that was more emotive, something that would capture the higher level 'why' behind it. For this, we used this *belief* that we'd seen at the heart of the organization: that 'every child has the right to be safe, curious, and happy.' It sort of seems obvious in hindsight, but it turned out to be important to establish as a starting point for the group.

CYNTHIA PRATOMO (WOLFF OLINS): The third part of the story was their vision for the future, and de-facto rallying cry: "We will not let up until every child is free to simply be a kid" or its shorter form "Until every child can be a kid." We felt like being a kid is the purest, most innocent form of childhood. It's what a child is allowed to do if their rights to safety, curiosity, and happiness are defended.

SAM LIEBESKIND (WOLFF OLINS): These three ideas went on to become the core of the brand manifesto we wrote (Figure 14.1). The idea of the manifesto – something we usually write for all of our clients – was to capture not just the purpose statement, but the bigger spirit around it. We teamed up with copywriter Steven Phillips Horst to get it exactly right.

We believe that every child has the right
to be safe, to be curious, to be happy.

But every day, for children across the world,
sexual abuse shatters those rights.

It is a global, invisible emergency –
Aggravated by technology, democratized by the internet.

Technology is a powerful tool. We choose to use it for good.

Thorn builds technology to
defend children from sexual abuse.

We're joining forces with the sharpest minds
from tech, non-profit, government and law enforcement.

Stopping the spread of child sexual abuse material.
Standing up to child traffickers.
Uncovering new kinds of abuse, and fighting those too.

We are an unstoppable force
on one of the most serious missions of our time.
And we will not let up until every child
is free to simply be a kid.

Figure 14.1 Thorn brand manifesto

We often talk about an organization needing to have one single statement that's the 'brand purpose,' but here we have three ideas that work as a set – each existing at a slightly different altitude of abstraction, and each useful for different situations. On the functional level – maybe you could call it 'what they're doing' – Thorn exists "to build technology to defend children from sexual abuse." But they're also united in this belief that "every child has the right to be safe, curious, and happy" and have this bigger, more emotive purpose and timeline for their work about creating a world where "every child is free to simply be a kid." My point is: I don't think a purpose-led brand needs to have just one simple phrase that everyone repeats all the time, everywhere. A kit of connected thoughts can be great, as long as they're all centered around the same concept, while each being distinct enough to be dimensionalizing, not redundant.

Expressing the ideas visually

SAM LIEBESKIND (WOLFF OLINS): You can have the greatest idea or story in the world, but if you can't express it in a way that connects with people emotionally and gets them jazzed about what you're doing, it'll fall flat.

SARAH POTTS (THORN): Before the change in visual identity, Thorn just felt too dark. We'd been using a visual metaphor depicting children as superheroes (Figure 14.2), but it was an easy aesthetic to mimic, and we knew we needed something that was as specific visually as we were strategically. It wasn't enough to not be heavy, it needed to be uplifting.

Figure 14.2 Thorn's logo and imagery style before the project

CYNTHIA PRATOMO (WOLFF OLINS): We started thinking about a new visual identity with a few considerations:
- It should express the strategy and story, building on Thorn's bigger purpose.
- Thorn is both a non-profit and a tech company – we wanted to build an expression system that pulled ideas, symbols, and styles from both worlds.

- It needed to feel active: Thorn is a group of builders, not just thinkers/talkers. Their previous design expression – with a serif, lower-case typeface – was literary and a little bit soft, and we saw them as having a strong, unapologetic presence in real life.
- We wanted to establish them as a peer to the big tech giants – to have that sense of maturity and scale, like something that could endure. Not to feel like a lightweight startup.
- The expression also needed to capture the passion and empathy of the team and partners: this is a group of people who were making sacrifices in their lives, to protect these kids. So the expression couldn't feel cold or mechanical.

KATE RINKER (DESIGN @ WOLFF OLINS): We also didn't want to make Thorn too 'premium' feeling or glossy – because that's not what they're like. They're a scrappy team, willing to roll up their sleeves and do the work.

JAN EUMANN (DESIGN DIRECTOR @ WOLFF OLINS): There were also some very practical considerations. We wanted to build something that was hard-working, that the Thorn team could use easily, and right away. Unlike some of our bigger corporate clients, Thorn didn't have a huge graphic design department. So we sat down with Sarah before designing anything to understand their workflows and skills. This informed some of our decisions later on. For example, we knew they'd be using Google Slides a lot so we'd need to pick a typeface that was part of the Google kit. Little details like this go a long way in building a visual system that works hard for the organization.

KATE RINKER (WOLFF OLINS): We started with about two weeks where we were just exploring a few different graphic routes, each pushing the level of abstraction in a different way. One route was imagining Thorn as 'a light in the darkness,' another was playing on the idea of creating a 'safe space,' and the last one was a 'swarming thorns' concept.

SARAH POTTS (THORN): Seeing these different routes really helped us realize that since Thorn as an organization wasn't pivoting to something entirely new – we were just re-framing what we were doing, and expanding the focus – introducing a new visual expression that was dramatically different from our past would send the wrong signal, potentially confusing our partners, donors, and people in law enforcement.

JAN EUMANN (WOLFF OLINS): Also, we came to realize that idea of a 'thorn protecting a rose' was already such a strong metaphor captured in the name, and that adding another concept on top of it would dilute the power of the whole thing and feel like it was competing.

KATE RINKER (WOLFF OLINS): There are a lot of times where designers really want to be clever, but it can often be more powerful to be humble and realize the right answer is the really obvious one. We were trying so hard that we missed that at first.

CYNTHIA PRATOMO (WOLFF OLINS): So we ultimately decided the identity should still be centered around a 'thorn' pretty explicitly, but there were

Figure 14.3 Thorn logo and watermark

a few key ideas from the new story that added dimensions to it. The first was saying that 'it takes more than one thorn to protect a rose' – in other words, the power of Thorn is its network of partners and volunteers working together. The design system we created could be applied in a singular way or in a group of thorns to express the different people working together as a force (Figure 14.3). This sense of dynamism was so true to the organization.

In addition to the thorn mark derived from the name, the other core thought that inspired the design system was the spirit of "until every child is free to be a kid." This informed the overall feel: that Thorn is not just about being stealthy or tough or feeling like a black-ops SWAT team, but that they bring a sense of hopefulness and optimism. For example, this color palette was a combination of warm and cool, representing Thorn's compassion and strength.

CRISSY FETCHER (DESIGN @ WOLFF OLINS): The idea "until every child is free to be a kid" also had a strong influence on how we thought about photography, and brought a new life and dimension to the system. We made a very conscious decision that photographs would not depict sad children or children with grown-ups. We also wanted to shift away from depicting 'children as superheroes' – which felt a little forced, a little artificial – to showing a diverse set of children in more natural, active, spontaneous situations, in-the-moment, happy, and carefree (Figure 14.4). Just being kids!

ANKUR NAIK (WOLFF OLINS): Once we had a system we all felt great about, we took it to Ashton to see if it felt right for him. This was a big moment to move forward together at all levels, from daily executors to the co-founder.

THORN

Figure 14.4 Just being kids

JULIE CORDUA (THORN): We are lucky to have a co-founder who has a strong vision, and a strong intuition for when something works. With the months of collaboration that had gone into preparing our brand refresh I was really confident that we were on the right track, and catching him up on where we were confirmed all the steps we took along the way. He liked the direction, and pushed us to say if we loved it, because this brand was a new tool to push us to meet our next big organizational goals.

CYNTHIA PRATOMO (WOLFF OLINS): I think the design system we ultimately got to is a perfect metaphor for how their organization is designed, and what they're in the world to do. Because we were able to get really clear about what Thorn actually did and how they worked – ideas like 'build' and 'defend' – we could visually express the organization and its purpose in the right way: what the design elements were, and how they all moved and behaved.

CRISSY FETCHER (WOLFF OLINS): To put the finishing touches on it all and fully build out a toolkit with the people who would be using it every day, we invited a few members of the Thorn team to work out of our office for a week. We did daily work sessions together to figure out the cracks in the system and work out the details.

ANKUR NAIK (WOLFF OLINS): Ultimately, we delivered a whole 'brand toolkit' – designed in Google Docs to be easily usable by Thorn's scrappy team and their partners. It included not just the visual identity and assets that people would need to execute the design system, but also Thorn's core beliefs, purpose, story, and audiences so everyone new to the organization would be able to get up to speed quickly.

Thorn Reflections

SARAH POTTS (THORN): We walked away with exactly what we needed. We had new key phrases to use as touchstones both internally and externally that aligned everyone working on this challenge to the same goal. When we say "until every child can be a kid," people understand immediately. They don't need to know about the size of the problem, or the severity of the issue, they need to understand the vision, and then we can inspire them to join us.

JULIE CORDUA (THORN): When we revealed the final brand outline to staff, it was really powerful. Everyone experienced the manifesto and the visual identity coming together in a way that felt completely natural. We had our purpose from the start, but the challenge was finding a partner who would take in all the nuances and, respecting the value of every angle, synthesize our work into a simple message we could share in any situation. Wolff Olins did just that.

SARAH POTTS (THORN): We immediately put the new brand to use for a hackathon we were hosting in NYC in IAC's beautiful headquarters. Wolff Olins made an incredible series of animations for one of the largest high-resolution video walls in the world (120 feet long!) And it was the perfect larger-than-life scale to launch. The whole room felt light, filled with energy and purpose.

SARAH GARDNER (THORN): Having the space to really dig into who we had become, and where we were headed, was a powerful journey we went on with the Wolff Olins team. I was excited for the brand refresh, but didn't imagine it would be as powerful as it was. Having close relationships with the people who have invested in us from the beginning, I needed them to understand how this was a continuation of the story, not a departure from it, and Wolff Olins delivered just that. We're able to use the images and the language immediately in our work and could see how well it resonated.

JULIE CORDUA (THORN): People are now able to understand the big picture impact we're trying to make much quicker, which gives us a jumping off point to speak to all the different pillars of our work.

KATE RINKER (WOLFF OLINS): We always hoped that brand thinking and design could do a lot of work in inspiring everyone inside Thorn. The stuff they're dealing with is super heavy and can be discouraging, so our goal was that this brand would remind them what they were doing it all for.

SARAH POTTS (THORN): And we'll keep building on what we started with Wolff Olins. They started us off with a suite of tools that our team and our partners are using every day. We use it to onboard new hires, to inspire our fundraising campaigns, and to orient our partner marketing to our shared values.

Wolff Olins reflections

SAM LIEBESKIND (WOLFF OLINS): We'll leave you with the five biggest lessons we took away from this project:

Having a clear sense of purpose is important for every organization

I think it's important that every organization has a purpose – otherwise, as a user, employee, participant – I don't know what I'm joining or supporting. The purpose doesn't always have to be lofty or super emotional, but everyone should have a point of view to guide what they're doing. And this kind of thinking isn't just for non-profits! Every company should tell and re-tell stories about where it came from and why it was started, and also be able to articulate a vision for its future and the world it's trying to create. These kinds of stories have incredible power to mobilize people.

Moving beyond the 'purpose statement' helps bring purpose to life

Ultimately having a clearly articulated purpose is great, but that's not enough to guide people. It's also important to have a core set of beliefs everyone agrees on and to codify a clear philosophy and style on how you plan to operate. Together, this set of coherent ideas, language and visual elements can inform what you do, how you look and feel, and in time, what you stand for in people's minds.

The best visual identities are purposeful

Creating a design system without a purpose is really hard. We've had to do it before on other projects, but with no purpose, it's such a wide canvas, and it becomes extremely subjective. Purpose gives the approach much more rigor, and allows you to determine if you're on the right path. If the design concept doesn't tie to the purpose, it's just not right.

Purpose-led brands require strong leaders

I don't think you can create a purpose-led brand if you don't have a CEO who truly believes. In this case, we had a true partnership with Julie and Sarah and the whole team. The work of a company like Wolff Olins is only as good as our clients, and in this case, they were fantastic.

Purpose should be created with input from everyone

Purpose-led brands are also only really powerful if everyone believes in what the purpose is, so when designing a process to put purpose at the center of an organization, getting input from employees and partners is incredibly important – and often a huge unlock! It can't just be about getting buy-in after the fact. The biggest lesson I took away from this project is how important it is to bring along the whole organization in a process like this, especially the design-minded people. In hindsight, this makes total sense. Something this fundamental to the organization has to include everyone in some way.

Ultimately, this project really showed us that purposeful design and honest, emotional storytelling can really drive change for an organization.

Team

Thorn: Julie Cordua, CEO; Sarah Gardner, Director of Development; Sarah Potts, Marketing and Communications; Douglas Graves, Design & Software Engineer.

Wolff Olins: Mila Linares, Cynthia Pratomo, Sam Wilson, Jan Eumann, Sam Liebeskind, Ankur Naik, Simon Blanckensee, Crissy Fetcher, Kate Rinker, Liz Benson, Steven Phillips-Horst and Brian Boylan.

15 Ben & Jerry's

Continuing to turn values into value through Linked Prosperity

Rob Michalak

Rob Michalak is the Global Director of Social Impact for Ben & Jerry's. From 2006 to 2017, Rob led a process of reinvigorating Ben & Jerry's Social Mission, following the acquisition of Ben & Jerry's by Unilever in April of 2000. The goal of the process was to ensure that Ben & Jerry's Social Mission thrives in balance with the company's Product and Economic Missions. His current focus is on identifying how Ben & Jerry's can achieve better outcomes from the Social Mission initiatives the company is investing in and prioritizing. Ben & Jerry's Social Mission works to create innovative ways that the business can apply its many resources to achieve positive social, economic, and environmental change in the world and make progress on the company's sustainable corporate concept of 'Linked Prosperity,' which is the ambition that as the company prospers, its stakeholders prosper too.

★ ★ ★

In 1978, two rather unconventional guys set up an ice cream scoop shop in a renovated gas station in Burlington, Vermont. By 1980, they rented space in an old spool and bobbin mill nearby so they could pack and deliver pints of their ice cream to local grocery stores and Mom and Pop shops around town. As their business grew, so did their community. These old friends were proud of what they were building and from the start they wanted their success to be linked to that of their partners, farmers, employees, and customers. With this vision as a cornerstone, they continued to build their company based on values, courage, commitment, transparency, faith, humility, and a good dose of humor. These two guys were Ben Cohen and Jerry Greenfield, co-founders of Ben & Jerry's.

You've probably heard of Ben and Jerry, but you might not know about Bernie. Bernie Glassman, a space-age aeronautical engineer turned Buddhist Zen Master, had a bakery in Yonkers, New York by the name of Greyston Bakery. From its start, Greyston was a local, purpose-driven business making wonderful cakes for high-end restaurants in the New York City area. Greyston did things a bit differently from most. It hired people with barriers to employment – a practice it called 'open hiring' – and its application process required no resume. They cared not about who you were yesterday, but rather about who you are today, and who you could be tomorrow.

In the late 1980's, Ben & Jerry's was looking for a thick brownie wafer that could be used for a decadent ice cream sandwich. Ben serendipitously met Bernie at a gathering of socially responsible enterprises, and for both, the concept of a mission-driven ice cream maker working with a mission-driven bakery was a no-brainer. Greyston committed to baking up a couple of tons of brownie wafers for Ben & Jerry's new ice cream sandwich.

The first shipments of brownies were baked in Yonkers, but hastily packed before cooling properly. By the time they arrived in Vermont, what had been brownie wafers had melded into two tons worth of fifty-pound brownie blocks. Those weren't going to be easy to turn into ice cream sandwiches. So, it was time for a little resourceful innovation. Instead of sending the brownies back to Greyston (which really couldn't afford the loss of a shipment that size at the time), the Ben & Jerry's team started chipping the brownie blocks into brownie chunks that could be mixed into a pint of ice cream.

And with that, in 1990 Ben & Jerry's Chocolate Fudge Brownie was born.

The flavor sold well, which meant Ben & Jerry's soon needed more brownies. More brownies meant more bakers, allowing Greyston to hire and train more people from the Yonkers community who couldn't otherwise find jobs. Between 1990 and 2018, Greyston created over 3,000 brownie-baking jobs, generating about $65 million in payroll and providing benefits to about 19,000 families through the Greyston Foundation.

Imagine saving the world through chocolate brownies and ice cream. Hyperbole? Well, maybe. But even if we're not saving the world, the humble brownie is a great example of what is at the center of Ben & Jerry's purpose-driven business model, which, when done well, can create a lot of good.

Our Linked Prosperity model

The Greyston Bakery story is a great example of the Ben & Jerry's business model in action. As we see it, there are three core pillars of our business (Figure 15.1). We serve the first pillar, our Product Mission, by making a great flavor (in this case, Chocolate Fudge Brownie). The second pillar, our Economic Mission, is achieved through high sales numbers (special thanks to our many fans who have loved and bought this flavor over the years!). And the third pillar, our Social Mission, is accomplished in this case through Greyston's hiring of more people with barriers to employment and contributing to families within the community.

These three pillars – Product, Economic, and Social – hold up our business model vision: we are dedicated to a "sustainable corporate concept of Linked Prosperity."

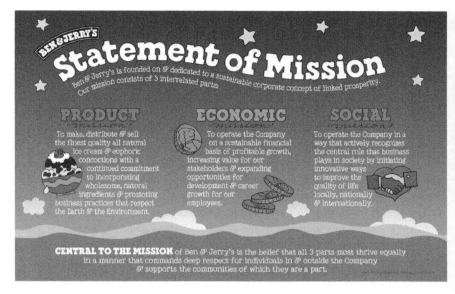

Figure 15.1 The three pillars of Linked Prosperity

The idea is as simple as it is radical. As a company prospers, all those touched by the company must also prosper – including employees, suppliers, customers, communities, and everyone else within our value chain.

We've been working on how to best practice Linked Prosperity throughout every aspect of our business ever since we first wrote our mission in 1988. Good examples include our livable wage policy, our ongoing support for family dairy farms and sustainable agricultural practices, our support for smallholder agricultural producers around the world through the purchase of Fairtrade-certified ingredients, and our values-led sourcing partnerships with social enterprises. In addition to these corporate policies and practices, we see our franchised scoop shop model as allowing Ben & Jerry's to deliver on Linked Prosperity at a more local level: locally-committed owner-operators are empowered to engage with their communities and foster mutually beneficial relationships. Each year, Ben & Jerry's scoop shops help to raise money for local charities but also actively engage in providing direct benefits to the community through a variety of activities. On one special day in the spring of each year, Ben & Jerry's scoop shops globally celebrate their local communities on Free Cone Day. The day creates important levels of awareness for local non-profits and raises tens of thousands of dollars for local charities, not to mention provides about two million free scoops of ice cream to our fans, whom we deeply appreciate all year round.

You might be thinking, "That's a nice idea, but at the end of the day, business is business – does this Linked Prosperity business model actually work?" To that I'd say a resounding yes: doing good for the community is also good for business. We know that people have deeper, more loyal connections to businesses that have shared values. They will stick with those companies longer, through good and bad times, helping to smooth out rough patches along the way. We've seen that through the dramatic moments in the global economy of the recent past. Our internal research supports this, telling us that Ben & Jerry's fans who know and understand our values-led business model are more than twice as loyal than those who don't know about it. The Millennial generation in particular favors authentic, purpose-driven businesses, and its members are twice as loyal to us as they are to other companies. The next generation up, Generation 'Z' (or 'Zennials,' as some cleverly call them) are demanding even more from purpose-driven businesses and expect authentic, transparent relationships with the businesses they will support.

Linked Prosperity is a business model. It's not PR. And it's not philanthropy. This means as we continue to grow our business, we will continue to grow our social impact. And that's something pretty awesome.

Acting on values

Our Linked Prosperity mission provides a clear, orienting vision for the impact we want to achieve as a business. It is, has been, and will continue to be our purpose. Excitingly, many companies today, especially in the United States, are taking up the idea of 'purpose' and seeing the value in orienting a business around a better future rather than merely around a better bottom line. But while purpose is a good thing to aspire to, its far off, utopian ideals can often become difficult to reconcile with the financial 'bottom line,' which demands more immediate, tangible results. The result is a gap between what we want to accomplish as a business tomorrow and the decisions we make as a business today.

To hold ourselves accountable for continuing to *act* on our three-part mission every day, in 1997 we created our Progressive Values statement (Figure 15.2). It acknowledges that capitalism, as practiced, doesn't create opportunities equally, nor does its pursuit of productivity recognize negative environmental consequences. As an agriculturally based global business participating in both the global economy and in the industrial food systems, we need to take responsibility for our part in creating solutions to the issues of growing social inequality and climate change that these systems worsen. For us, this means taking continued action to reduce our carbon footprint, address the unjust consequences of climate change throughout our value chain, and help to re-shape public discourse around the issues of equity, race, and class. Reaffirming this commitment, in 2012 (after a quarter-century of pioneering socially thoughtful and responsible business practices) we were excited to join the B Corp movement – what was then a new type of corporation that used the power of business to solve social and environmental problems.

Our Progressive Values statement commits us to acting consistently to minimize, mitigate, and avoid these twin social and environmental challenges, but we also

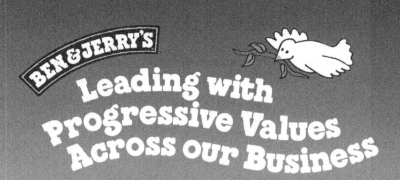

Leading with Progressive Values Across our Business

We have a progressive, nonpartisan social mission that seeks to meet human needs & eliminate injustices in our local, national, & international communities by integrating these concerns into our day-to-day business activities. Our focus is on children & families, the environment & sustainable agriculture on family farms.

- Capitalism & the wealth it produces do not create opportunity for everyone equally. We recognize that the gap between the rich & the poor is wider than at any time since the 1920's. We strive to create economic opportunities for those who have been denied them & to advance new models of economic justice that are sustainable & replicable.

- By definition, the manufacturing of products creates waste. We strive to minimize our negative impact on the environment.

- The growing of food is overly reliant on the use of toxic chemicals & other methods that are unsustainable. We support sustainable & safe methods of food production that reduce environmental degradation, maintain the productivity of the land over time, & support the economic viability of family farms & rural communities.

- We seek & support nonviolent ways to achieve peace & justice. We believe government resources are more productively used in meeting human needs than in building & maintaining weapons systems.

- We strive to show a deep respect for human beings inside & outside our company & for the communities in which they live.

Figure 15.2 Leading with progressive values

realize that to achieve greater impact and to hold ourselves to greater accountability, we need to apply a strategic focus to our actions.

This is where our rolling three-year 'Better World' visions come in. When we consider climate change and social equity, much of what we're working on will take many decades to move the needle significantly. But working in three-year cycles and constantly adjusting our goals as needed along the way allows us to move forward in incremental, tangible ways. As we close in on the current multi-year targets, we start drafting the next iteration before reaching the actual target year. This means that we never really arrive at the destination: we are always on the journey there, always pushing out our horizon to achieve more.

We are already deep into the '2020' iteration of the three-year vision, which outlines the following priorities:

> Use our influence as a buyer and producer to increase awareness of and encourage stakeholders in our supply chain, other similarly situated businesses, and fans to adopt and/or support policies and practices that help to reduce the negative impacts of climate change specifically on vulnerable, marginalized, and disenfranchised communities.

> Use our influence and impact as a food company and major economic and cultural engine to advance opportunities, access, and inclusion for marginalized and under-resourced populations across the five pillars of social equity – economics, education, social capital, civic participation, and cultural pluralism – in the food system.

These statements highlight our role as both purchaser and producer, and call for us to consciously use the influence we wield in both positions to deliver against our vision. The scope of *how* we deliver is specific enough that it gives clear direction to our activity, but also broad enough that every aspect of our business is involved in the effort – from supply chain experts to marketing gurus, everyone has a part to play.

Though we have undertaken many, many initiatives over the past several years to act on this iteration of the vision, I want to highlight a few in this chapter to bring to life how our actions ladder up to Linked Prosperity.

Positive peer pressure: reducing our carbon footprint

When we first launched the 2020 vision, we started by revisiting scientists' findings on the extent of climate degradation so far and the scope of change that will be needed to ameliorate it. Climate change experts agree that collectively, we as a planet need to reduce the absolute carbon levels in the world by 80 percent by 2050. That's a lot. With this larger goal in mind, we asked ourselves: what do *we* need to do at Ben & Jerry's to make that happen?

We did a lifecycle analysis on our products using a pint of ice cream as our unit of measurement and determined that there's about three pounds (1.6 kilograms) of equivalent carbon in a pint of Ben & Jerry's. To do our part in reducing carbon levels to what scientists suggest is needed, we did the math and set the goal to reduce our carbon-per-pint to just under two pounds by 2025 and to a little over a half pound by 2050. To fund this carbon footprint reduction work, we put an internal 'fee' on our carbon emissions and draw from that pool of money set aside specifically for these reduction efforts. It's this type of concerted, intentional action that's necessary to move the needle – or at least keep the needle from rising more than two degrees Celsius by 2050.

But this is just part of our effort on this front. Many companies that make public claims that they are 'climate friendly' or 'climate neutral' focus on reducing emissions directly under their control (emissions from a company's use of fossil fuels, for example, or related to energy purchase). However, the bulk of a company's carbon footprint actually comes from another source: the *indirect* emissions that come from a company's supply chain, which is controlled by others.

This is where we use our influence as a buyer to make good on our vision *"to encourage stakeholders in our supply chain . . . to adopt policies and practices."* We've proposed ambitious indirect emission reduction goals in line with what the accepted science says is needed if we are to stave off the worst impacts of climate change. To date, our efforts to reduce these indirect greenhouse gas emissions have been mostly through investments in on-farm technologies and management systems that reduce emissions primarily as a result of better manure management – we help to subsidize the costs to farmers for actual on-farm technologies such as bio-digesters and manure separators, and we invest in a field team and experts to help farmers implement improved management practices that result in greenhouse gas reductions.

Beyond these management efficiency techniques, we believe that the greatest potential for reducing emissions lies in drawing down carbon from the atmosphere into the soil and we are investing in participating in the development of this science. If proven, carbon sequestration through regenerative agricultural practices might even enable our dairy farms to become net carbon sinks, which is the ultimate goal. Our plan is to continue working with leading organizations and experts to forge a plan going forward on this exciting front.

In providing all of this support to the farming community that supplies Ben & Jerry's, we are supporting them to become more environmentally, economically, and socially sustainable farms, which in turn strengthens the core of our supply chain. However, tackling indirect emissions is one of many initiatives that look beyond our individual company to the broader and more complex system in which we work. It's an endless process and we haven't covered everything in our value chain yet, but it's our intention to eventually do so.

Practicing what we preach: fighting for social equityfrom the inside out

While we've long been a proponent for equity and social justice, we know that to stand up for these issues in the world we need to critically examine the ways in which our values manifest internally in our company culture. Our re-commitment to social equity with the 2020 Vision, therefore, began by looking within. Ben & Jerry's is working with Race Forward, a leading organization equipped to provide technical assistance and capacity support, to help us continue to deeply integrate social equity into the company culture. Race Forward will work through a collaborative, multi-year process to help us develop and adopt a progressive, company-wide understanding and frame for social equity that informs and supports the ongoing development of internal programs, policies, and practices. Among these, we are expanding and elevating the knowledge among staff and leadership, while also building on existing initiatives to create new pathways that increase racial and cultural diversity within the company. And beyond being the right thing to do, we know a more diverse, inclusive company makes us a more successful, profitable company. There have been countless studies recently, including McKinsey's *Diversity Matters* research from 2015, that proves this point.

Externally, we have paid close attention to recent events that push the boundaries of how society is dealing with social equity, as well as the oftentimes hostile narratives that surround this set of issues. In our advocacy work, we listen to and tap into these conversations, ultimately seeking to enhance people's understanding of equity-based issues and inspire them to act on those issues.

To this end, our advocacy work in the United States focuses on issues of racial, economic, and environmental justice. Though this work will continue for years to come since it is steeped in centuries of evolution, we redoubled our efforts to address these systemic issues when we began working with the new Poor People's Campaign in 2017 and 2018 – a movement based on a campaign Dr. Martin Luther King, Jr. started in 1968 shortly before his life was tragically taken.

The Poor People's Campaign is a "national call for moral revival," seeking to galvanize Americans to unite in moral courage across our differences to fight poverty, racism, militarism, and ecological destruction – the root causes of inequality. We've supported this important work at the regional and national level. At the regional level, we've strategically supported our scoop shop franchises where the Campaign will be active, encouraging local engagement. At a national level, we've begun using our tools and communications channels to advance and amplify the larger strategy of the Campaign. We are proud to be a platform for and participant in this work aiming to build lasting and broad-based political power for the poor and disenfranchised.

The same ethos goes for our European communities, where we want to address the current issues that create social inequities. Our biggest recent effort has been our Together for Refugees campaign. Currently, over 65 million people are displaced around the world and European governments are simply not doing enough to help these people find safety and prosper in their new communities. Improving the lives of refugees and asylum seekers in Europe and elsewhere will be an uphill battle because it is so complex and fraught with tension points at several levels. Any party entering into this territory will surely find that the *good* is better than the *perfect*, especially since no actor on this stage can reach perfection – certainly not on their own. While policy efforts are important to frame standards and commitments of states, we believe that real change will only come with changes in the attitudes of local societies toward people arriving in their communities and improving dialogue between them. Addressing this is a long, hard, but essential, road to travel and it will be a key reflection for our future strategy. Perseverance. Resilience. Steps forward.

By directly confronting the greatest social inequities of our times alongside our ambitious and fearless partners, we are working to address root causes of historic problems. By advocating constructive and proactive approaches to resolving social inequities, we believe we can constructively reset the balance so that more people can participate at more productive, empowered levels in society creating a higher quality of life for more and more people throughout the world. This same idea lived at the very core of the Linked Prosperity model back when Ben met Bernie and bought some brownies. And it will continue to be the cornerstone of our business.

Conclusion

There's an African proverb that says, "If you want to go fast, go alone. If you want to go far, go together." We are trying to tackle some of the most challenging issues facing the world today, and we are fully aware that we cannot do this overnight, in a week, or even in a year – and we sure cannot do it alone. It's going to take time, and it is only going to be possible if millions of people continue to come together and mobilize to demand positive change in the world. We believe that business, with all of its immense resources, is currently the most powerful force in the world to effect positive change socially, environmentally, and economically. We need businesses to step up to this role, one requiring intentional, purpose-driven models that bring added value through principled values.

We understand that ice cream alone can't change the world, but the people who share our values and come together around them can. And together over the course of time, we continue to make significant strides in social, economic, and environmental justice. To other companies, we seek to demonstrate that operating a values-led business model based on the concept of Linked Prosperity – where all stakeholders connected to the business, and their communities, are treated equitably and benefit from business success – can be profitable and thrive in today's marketplace.

Conclusion

Jonathan Jackson

Jonathan Jackson is a Co-Founder and former Head of Corporate Brand at Blavity Inc., the largest media company for black Millennials, which maintains five unique sites covering travel, lifestyle, beauty, technology, and culture. He is a 2019 Nieman-Berkman Klein Fellow at the Nieman Foundation for Journalism and the Berkman Klein Center for Internet and Society at Harvard University. His research centers around the emergence of black media in the digital age and examines new ways to measure black cultural influence in the U.S. and abroad, including its effects on media and advertising.

★ ★ ★

Growing up, my mom used to tell me the same thing at any major life milestone. She would look into my eyes, grab my hand, and quietly affirm in the way only a mother can: "Jonathan, remember that your decisions determine your destiny."

One of the best decisions I ever made was joining the Blavity Inc. founding team. I first learned of the idea from Morgan DeBaun, a polymathic, entrepreneurial black woman from Saint Louis, who convinced me of a new vision for a media company. The premise of this company was to tell the stories and perspectives that we knew were true, but never saw ourselves in. These stories carry the full weight of a lineage that is scattered but never separate. Apart but together, with bonds that are unbroken by time and distance, full of nuance, power, and dignity. These stories are how I see the world. They're who I am, and what I care about. I, along with Jeff and Aaron, my other co-founders, believed wholeheartedly that Morgan's idea for a new kind of media landscape was needed in the world, and that collectively we could make it into a reality.

My past few years have been spent building and growing Blavity Inc., the largest on-and offline community for black Millennials. As a team, we have done much more than the possible, and have built a company more influential than we ever could have imagined at our humble beginnings. With a recent Series A funding round, Blavity will be a persistent force, and continue to grow and expand. As it does, under the leadership of Morgan, Jeff, and Aaron, it will not lose sight of why it started, and who we committed to being.

We said we were going to be a voice for black Millennials. We said we would build something we needed that we didn't have. We said we would use the tools most accessible to us to construct a new idea of what was possible. We said we would blow up the silos, and be a media company with multiple revenue streams that could be influential online and resonate offline, all without losing the touch and intentionality of community. Even without intentional labeling or articulation, we were endeavoring to move and deliver with 'purpose' what we had committed to.

We were, as much as we could be, exactly who we said we were. The experience of Blavity Inc., matched up to the promises we made. Before the capital, the awards, the accolades, the sold out events, or the funding, we built trust and consistency. The unscalable things – like individually reaching out to creators to highlight their work or responding manually to every email we could – were our calling card and our key differentiator. That journey continues, but it is informed by the choices that were made long before our first customer or user. The intentionality guiding how Blavity has grown was sharpened by purpose and a tireless commitment to act on it. The decisions of this company, in other words, determined its destiny, and will continue to in its bright future. Per usual, Mom was right.

The climate we live in is tumultuous and has created a new engagement where brands are speaking directly to consumers and consumers are speaking back with their wallets, opinions, and attention. Within this context, brands are the sum total of the promises they keep – a composite of the decisions they make. You can be who you say you are, but only if you decide that you will choose your values over the comfort of complacency.

My aim in this concluding chapter is to offer a few inter-connected questions on the topic of this book. As a young leader in the space, the questions below are what matter to me, and many of the rooms I am invited into or hold space in.

How do we challenge the systems we exist in and contribute to?

Everything is intersectional, so learning how to engage with systems is critical for companies who want to thrive in the changing global ecosystem. This is non-negotiable. If part of your brand is associated with good, to deliver you need to know the system you are a part of.

The obvious example here is understanding your role in relationship to the environment. Recycling is not about what you put in a bin so much as it is how you think about your imprint on the environment, and where you sit in the supply chain of waste. Sustainability also has a social component, and so how you bus your employees to headquarters – and how those busses create congestion in the city or affect living patterns – are just as important as recycling. Everything is interconnected, and understanding this helps preempt challenges and navigate existing crises or future ones.

Beyond considering your current engagement in the global ecosystem, you must understand your own organizational system and the role it plays in affecting people's – especially employees' – lives. The places you work inside of, and the structures that govern them, may predate you, but that doesn't absolve you from the need to interrogate them, the same way you would a product launch or a new initiative.

History is not about comfort, but it can be a guidepost about what to avoid so that we do not repeat our past mistakes. Even if the intentions were not malicious, the responsibility for working toward a better system – whether social, environmental, or organizational – falls on you, whether or not you make that promise as part of your purpose. As part of the system, you *will* be part of its problems. And therefore you must be part of the solution.

How do we value our greatest resource: our employees?

The way we live informs how we work and produce value. Rest and rejuvenation have to be facilitated by the spaces we are in, so the best can come out of us. That's both humane and profitable. Awareness is the beginning of how organizations re-structure themselves, their practices, and their frameworks to embolden people to make informed choices that better their lives, both in and outside of the workplace.

People are valuable because they exist, not because they work for you. They should be made better by their time spent in service of your brand, especially if they are applying their talents to the growth of your organization. Recognizing this harmony and your place in it, can help you get the most out of your most important resource: human capital.

What is our role in political discourse and civic engagement?

Where a brand and company operate, is exactly where their narrative will be created. Companies cannot avoid being part of these stories and expect to remain unscathed. Companies must integrate with communities and cities to empower new ways to give back to these populations. There is an opportunity for brands to listen to issues that exist at the center of people's lives and communities. Learn those stories and help tell them, instead of inserting your own narrative into an existing conversation. Brands do not have to be the primary actor to be effective advocates.

Not every brand is equipped to speak clearly and effectively on political discourse, but all can have codes of operations that force them to 'do no harm' as a prerequisite for being in a market. 'Doing no harm' doesn't mean not doing anything – it requires active measurement and calibration of your outcomes and alignment toward goals that are focused on change and impact.

How we design our future is a shared interest. Companies have a space in that dialogue, and with purpose they can begin to construct their role in bringing about a future that benefits all their stakeholders.

To answer these questions, you, brands, must realize that you are by default part of a local and global community. Recognizing this makes your work a lot harder – it raises a lot more dimensions to the decisions you make. But it is also an incredible opportunity to make inroads and channels inside these communities. This begins with being thoughtful about where you do business, and how you go about it. Your relationships with vendors, the individuals who serve food in your cafeteria, how and where your employees live in proximity to your offices, are all parts of this deeper conversation. You must take seriously your imprint on the various communities you touch – many of which have been systematically denied, subjugated, and penalized from access to basic resources that would improve the quality of their lives in meaningful ways. If you are going to be part of these communities, you need to *decide* to work for them.

And to work for them, you must *know* their constituents. You must understand the lives, with all their nuances, of the people you serve. But at the same time you must move past the nominal conversations and visual efforts that simply highlight differences, and instead begin to understand what those differences reflect about the reality of how people are living. You need to begin nuanced and uncomfortable interrogations of how and why the people closest to the issues you are looking to solve are not involved in the conversations. To understand where people are, you have to see from where they are, and what that means. That begins with listening intently to understand.

Below you'll find selections from young, global thought leaders who exemplify the need to couple experience with vision. Each frames the world they live in and how they experience it based on their background. Each represents the kind of sophisticated consumer, contractor, executive, and community leader you will encounter across the market, if you haven't already. Each lives at various intersections that inform their work and their lives. Each has built influence through their deep roots in and service to a community, fortified through integrity and consistency. Together, they represent the voices of tomorrow's leaders. They are dynamic, prescient, and refract the world as it is – and they refuse to bend because they may be overlooked or relegated to an afterthought.

★ ★ ★

Karen Mok, Community Designer and Co-Founder, The Cosmos

I deserve brands who speak to my identity as a woman, a minority, a daughter of immigrants, and a child of the American South. I deserve brands that represent the full and contradictory spectrum of the American experience. I want brands to recognize that I do not fit into clean demographic personas: I am a Millennial Asian-American outraged by the injustices that people of color still face in America. I'm a streetwear connoisseur and a minimalist and partial to rosé. I've been a techie, management consultant, and investor. I don't want to choose one brand for each facet of my identity – if you want my lifetime value, acknowledge my multidimensional life.

I deserve to engage with brands that understand activating my buying power is not about effectively targeted posts, but rather giving me the proof points to believe the brand will thoughtfully engage with my community and its causes. I deserve to engage with brands that understand the definition of brand has expanded to include personalities, hashtags, and social movements. Rupi Kaur, The Pussy Hat Project, and #SayHerName are movements and personalities and brands; it's not important to me which comes first. They have something to say that resonates with my identity, and I am listening, and I am pulling out my credit card to support. This is what my buying power feels like.

I want a brand to commit to minorities not just as a zeitgeist marketing persona, but as agents of economic and cultural influence. I don't want a 'feel good' commitment that checks the box; I want brands to talk business with me, and I want to do it outside of the ethnic aisle. I want brands to promote minority leaders internally to lead product development, deploy working and long-term capital to minority entrepreneurs, and launch campaigns with grassroots communities of color.

Forging a relationship with a minority consumer for venture returns or PR recovery is not the same as a long-term commitment to the cultural and economic influence of Black, Hispanic, and Asian communities. In fact, the obligation of venture returns is often at odds with the slower, nuanced pace that cultural change requires. The commitment and self-awareness required for a brand to navigate the growing representation of minorities and the bias, oppression, and violence that black and brown communities still face in America is not to be taken lightly. But as brand expert Douglas Holt argues, brands that speak to these complex truths and guide humanity through paradigm shifts become icons.

I deserve brands that see the business and human value of a more equitable and just society. The motivation for my ask goes deeper than my palatable Millennial social consciousness; this is about a lifetime of not seeing my identity represented in the brands I want to support. I am an empowered woman, minority, daughter of immigrants, and child of the American South, but I'm still underpaid, reduced to an outsider, and unlikely to ever be promoted to an executive. I deserve a brand that wants to tell my story.

Karen Mok is the Co-Founder of The Cosmos (jointhecosmos.com), which produces content and experiences for Asian women to flourish and thrive. She has led international expansion for Stripe, a $9B tech company, invested and trained entrepreneurs in Asia, and helped companies like Google, The Rockefeller Foundation, and The Omidyar Network think about inclusive impact. She was born and raised in Charleston, South Carolina and started her first brand, a greeting card company, at age 16.

Jason Touray, Founder and CEO, Black Unicorn

I was a bright kid with some charm and some sporting prowess. I was also a black London boy from a poor family who learned to survive trauma and abuse. So, beneath the surface of charm, I was angry and could be hyper-masculine when triggered. Aged 16, I was on the edge of either fulfilling my potential or losing my way, similar to so many others like me. Then I had my first encounter with a purpose-led brand. That brand was a school and it is called Christ's Hospital.

CH is an unusual public boarding school because of its origins and its purpose. Founded in 1552 by King Edward VI to care for orphaned children in The City of London, CH now provides more bursaries than any other independent boarding school. Kids assessed as being in high need, or as high potential but with low (economic) means, are prioritized. I was offered a place to study A Levels at CH. At that time, nearly 70 percent of kids paid none of the £35,000 annual fees. That's what I call a purpose-led brand!

It provided me with an escape from the chaos that many poor kids from London grow up in. I suddenly lived in an environment that eliminated the need and frequency for me to be such a dickhead. CH introduced me to genuine friendships. Some of the most significant were with fellow black boys. Significant because these friendships differed from the hyper-masculine (and sometimes toxic) friendships that many poor black boys have when navigating life in cities like London.

I learned the confidence to feel as though I belong in all spaces, no matter how unfamiliar, elite, or boujee. Nothing teaches you that type of confidence like a public school does (and few people need that lesson like a poor black kid). CH changed my life. Academically and professionally, it set me on a positive trajectory that I likely wouldn't have been on otherwise. As a human, it set me on the path to defining my brand purpose; to not do things that mean nothing to me and to be of service to other people (especially people who have faced challenges similar to the ones I have).

Have a reason for existing beyond simply making money. Unashamedly do the things that make a positive impact, the things that add value, that tear down barriers, and that create experiences that resonate with the people you want to reach. Be for someone, not for everyone. Do it because it's the right thing. Embrace your world view and experiences and allow them to define who you are and what you do. That's how we all win.

This is the age of brands that democratize their industries. Traditional brands don't call the shots. We do, and we choose the purpose-led. Whether you're a for-profit company, a charitable organization, a self-employed individual, or a person putting your world view and experiences out there, we choose you. We are inclusive. We lean into the awkward conversations about the state of the world. We do good and no unnecessary harm. We create solutions that serve people like us. Our tribe supports us for what we do with their hard-earned money.

Jason was fortunate enough to realize early in his career that he wasn't born to do things that mean nothing to him. He's had the privilege to help hundreds of people to do work that is meaningful to them and fulfil their potential.

Then: People Guy @ Casper and @ WeWork before that.

Now: Founder & CEO @ Black Unicorn, People Guy and Ambassador @ Huckletree, Mentor @ Backstage Capital and Advisory Board Member @ colorintech.

Melissa Kimble, Founder, #blkcreatives

Community isn't about money, it's about moments.

As a child, I arrived at my love and my passion that would eventually turn into my career, by way of my community. When I was still a toddler, it was my mother who taught me how to read, instilling the importance of education and learning into me. When I came across an old, discarded collection of hip-hop magazines in my grandmother's house at age seven, I discovered the intersection of media and culture. In the fifth grade, my English teacher's daily writing prompts inspired my creative freedom and love of storytelling. She helped me ask the question that has driven my work: *Why is my story so important in the context of brands and their audiences?*

What matters most to your audience is service, honor, and commitment: service to themselves and their families, honor to their neighborhoods and their respective cultures, and commitment to leaving a legacy that allows us to see the best in ourselves despite how much our society says otherwise. These things are important to keep in mind as we enter into a new age in our country.

According to the U.S. Census Bureau's 2017 National Population Projections, the nation will become 'minority white' in 2045. During that year, whites will comprise 49.9 percent of the population in contrast to 24.6 percent for Hispanics, 13.1 percent for blacks, 7.8 percent for Asians, and 3.8 percent for multiracial populations. Diversity and inclusion is a trending topic now, but in a little over 25 years, population numbers will force it into a societal norm – and a consumer demand when interacting and engaging with brands. Our world is changing. Does your company reflect that?

Moments within our villages and our families are what shape the world around us and our contributions to it, not profit margins and ROI. You, dear brand practitioner, now have the opportunity to start thinking about what's truly important to your audience.

Our presence isn't a commodity, and our culture and community is not for sale. Your support on the issues, challenges, and systemic barriers that plague our communities, is always welcomed, but only if given with the right awareness and intentions.

If your brand wants to grow and evolve with the times, you must find authentic ways to get in touch with multicultural audiences in a way that builds connection, trust, and mutual respect.

You can't just champion inclusion. You need to support the existing companies, brands, organizations, and people that are doing the work on the ground. That means going beyond numbers and 'influence' on the vanity level and digging deeper into those who are mission-driven and looking to make an impact on generations to come.

Melissa Kimble is a digital media strategist and writer who believes in using the Internet to serve the greater good. As the Founder of #blkcreatives, a community that advocates for Black genius across Creative industries, Melissa is intentional about creating impactful spaces and experiences at the intersection of culture, creativity, and careers.

Bianca Laurie, Founder, C/E Suite

No longer are we pigeonholed into a narrow view of what the world and future looks like. As brands evolve and position themselves for longevity, they're going to have to be inclusive. You'll no longer be surprised that your products are being worn and experienced by those who are able-bodied and those who have disabilities – that your brand is experienced by men and women, and those who don't conform to either of those labels. Brands understand that there's a range in who touch their work, from the young girl that finds her space of comfort in the chaos of her home to the young woman articulating her power. Who we are must be considered worthy, seen, and enabled. You have the space to do more through your messages and products.

The products we use enable us to capture our protest and feeling. Brands of the future will realize that community, as told through their users, represents something beyond. They will use the narratives of their mission to speak up.

I think about aspiration, integrity, and community. Legacy. I'm reminded that brands often are the aspiration, the guides, and markers. Often reflecting what is but also defining and inspiring what could be – saying the things that we can't say or articulating the power we want to see; becoming the space where we are connected; inviting us into the nuance of their evolution.

Brands of the future are responsible. While we think of picking up an item or a piece of clothing, there's a level of trust that comes about in that experience. With vast levels of income inequality brands are not aloof to the social dynamics and culture chasms that take place. Brands of the future are thoughtful and understanding that these are actual people that you are impacting. That people are meeting and connecting with so many things in the world – the good and the bad. They understand that their brands often go beyond utility. The global reach of your brand and the humanity of those that experience it globally. That in a space where attention and time spent can be weaponized or a catalyst for good, brands are aware of this new reality.

Brands of the future are the place we find space to be united in our difference but amplified in our unique nature. Brands of the future to me represent a space that I can see myself but also be myself. So to me, thinking through this notion of brands of the future, they're reminded of the people that they serve. They reflect the opportunities that can be invoked and cultivated not just for one type but all. I want to see myself. A nuanced self – a tech loving, Caribbean, black woman, pseudo introvert, nature loving, and still figuring it out self.

While you can be anything, brands of the future should be extensions and enablers of ourselves and all that represents.

Bianca is the founder of The C/E Suite a management consultancy focused on activating inclusive company growth. Her work places special emphasis on diversity and inclusion, building tools and services that propel social innovation within the tech space. Bianca has worked at Pinterest, a16z (Andreessen Horowitz), CODE2040, LinkedIn, Startup America, and The White House.

Janel Martinez, Entrepreneur, Journalist, Founder, Ain't I Latina?

No one racial or ethnic group, gender identity, disabled or able-bodied, or socio-economic class, is monolithic. Identity is complex and layered, which makes it all the more interesting to unpack, learn, and understand the nuances of. As a brand, you must do this unpacking, learning, and understanding to speak authentically to a given audience.

Understanding nuance equates to longevity; life or death for your brand. If you're invested in building a brand of the future that can effectively speak to the ever-evolving human race, nuance is the key. You reading this is a confirmation that you're a step ahead of your competitors. You care, not just about your top-line growth (I mean, who doesn't want to bring in more revenue?) but tapping a new audience, and providing effective content creation and storytelling overall.

The topic of nuance, a subtle distinction or variation, can go in various directions. For the purpose of this, I'm focusing on race and ethnicity. Before the age of six, I was familiar with the impact of both terms – and how they're perceived in the United States – as a young woman who is Black Latina. Racially, I'm Black, but ethnically I'm Afro-Latina or more commonly digested as Latina.

The media's failure to tackle Latinx representation inclusively has led to decades of misinformation, stereotypical misrepresentations, and a missed opportunity for brands. As a consumer, it's virtually impossible for me to see my entire identity represented in advertisements, TV, streaming shows, or magazines. This growing frustration led me to launch *Ain't I Latina?*, a platform that celebrates and highlights Afro-Latinas, in December 2013. Since our start, we've grown an in-person and online community of more than 20,000 people, the majority of whom identify as Afro-Latina. After reviewing demographic data and speaking with our tribe of Afro-Latinas, it's clear why our content resonates with them and why they feel embraced within our community: we speak directly and authentically to our unique lived experiences. That impact has placed pressure on other Latinx media brands to cover the Afro-Latinx experience. There's been a sizable uptick in coverage of

Afro-Latinxs in both English-language and several Spanish-language outlets since that time.

Many companies see the growing numbers of Latinxs as a chance to market to us. But a blanketed, one-size-fits all approach will cost you money and trust.

You need to create with nuance, and when it comes to creating with this nuance in mind, here are three things branding professionals should consider:

1. *Listen to understand, not respond.* Become an active listener. Listen to actually grasp the message being communicated without racking your brain on what you're going to say or do next. You're not the expert here. When creating content for an audience, get a pulse on the conversations being had online or in-person within that community, and invite that audience in as co-creators. It's by listening attentively that you'll begin to pick up on the audience's values, concerns, likes and dislikes, among other things.
2. *Include the perspective of those from the demo you're reaching.* Speaking of co-creators, employ individuals from the audience you're trying to reach to help you develop your campaign. You may default to what you know when it comes to developing campaigns, but how has that worked for you in the past? No one can speak as authentically to a specific audience like its own members. Even within that group, each person won't have the same experience but you'll begin picking up on overarching themes.
3. *Learn from your mistakes.* You won't get it right all the time. Admit when you f*ck up, review what went wrong, and try again.

Janel Martinez is an entrepreneur, multimedia journalist, and founder of AintILatina.com. The Bronx, NY native, she is a frequent public speaker discussing media, tech, entrepreneurship, culture, and identity, as well as diversity at conferences and events for Bloomberg, NBCU, Oath, SXSW, and more. She's appeared as a featured guest on national shows and outlets, such as BuzzFeed, ESSENCE, NPR, and Sirius XM, and her work has appeared in Univision Communications, NBC, and HuffPost.

Further reading

Like any further reading list, this one is designed as a launch pad for the curious reader. You'll notice quite quickly though that it's not broken down by some of the topics you might expect (there is no section with further reading 'on purpose' or 'on management strategy,' for example). A simple Amazon search can bring up a lengthy, and valuable, reading list on those topics, which I encourage you to explore – there is a lot to learn from this industry hive mind.

Our list instead orients around some of the higher-order questions at the heart of the whole purpose conversation: what's happening in the world? Who are we as people and what is this life all about? Where do the organizations we build slot into all of this?

Exploring these questions requires looking beyond the business aisle bibliography. Anthropology, systems thinking, history, consumer theory, psychology, comedy, literature, and many, many other corners of inquiry can help us think more elastically, challenge our own frames of reference, and bring fresh inspiration to our practice of purpose.

Collected here is a curated list of books, academic publications, blog posts, popular culture artifacts, podcasts, and articles crowdsourced from the contributors to this collection. Even if not immediately obvious, we feel each source brings new dimension to the organizational purpose conversation. The constellation between these ideas is yours to draw.

On thinking

Berlin, Isaiah and Michael Ignatieff. *The Hedgehog and the Fox: An Essay on Tolstoy's View of History*. Edited by Henry Hardy. Princeton: Princeton University Press, 2013.

Boulton, Jean G., Peter M. Allen, and Cliff Bowman. *Embracing Complexity: Strategic Perspectives for an Age of Turbulence*. 1st edition. Oxford: Oxford University Press, 2015.

Gaddis, John Lewis. *On Grand Strategy*. New York: Penguin Books, 2018.

Langer, Ellen. *Mindfulness*. Boston: Da Capo Lifelong Books, 2014.

Meadows, Donella H. *Thinking in Systems: A Primer*. Edited by Diana Wright. White River Junction, VT: Chelsea Green Publishing, 2008.

Patrizi, Patricia, Elizabeth Heid Thompson, Julia Coffman, and Tanya Beer. 'Eyes Wide Open: Learning as Strategy Under Conditions of Complexity and Uncertainty.' *The Foundation Review* 5, no. 3, 1 January 2013. https://doi.org/10.9707/1944-5660.1170.

On what's happening in the world

Beard, Mary. 'The Public Voice of Women.' *London Review of Books*, March 20 2014.

Christian, David. *Origin Story: A Big History of Everything*. New York: Little, Brown and Company, 2018.

Fields, Joshua. 'Is Civilization on the Verge of Collapse?' Medium Blog. 10 July 2018. https://medium.com/@joshfields/is-civilisation-on-the-verge-of-collapse-14ffa9cac6e4.

Giridharadas, Anand. *Winners Take All: The Elite Charade of Changing the World*. New York: Penguin Random House, 2018.

'Global Phase Shift with Daniel Schmachtenberger.' *Future Thinkers Podcast*, Episode 36, February 11 2017. https://futurethinkers.org/daniel-schmachtenberger-phase-shift/.

Godin, Seth. *We Are All Weird: The Rise of Tribes and the End of Normal*. London: Portfolio, 2011.

Harari, Yuval Noah. *Homo Deus: A Brief History of Tomorrow*. New York: Harper, 2017.

Harari, Yuval Noah. *21 Lessons for the 21st Century*. Spiegel & Grau, 2018.

Heimans, Jeremy and Henry Timms. *New Power: How Power Works in Our Hyperconnected World – and How to Make It Work for You*. New York: Doubleday, 2018.

Menand, Louis. 'Francis Fukuyama Postpones the End of History.' *The New Yorker*, August 27 2018. www.newyorker.com/magazine/2018/09/03/francis-fukuyama-postpones-the-end-of-history.

Raworth, Kate. *Doughnut Economics: Seven Ways to Think Like a 21st-Century Economist*. White River Junction: Chelsea Green Publishing, 2017.

Senge, Peter *et al. The Necessary Revolution*. New York: Broadway Books, 2008.

Tepper, Jonathan and Denise Hearn. *The Myth of Capitalism: Monopolies and the Death of Competition*. Hoboken: John Wiley & Sons, 2019.

Tolentino, Jia. 'Where Millennials Come From.' *The New Yorker*, November 27 2017. www.newyorker.com/magazine/2017/12/04/where-millennials-come-from.

On people and the pursuit of happiness

Alderman, Naomi. *The Power*. New York: Little, Brown and Company, 2017.

Arnould, Eric J and Craig J. Thompson. 'Consumer Culture Theory (CCT): Twenty Years of Research.' *The Journal of Consumer Research* 31, no. 4, March 2005: 868–88.

Block, Peter. *The Answer to How Is Yes: Acting on What Matters*. San Francisco: Berrett-Koehler Publishers, 2003.

Bock, Laszlo. *Work Rules!: Insights from Inside Google That Will Transform How You Live and Lead*. New York: Twelve, 2015.

Bourgois, Philippe. *In Search of Respect: Selling Crack in El Barrio*. Cambridge: Cambridge University Press, 2003.

Csikszentmihalyi, Mihaly. *Flow: The Psychology of Optimal Experience*. New York: Harper Perennial Modern Classics, 2008.

Du Bois, W. E. B. *The Souls of Black Folk*. New York: Dover Publications, 1994.

Frankl, Viktor. *Man's Search for Meaning*. Boston: Beacon Press, 1959.

Gadsby, Hannah. 'Hannah Gadsby: Nanette.' *Netflix Special*. 2018.

Holiday, Ryan. *Ego Is the Enemy*. New York: Portfolio, 2016.

Lewis, Sarah. *The Rise: Creativity, the Gift of Failure, and the Search for Mastery*. New York: Simon & Schuster, 2015.

Lofton, Kathryn. *Consuming Religion*. Chicago: University of Chicago Press, 2017.

Moore, Wes. *The Work: Searching for a Life That Matters*. New York: Spiegel & Grau, 2015.

Newport, Cal. *Deep Work: Rules for Focused Success in a Distracted World*. New York: Grand Central Publishing, 2018.

On organizations

Chatterji, Aaron K. and Michael W. Toffel. 'Divided We Lead: CEO Activism has Entered the Mainstream.' *Harvard Business Review*, March 22, 2018. https://hbr.org/2018/03/divided-we-lead.

Collins, Jim and Jerry I. Porras. *Built to Last: Successful Habits of Visionary Companies*. New York: HarperBusiness, 1994.

Geertz, Clifford. 'Ethos, World View, and the Analysis of Sacred Symbols.' In *The Interpretation of Cultures: Selected Essays*, 126–141. New York: Basic Books, 1973.

Grayson, David and Jane Nelson. *Corporate Responsibility Coalitions: The Past, Present, and Future of Alliances for Sustainable Capitalism*. Stanford: Stanford Business Books, 2013.

Holt, Douglas B. *How Brands Become Icons: The Principles of Cultural Branding*. Boston: Harvard Business School Press, 2004.

Koehn, Nancy. *Forged in Crisis: The Power of Courageous Leadership in Turbulent Times*. New York: Scribner, 2017.

Lawrence, Anne T. and James Weber. *Business and Society: Stakeholders, Ethics, Public Policy*. New York: McGraw-Hill Education, 2016.

Mackey, John and Raj Sisodia, *Conscious Capitalism: Liberating the Heroic Spirit of Business*. Boston: Harvard Business School Press, 2014.

Millman, Debbie and Rob Walker. *Brand Thinking and Other Noble Pursuits*. New York: Allworth Press, 2013.

Senge, Peter. *The Fifth Discipline: The Art & Practice of the Learning Organization*. New York: Doubleday, 2006.

'The Business Case for Purpose.' Harvard Business Review Analytic Services Report. https://hbr.org/resources/pdfs/comm/ey/19392HBRReportEY.pdf.

Useem, Jerry. 'What Was Volkswagen Thinking?: How Corporations Become Evil.' *The Atlantic*, December 21 2015. www.theatlantic.com/magazine/archive/2016/01/what-was-volkswagen-thinking/419127/.

Williams, Freya. *Green Giants: How Smart Companies Turn Sustainability into Billion-Dollar Businesses*. New York: AMACOM, 2015.

Leaders on north star purpose

Chouinard, Yvon. *Let My People Go Surfing: The Education of a Reluctant Businessman*. New York: Penguin Books, 2006.

Fink, Larry. 'Larry Fink's Annual Letter to CEOs: A Sense of Purpose.' *BlackRock*, 2018. www.blackrock.com/corporate/investor-relations/larry-fink-ceo-letter.

Kamprad, Ingvar. 'The Testament of a Furniture Dealer.' *Ikea*. 20 December 1976. www.ikea.com/ms/fr_FR/media/This_is_IKEA/the-testament-of-a-furniture-dealer-small.pdf.

Knight, Phil. *Shoe Dog: A Memoir by the Creator of Nike.* New York: Scribner, 2018.

Musk, Elon. 'The Secret Tesla Motors Master Plan (Just Between You and Me).' *Tesla.* 2 August 2006. www.tesla.com/blog/secret-tesla-motors-master-plan-just-between-you-and-me.

Page, Larry and Sergey Brin, 'Letter from the Founders.' *The New York Times*, 29 April 2004. www.nytimes.com/2004/04/29/business/letter-from-the-founders.html.

Schultz, Howard and Dori Jones Yang. *Pour Your Heart into It: How Starbucks Built a Company One Cup at a Time.* New York: Hyperion, 1997.

Zuckerberg, Mark. 'Bringing the World Closer Together.' 22 June 2017. www.facebook.com/notes/mark-zuckerberg/bringing-the-world-closer-together/10154944663901634/.

Notes

Introduction

1 I'm very grateful for the help of Margo Manocherian, Frank Oswald, English Taylor, Natalie Shell, Amanda Roosa, and Jonathan Jackson in helping me shape this introduction. For legibility, I've left a paper trail of the key ideas and influences that have informed this point of view in the footnotes.

2 The business and economic theory of Milton Friedman, a Nobel-prize winning economist, has dominated the last 70 years. Friedman is repeatedly referenced and refuted in this volume because of his axiom that the ultimate goal of business is always to maximize profits for shareholders and owners, and any 'social responsibility' of business serves the bottom-line – a point of view best captured in 'The Social Responsibility of Business is To Increase Profits,' *The New York Times Magazine*, 13 September 1970.

3 J. Collins and J. Porras, *Built to Last* (Random House, 2002), xxi.

4 L. Fink, 'Larry Fink's Annual Letter to CEOs: A Sense of Purpose,' *BlackRock*, 2018, www.blackrock.com/corporate/investor-relations/larry-fink-ceo-letter.

5 Though I don't discuss these 'realities' in detail in this introduction, the will be covered throughout the book. However there are many great, accessible reads highlighted in the further reading section that cover these dynamics. Of these recommendations, my personal favorites are: J. Heimans and H. Timms, *New Power: How Power Works in Our Hyperconnected World – and How to Make It Work for You* (Doubleday, 2018); K. Raworth, *Doughnut Economics: Seven Ways to Think Like a 21st-Century Economist* (Chelsea Green Publishing, 2017); Y. N. Harari, *21 Lessons for the 21st Century* (Spiegel & Grau, 2018).

6 Many discuss the need to update organizational systems of business. Some of my personal favorites come from my own communities of IDEO and Oxford: T. Brown, *Change by Design* (Harper Collins, 2019); 'A Sense of Purpose,' *Saïd Business School*, 23 October 2018, www.sbs.ox.ac.uk/news/sense-purpose.

7 There are many definitions of purpose that offer variations on this theme. The one referenced most frequently by contributors can be found in 'The Business Case for Purpose,' *Harvard Business Review Analytic Services Report*, https://hbr.org/resources/pdfs/comm/ey/19392HBRReportEY.pdf.

8 Purpose has also been stretched to emphasize a more personal, rather than organizational, prerogative – employed to evoke either the leader's mandate as they steer

their corporate ship, or the employee's motivation to arrive at the office earlier in the morning and stay later into the evening.

9 J. Mackey and R. Sisodia, *Conscious Capitalism: Liberating the Heroic Spirit of Business* (Harvard Business School Publishing, 2014).

Chapter 1

1 This chapter is a modified and updated version of one originally printed in Freya's book *Green Giants: How Smart Companies Turn Sustainability into Billion-Dollar Businesses* (AMACOM, 2015).

2 'Putting Purpose into Marketing,' *World Federation of Advertisers and Edelman*, 7 March 2013, www.wfanet.org/en/global-news/brands-will-increasingly-need-purpose-say-worldu2019s-biggest-marketers?p=32; 'The Business Case for Purpose,' *Harvard Business Review Analytic Services Report*, https://hbr.org/resources/pdfs/comm/ey/19392HBRReportEY.pdf.

3 This research was conducted by Jason Denner, POINT380, for *Green Giants*. For an overview of research methodology, see F. Williams, *Green Giants*, 257–258.

4 J. Collins and J. Porras, *Built to Last: Successful Habits of Visionary Companies* (HarperCollins, 2004).

5 'The Business Case for Purpose.'

6 M. Friedman, 'The Social Responsibility of Business Is to Increase its Profits,' *New York Times Magazine*, 13 September 1970.

7 *Ibid.*

8 *Ibid.*

9 D. West, 'The Purpose of the Corporation in Business and Law School Curricula,' *Brookings,* 19 July 2011, www.brookings.edu/research/the-purpose-of-the-corporation-in-business-and-law-school-curricula/.

10 I. Kamprad, 'The Testament of a Furniture Dealer,' 20 December 1976, www.ikea.com/ms/fr_FR/media/This_is_IKEA/the-testament-of-a-furniture-dealer-small.pdf.

11 *Ibid.*, 2.

12 *Ibid.*, 8.

13 *Ibid.*, 8.

14 Author interview, 2015; R. LaFranco, 'Kamprad is Europe's Richest Man in Global Daily Ranking,' *Bloomberg*, 4 March 2012, www.bloomberg.com/news/articles/2012-03-05/kamprad-is-europe-s-richest-in-billionaire-index.

15 J. Collins, *Good to Great: Why Some Companies Make the Leap . . . and Others Don't* (HarperCollins, 2001), 90.

16 *Ibid.,* 91.

17 E. Musk, 'The Secret Tesla Motors Master Plan (Just Between You and Me),' *Tesla*, 2 August 2006, www.tesla.com/blog/secret-tesla-motors-master-plan-just-between-you-and-me.

18 F. Lambert, 'Tesla Reaches Model 3 Production Milestone and Record 7,000-car Week Total Production, Says Elon Musk,' *Electrek,* 1 July 2018, https://electrek.co/2018/07/01/tesla-model-3-production-milestone-record-total-production-elon-musk/.

19 'Ingka Holding B.V. and Its Controlled Entities Yearly Summary FY17,' *IKEA*, www.ikea.com/ms/da_DK/pdf/yearly_summary/ikea-group-yearly-summery-fy17.pdf.

20 R. Safian, 'Generation Flux's Secret Weapon,' *Fast Company*, 14 October 2014, www. fastcompany.com/3035975/generation-flux/find-your-mission/.

21 *Ibid.*

22 'Watch Jerry Seinfeld Rip the Ad World While Getting Advertising Award,' *Time: Money*, 3 October 2014, http://time.com/money/3461169/seinfeld-advertising-clio-award/.

23 J. Amortegui, 'Why Finding Meaning at Work is More Important Than Feeling Happy,' *Fast Company*, 26 June 2014, www.fastcompany.com/3032126/how-to-find-meaning-during-your-pursuit-of-happiness-at-work.

24 '2014 Business as Unusual: the Social and Environmental Impact Guide to Graduate Programs – for Students by Students,' *Net Impact*, https://netimpact.org/sites/default/files/documents/business-as-unusual-2014.pdf.

25 A. Kaufman, 'Tesla Owners' Full-Page Newspaper Ad Gets Elon Musk's Attention,' *HuffPost*, 8 August 2014, www.huffingtonpost.co.uk/entry/tesla-newspaper-ad_n_5705381.

26 'Promoting National Security has Never Been So Much Fun,' *Tesla*, 7 August 2009, www.tesla.com/en_GB/blog/promoting-national-security-has-never-been-so-much-fun?redirect=no.

27 *Ibid.*

28 *Ibid.*

29 'Brandshare 2014,' *Edelman*, www.edelman.com/insights/intellectual-property/brandshare-2014/.

30 'Executive Summary: 2015 Edelman goodpurpose Study,' *Scribd*, www.scribd.com/doc/90411623/Executive-Summary-2012-Edelman-goodpurpose-Study.

31 *Ibid.*

32 *Ibid.*

33 *Ibid.*

34 E. Whan, 'Why Companies Must Win the Trust of Aspirational Consumers,' *GreenBiz*, 20 June 2014, www.greenbiz.com/blog/2014/06/20/why-companies-must-win-trust-aspirational-consumers.

35 'From Obligation to Desire: 2.5 Billion Aspirational Consumers Mark Shift in Sustainable Consumption,' *CSRwire*, 3 October 2013, www.csrwire.com/press_releases/36215-From-Obligation-To-Desire-2-5-Billion-Aspirational-Consumers-Mark-Shift-in-Sustainable-Consumption.

36 'Aspirational Consumers are Rising. Are Brands Ready to Meet Them?,' *GlobeScan*, 6 June 2016, https://globescan.com/aspirational-consumers-are-rising-are-brands-ready-to-meet-them/.

37 'Meaningful Brands,' *Havas Media*, 2 January 2017, www.havasmedia.com/meaningful-brands.

38 'The Jack Welch MBA,' *The Economist*, 23 June 2009, www.economist.com/business/2009/06/23/the-jack-welch-mba.

39 G. Colvin, 'Ultimate Manger in a Time of Hidebound, Formulaic Thinking, Jack Welch Gave Power to the Worker and the Shareholder. He Built One Hell of A Company in the Process,' *Fortune*, 22 November 1999, http://archive.fortune.com/magazines/fortune/fortune_archive/1999/11/22/269126/index.htm.

40 'Welch Condemns Share Price Focus,' *Financial Times*, 12 March 2009, www.ft.com/intl/cms/s/0/294ff1f2-0f27-11de-ba10-0000779fd2ac.html?siteedition=intl#axzz3MYzB6tfa.

41 L. Fink, 'Larry Fink's Annual Letter to CEOs: A Sense of Purpose,' *BlackRock*, 2018, www.blackrock.com/corporate/investor-relations/larry-fink-ceo-letter.

Chapter 2

1 M. Ray, 'Pepsi Showed the Ultimate Downside of In-House Creative: A Lack of Perspective,' *Adweek*, 6 April 2017, www.adweek.com/brand-marketing/pepsi-showed-the-ultimate-downside-of-in-house-creative-a-lack-of-perspective/.
2 L. Fink, 'Larry Fink's Annual Letter to CEOs: A Sense of Purpose,' *BlackRock*, 2018, www.blackrock.com/corporate/investor-relations/larry-fink-ceo-letter.
3 E. Schurenberg, 'Richard Branson: Why Customers Come Second at Virgin,' *Inc. com*, 30 November 2017, www.inc.com/eric-schurenberg/sir-richard-branson-put-your-staff-first-customers-second-and-shareholders-third.html.

Chapter 3

1 R. Parloff, 'This CEO is Out for Blood,' *Fortune*, 12 June 2014, www.fortune.com/2014/06/12/theranos-blood-holmes/.
2 K. Auletta, 'Blood, Simpler: One Woman's Drive to Upend Medical Testing,' *The New Yorker*, 15 December 2014, www.newyorker.com/magazine/2014/12/15/blood-simpler.
3 R. Parloff, 'This CEO is Out for Blood.'
4 J. Mackey and R. Sisodia, *Conscious Capitalism: Liberating the Heroic Spirit of Business* (Harvard Business School Publishing Corporation, 2014), 7.
5 K. Auletta, 'Blood, Simpler: One Woman's Drive to Upend Medical Testing.'
6 G. Cierra, 'Healthcare is the leading cause of bankruptcy: Elizabeth Holmes @ TEDMED 2017 [sic],' *YouTube*, 1:47–3:16, www.youtube.com/watch?v=9B_oJM Qk754&t=172s. Interestingly, the original video no longer appears on the TEDMED website.
7 J. Carryrou, *Bad Blood: Secrets and Lies in a Silicon Valley Startup* (Alfred A. Knopf, 2018), 107.
8 V. Frankl, *Man's Search for Meaning* (Washington Square Press, 1984), 133; original English edition (Beacon Press, 1959).
9 J. Fox, 'The Social Responsibility of Business Is to Increase . . . What Exactly?,' *Harvard Business Review*, 18 April 2012, www.hbr.org/2012/04/you-might-disagree-with-milton.
10 J. Collins and J. Porras, *Built to Last: Successful Habits of Visionary Companies*, (Harper Business, 1994), 8.
11 *Ibid.*, 48, cf. 73, 76.
12 K. Freeman, P. Spenner, and A. Bird, 'Three Myths about What Customers Want,' *Harvard Business Review* (online), 23 May 2012, www.hbr.org/2012/05/three-myths-about-customer-eng.
13 P. Hill, and N. Turiano, 'Purpose in Life as a Predictor of Mortality Across Adulthood,' *Psychological Science* 25, no. 7 (2014): 1482–1486.
14 L. Page and S. Brin, 'Letter from the Founders,' *The New York Times*, 29 April 2004, www.nytimes.com/2004/04/29/business/letter-from-the-founders.html.
15 R. Safian, 'Facebook, Airbnb, Uber, and the Struggle to Do the Right Thing,' *Fast Company*, 11 April 2017, www.fastcompany.com/40397294/facebook-airbnb-uber-and-the-struggle-to-do-the-right-thing.

16 S. Shane, and D. Wakabayashi, "'The Business of War": Google Employees Protest Work for the Pentagon,' *The New York Times*, 4 April 2018, www.nytimes.com/2018/04/04/technology/google-letter-ceo-pentagon-project.html.

17 S. Pichai, 'AI at Google: Our Principles,' 7 June 2018, www.blog.google/topics/ai/ai-principles/.

18 E. Stack, 'I Run Dick's Sporting Goods. It's Congress's Turn to do Something About Guns,' *The Washington Post*, 21 March 2018, www.washingtonpost.com/opinions/i-run-dicks-sporting-goods-its-congresss-turn-to-do-something-about-guns/2018/03/21/3dd1b040–2c3f–11e8-b0b0-f706877db618_story.html?utm_term=.c5e9be521673.

19 E. Griffith, 'Theranos and Silicon Valley's "Fake it Till You Make It" Culture,' *Wired*, 14 March 2018, www.wired.com/story/theranos-and-silicon-valleys-fake-it-till-you-make-it-culture/.

20 B. Mole, 'Check Out This Surreal Chat with Theranos Investor Who Says He's "Thrilled,"' *ArsTechnica.com*, 12 May 2018, www.arstechnica.com/science/2018/05/check-out-this-surreal-chat-with-theranos-investor-who-says-hes-thrilled/.

21 H. Schultz and D. J. Yang, *Pour Your Heart into It: How Starbucks Built a Company One Cup at a Time* (Hyperion, 1997), 5.

22 J. Jargon and R. Feintzeig, 'Starbucks Closes for Antibias Training, Leaving Customers in Need of a Fix,' *The Wall Street Journal*, 29 May 2018, www.wsj.com/articles/starbucks-closing-8-000-stores-for-antibias-training-1527614019.

Chapter 4

1 I would like to give deep thanks to Maryam Banikarim, Carol Cone, and Hope Freeman for taking the time to speak with me about their deep knowledge in helping build purpose-led initiatives and organizations. Thanks also to my colleagues at Columbia Business School, Bernd Schmitt and Evangeline Lew, for providing me with feedback. And finally, I must give great thanks to my wife, Tegan Culler, for supporting me in all things, and especially for her wonderful editing review of this chapter.

2 J. Delingpole, 'When Lego Lost its Head – and How This Toy Story Got its Happy Ending,' *Daily Mail*, 18 December 2009, www.dailymail.co.uk/home/moslive/article-1234465/When-Lego-lost-head-toy-story-got-happy-ending.html.

3 M. Bonchek and C. France, 'How Marketers Can Connect Profit and Purpose,' *Harvard Business Review*, 18 June 2018, https://hbr.org/2018/06/how-marketers-can-connect-profit-and-purpose.

4 'The Business Case for Purpose,' *Harvard Business Review Analytic Services Report*, https://hbr.org/resources/pdfs/comm/ey/19392HBRReportEY.pdf.

5 *Ibid.*, 1.

6 'Millward Brown, in Partnership with Jim Stengel, Reveals the 50 Fastest-Growing Brands in the World and Uncovers the Source of Their Success,' *Business Wire*, 12 January 2012, www.businesswire.com/news/home/20120117005066/en/Millward-Brown-Partnership-Jim-Stengel-Reveals-50.

7 R. Shotton, 'Truthiness in Marketing: Is The Evidence Behind Brand Purpose Flawed?,' *The Drum*, 12 April 2017, www.thedrum.com/opinion/2017/04/12/truthiness-marketing-the-evidence-behind-brand-purpose-flawed.

8 'We Pioneer,' *Amazon Jobs*, www.amazon.jobs/en/working/working-amazon.

9 'Apple CEO on a Trump Presidency: "Apple's North Star Hasn't Changed,"' *Business Insider*, 10 November 2016, www.businessinsider.com/apple-ceo-tim-cook-memo-on-donald-trump-2016-11.

10 M. Zuckerberg, 'Bringing the World Closer Together,' *Facebook*, 22 June 2017, www.facebook.com/notes/mark-zuckerberg/bringing-the-world-closer-together/10154944663901634/.

11 'Purpose, Vision, Values, and Mission,' *Southwest*, http://investors.southwest.com/our-company/purpose-vision-values-and-mission.

12 'Our Company: The Business of Good Food,' *Chipotle*, www.chipotle.com/company.

13 Phone interview, July 3 2018.

14 'Insights for the 2018 Deloitte Millennial Survey,' *Deloitte*, 15 May 2018, www2.deloitte.com/insights/us/en/topics/talent/deloitte-millennial-survey.html.

15 'About,' *CVS Health*, https://cvshealth.com/about.

16 M. Egan, 'CVS Banned Tobacco. Now its sales are hurting,' *CNN Money*, 4 August 2015, https://money.cnn.com/2015/08/04/investing/cvs-earnings-cigarettes/.

17 N. Dvorak and D. Yu, 'Why CVS May Not Get Burned By Its Tobacco Decision (Part 1),' *Gallup*, 18 March 2014, https://news.gallup.com/businessjournal/167870/why-cvs-may-not-burned-tobacco-decision-part.aspx.

18 'Sustainable Living Plan,' *Unilever*, www.unilever.com/sustainable-living/.

19 'The 10 Principles of the UN Global Compact,' *United Nations Global Compact*, www.unglobalcompact.org/what-is-gc/mission/principles.

20 'How It Works,' *B Corporation Impact Assessment*, https://bimpactassessment.net/how-it-works/assess-your-impact.

21 D. Jergier, 'B Corp Status Gives California Agency Conscientious Bragging Rights,' *Insurance Journal*, 8 June 2015, www.insurancejournal.com/news/west/2015/06/08/370873.html.

22 'Why Is Benefit Corp Right for Me?,' *Benefit Corporation*, http://benefitcorp.net/businesses/why-become-benefit-corp.

23 'Consumer-Goods Brands That Demonstrate Commitment to Sustainability Outperform Those That Don't,' *Nielson*, 12 October 2015, www.nielsen.com/us/en/press-room/2015/consumer-goods-brands-that-demonstrate-commitment-to-sustainability-outperform.html.

24 'Shared Value Initiative,' www.sharedvalue.org/.

25 Phone interview, July 3 2018.

26 The Coca-Cola Company, 'Collaborating to Replenish the Water We Use,' *Coca-Cola Journey*, 29 August 2018, www.coca-colacompany.com/stories/collaborating-to-replenish-the-water-we-use.

27 'Solar Means Business 2017,' *SEIA*, www.seia.org/solar-means-business-report.

Chapter 5

1 'Purpose, Vision, Values, and Mission,' *Southwest*, http://investors.southwest.com/our-company/purpose-vision-values-and-mission.

2 For a great example of the power of Southwest's employees to act on values, see: M. Schwantes, 'The Unforgettable Story of a Southwest Pilot's Response to a Late,

Frazzled Passenger Is a Master Class in Leadership,' *Inc.*, www.inc.com/marcel-schwantes/when-you-think-of-what-makes-a-great-leader-does-this-trait-come-to-mind-it-rarely-does-unfortunately.html.

3 J Collins and J. Porras, *Built to Last: Successful Habits of Visionary Companies* (Harper-Collins, 2004).

4 'Millward Brown, in Partnership with Jim Stengel, Reveals the 50 Fastest-Growing Brands in the World and Uncovers the Source of Their Success,' *Business Wire*, 12 January 2012, www.businesswire.com/news/home/20120117005066/en/Millward-Brown-Partnership-Jim-Stengel-Reveals-50.

Chapter 7

1 Y. Harari, *Sapiens: A Brief History of Humankind* (New York: HarperCollins, 2015).

2 L. Gerstner, Jr., *Who Says Elephants Can't Dance?* (New York: HaperCollins, 2002) 134.

Chapter 8

1 J. Coffman, A. Aggrawal, and S. Wang, 'Restoring a Founder's Mentality Culture,' *Bain & Company*, 19 June 2017, www.bain.com/insights/restoring-a-founders-mentality-culture/.

2 M. Scott, 'What Uber Can Learn From Airbnb's Global Expansion,' *The New York Times*, 7 July 2015, www.nytimes.com/2015/07/08/technology/what-uber-can-learn-from-airbnbs-global-expansion.html.

3 *Ibid.*

4 *Ibid.*

5 M. Kircher, 'Uber CEO Replaces Infamous Core Values with Friendlier-Sounding List,' *New York Magazine*, 7 November 2017, http://nymag.com/selectall/2017/11/ubers-list-of-new-core-values-are-friendlier.html.

6 'How to Avoid F★★king Up Purpose,' *Kin&Co*, 27 January 2018, www.kinandco.com/wp-content/uploads/2018/01/KinCo_Fucking-Up-purpose_27thJan_More-high.pdf

7 *Ibid.*

8 J. Berman, 'The Three Essential Warren Buffett Quotes to Live By,' *Forbes*, 20 April 2014, www.forbes.com/sites/jamesberman/2014/04/20/the-three-essential-warren-buffett-quotes-to-live-by/#389a7cd56543.

9 'How to Avoid F★★king Up Purpose,' *Kin&Co*.

Chapter 10

1 This chapter reprints, with slight modifications, an original article by T. Ordahl, 'Revolutionizing the way we manage brand: the Brand Community Model' *Landor*, 8 February 2017, https://landor.com/thinking/revolutionizing-way-manage-brands-brand-community-model.

Chapter 11

1 '25 Largest US Foundations by Total Assets,' *National Philanthropic Trust*, www.nptrust. org/philanthropic-resources/25-largest-foundations-in-the-us-by-total-assets.

2 C. Sophie, 'Revealed: The World's 10 Largest Companies by Revenue,' *The Telegraph*, 19 July 2018, www.telegraph.co.uk/business/0/revealed-worlds-10-largest-companies-revenue/.

3 For a much more thorough explanation, it's best to go to the source: S. Earl, F. Carden, T. Smutylo, and M. Quinn Patten, *Outcome Mapping: Building Learning and Reflection into Development Programs* (IDRC Books, 2002).

Index